SLOW TRAVEL

North East Scotland

Including Aberdeenshire, Moray & the Cairngorms National Park

Local, characterful guides to Britain's special places

Rebecca Gibson

First edition published May 2023
Bradt Guides Ltd
31a High Street, Chesham, Buckinghamshire, HP5 1BW, England
www.bradtguides.com

Print edition published in the USA by The Globe Pequot Press Inc,
PO Box 480, Guilford, Connecticut 06437-0480

Text copyright © 2023 Bradt Guides Ltd
Maps copyright © 2023 Bradt Guides Ltd; includes map data © OpenStreetMap contributors
Photographs copyright © 2023 Individual photographers (see below)
Project Manager: Emma Gibbs
Cover research: Pepi Bluck, Perfect Picture

ISBN: 9781784779016

British Library Cataloguing in Publication Data
A catalogue record for this book is available from the British Library

Photographs
© individual photographers credited beside images & also those from picture libraries
credited as follows: Alamy.com (A); Shutterstock.com (S)

Front cover Dunnottar Castle (mauritius images GmbH/A)
Back cover Loch of Blairs (Brian Higgs/Friends of Blairs Loch)
Title page Gardenstown (VisitAberdeenshire)
Maps David McCutcheon FBCart.S

Typeset by Ian Spick, Bradt Guides, Ltd
Production managed by Zenith Media; printed in the UK
Digital conversion by www.dataworks.co.in

AUTHOR

With her wildlife background, outdoor writer and photographer Rebecca Gibson is used to exploring at a leisurely pace. She enjoys inspiring others to connect to the natural world and discover lesser-known places with immersive storytelling and images. Having spent years exploring the diverse landscape of North East Scotland, Rebecca has developed a particular fascination for its many  stone circles and Pictish carvings. She has a master's degree in Travel and Nature Writing and her work has been featured in a range of digital and print publications. You can follow her updates on 📷 and 📘 Rebecca On The Wing.

AUTHOR'S STORY

Is there a better way to get to know a new place than by writing a book about it? Unconventional perhaps, but I wouldn't have had it any other way. Having spent many summer holidays visiting family in central Scotland, I was keen to venture further north and the Moray Coast looked like the peaceful, wild place for me. I moved in February 2020, three weeks before the first Covid-19 lockdown began. Because I couldn't drive anywhere I had to explore on foot, so I unknowingly began my Slow travelling straight away.

Sampling homegrown food, coast paths and hidden castles one walk at a time, I connected with the North East instantly. With few famous locations and countless undiscovered ones, I knew it would be well-suited for a Slow Guide. My fresh-eyed perspective helped – I took everything in for the first time without any preference towards a particular location.

Once I discovered how abundant Pictish symbol stones and stone circles are in this area, I was determined to find as many as I could. Knowing they'd stood there for millennia just blew my mind. My favourites include the vast stone circle of East Aquhorthies just outside Inverurie and the diversely decorated Rhynie Pictish stones near Huntly.

I've learned so much while researching and writing this guide and I consider myself very lucky to have had the opportunity. To meet the specific demands of a Slow Guide, I've rummaged for places you wouldn't know about unless you take the time and effort to find them. Exploring my new home in this thorough and meaningful way has been so rewarding, and I hope I inspire you to visit this extraordinary corner of Scotland and fall for it like I did.

ACKNOWLEDGEMENTS

I've wanted to write my own book since I was nine years old. So, the first thank you has to go to my English teacher, Claire Gibbs, whose encouragement helped me realise that maybe I could be an author when I grew up.

Huge thanks to the team at Bradt for their guidance and support, particularly Anna Moores, Emma Gibbs, Claire Strange and Adrian Phillips. Thanks also to fellow Slow Guide writers Neil and Helen Matthews and Helen Moat, who gave me advice and reassurance when I didn't know where to start.

While researching this book I visited dozens of visitor attractions and I must mention Moira Gash, who kindly organised several of my visits. Thank you to all the fantastic accommodation providers, museum staff, small business owners, volunteers and friends across the North East who gave up their time to welcome me, take me on guided tours, offer their expertise or all of the above. There are far too many wonderful people to list here, but they include: Gabrielle Balfour, Allan Bantick, Dan Barnett, Robert Cumming, Douglas Cusine, Lisa Farley, Amanda Frazer, Catie Gandhi, Lisa Gardiner, Alex Giddes, Linda Gorn, Rhona Graham, Kim Grant, David Hanson, Tim Marshall, Liam McBride, Alan Milne, Kirsteen Mitcalfe, Bill and Lynn Pitt, Jen Price, Gill Reid, Alison Rose, Harry Scott, Carole and Matthew Short, Derek and Lorraine Toal, Steve Truluck, Ellie Turner, Lynne Watson and Cath Wright.

Massive thanks also to those who lent me their fresh eyes when mine had turned to sandpaper: David Hanson, Joan Megson, Rebecca Russell-Peach, Stephen Moss and my fellow wild woman, Jeni Bell.

Finally, Mum and Dad. Thank you for your unwavering faith in me – this book simply wouldn't exist without you.

CONTENTS

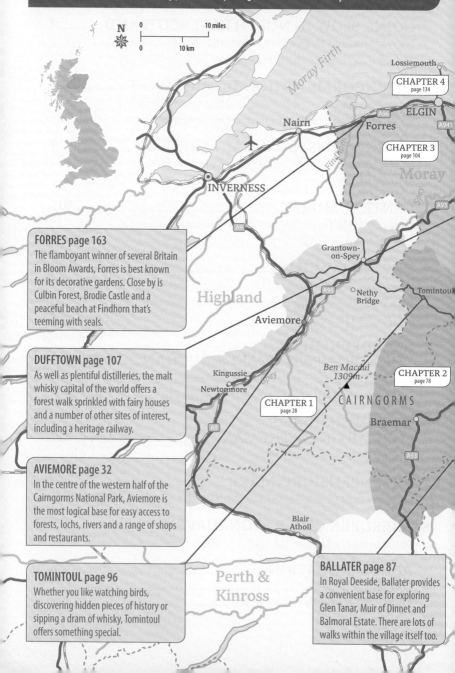

SUGGESTED PLACES TO BASE YOURSELF

These bases make ideal starting points for exploring localities the Slow way.

N

0 — 10 miles
0 — 10 km

Moray Firth

Lossiemouth

CHAPTER 4
page 134

ELGIN

Nairn   Forres

CHAPTER 3
page 104

Moray

INVERNESS

Grantown-
on-Spey

Tomintoul

Highland

Nethy
Bridge

Aviemore

Ben Macdui
1309m

CHAPTER 2
page 78

Kingussie

Newtonmore

CHAPTER 1
page 28

CAIRNGORMS

Braemar

Blair
Atholl

Perth &
Kinross

FORRES page 163
The flamboyant winner of several Britain in Bloom Awards, Forres is best known for its decorative gardens. Close by is Culbin Forest, Brodie Castle and a peaceful beach at Findhorn that's teeming with seals.

DUFFTOWN page 107
As well as plentiful distilleries, the malt whisky capital of the world offers a forest walk sprinkled with fairy houses and a number of other sites of interest, including a heritage railway.

AVIEMORE page 32
In the centre of the western half of the Cairngorms National Park, Aviemore is the most logical base for easy access to forests, lochs, rivers and a range of shops and restaurants.

TOMINTOUL page 96
Whether you like watching birds, discovering hidden pieces of history or sipping a dram of whisky, Tomintoul offers something special.

BALLATER page 87
In Royal Deeside, Ballater provides a convenient base for exploring Glen Tanar, Muir of Dinnet and Balmoral Estate. There are lots of walks within the village itself too.

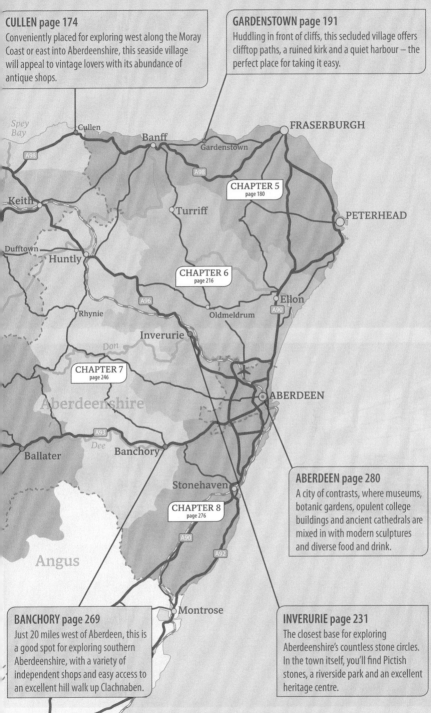

CULLEN page 174
Conveniently placed for exploring west along the Moray Coast or east into Aberdeenshire, this seaside village will appeal to vintage lovers with its abundance of antique shops.

GARDENSTOWN page 191
Huddling in front of cliffs, this secluded village offers clifftop paths, a ruined kirk and a quiet harbour – the perfect place for taking it easy.

CHAPTER 5
page 180

CHAPTER 6
page 216

CHAPTER 7
page 246

CHAPTER 8
page 276

ABERDEEN page 280
A city of contrasts, where museums, botanic gardens, opulent college buildings and ancient cathedrals are mixed in with modern sculptures and diverse food and drink.

BANCHORY page 269
Just 20 miles west of Aberdeen, this is a good spot for exploring southern Aberdeenshire, with a variety of independent shops and easy access to an excellent hill walk up Clachnaben.

INVERURIE page 231
The closest base for exploring Aberdeenshire's countless stone circles. In the town itself, you'll find Pictish stones, a riverside park and an excellent heritage centre.

GOING SLOW IN
NORTH EAST SCOTLAND

Stroll beneath Scots pines so ancient they once thrummed with the howls of wolves. Find cactus forests and gravestones for wizards in Scotland's third-largest city. Swirl a dram of whisky while admiring mountains diluted by distance, their peaks brushed over with snow. Across 200 miles of coastline, waves seep into sand and slap against jagged cliffs stippled with nesting seabirds. This is a landscape that offers whatever views you fancy, including heather-felted hills, treacle-toned rivers and fishing villages too small to access except on foot. Whether you're hankering for wilderness adventures or quirky urban discoveries, this region lends itself well to the leisurely pace of Slow exploration.

For the purposes of this book, North East Scotland refers to the triangular wedge above Dundee and east of Inverness. Aberdeenshire claims the right half of this chunk, bordered by the North Sea to the east and the Moray Firth to the north. From this north-facing coast, you can gaze at yawning ocean that will eventually reach Norway, Svalbard and the top of the world. Aberdeenshire is famed for its history, with a huge range of ruined castles, stone carvings and Neolithic structures. Forget tourist-clogged Stonehenge – I'm going to show you stone circles with no barriers, queues or even signs pointing the way.

The east-facing stretch of Aberdeenshire's coastline spans over a hundred miles from Fraserburgh down to St Cyrus. Along here, you can climb to the top of Kinnaird Head Lighthouse and look for killer

◀ **1** Uath Lochans, page 59. **2** Speyside Cooperage, page 111.

THE SLOW MINDSET

Hilary Bradt, Founder, Bradt Travel Guides

> We shall not cease from exploration
> And the end of all our exploring
> Will be to arrive where we started
> And know the place for the first time.
>
> T S Eliot, 'Little Gidding', *Four Quartets*

This series evolved, slowly, from a Bradt editorial meeting when we started to explore ideas for guides to our favourite part of the world – Great Britain. We wanted to get away from the usual 'top sights' formula and encourage our authors to bring out the nuances and local differences that make up a sense of place – such things as food, building styles, nature, geology, or local people and what makes them tick. Our aim was to create a series that celebrates the present, focusing on sustainable tourism, rather than taking a nostalgic wallow in the past.

So without our realising it at the time, we had defined 'Slow Travel', or at least our concept of it. For the beauty of the Slow movement is that there is no fixed definition; we adapt the philosophy to fit our individual needs and aspirations. Thus Carl Honoré, author of *In Praise of Slow*, writes: 'The Slow Movement is a cultural revolution against the notion that faster is always better. It's not about doing everything at a snail's pace, it's about seeking to do everything at the right speed. Savouring the hours and minutes rather than just counting them. Doing everything as well as possible, instead of as fast as possible. It's about quality over quantity in everything from work to food to parenting.' And travel.

So take time to explore. Don't rush it, get to know an area – and the people who live there – and you'll be as delighted as the authors by what you find.

whales in spring, or explore a windswept, Gothic ruin that's said to have inspired Dracula's castle. South of Aberdeen's knot of activity, experience a thrilling Hogmanay (New Year) fire festival in the otherwise peaceful town of Stonehaven, or look for puffins at RSPB Fowlsheugh, which literally means 'bird cliff'.

Moray (pronounced the same way as Andy Murray's surname) lies west of Aberdeenshire, and together they share the vast Moray Firth. This is arguably a part of Scotland few people are well acquainted with, although it includes the world's malt whisky capital: Dufftown. In this unassuming burgh, visitors can find a fairy village submerged in the woods, experience healing vibrations from singing bowls, or nibble scones on a heritage railway. Further north, on the Moray Coast, wildlife watchers are spoilt rotten with high chances of seeing bottlenose dolphins and seals. Seasonal visitors such as ospreys, long-tailed ducks and basking sharks often drop by too.

Twice the size of the Lake District, the Cairngorms National Park stretches across parts of Moray, Aberdeenshire and several other Scottish council areas. It holds great appeal to both summer and winter outdoor enthusiasts so can be busy, especially during school holidays. Despite this, it's easy to escape the crowds and find solitude on the banks of hidden lochans or bubbling streams stitched across neighbourhoods of pines and birches. Curiosity is rewarded with stone cairns, wood carvings and memorials tucked among the trees, not to mention mythical monsters lurking in the depths.

I've featured the western and eastern edges of the national park and stopped before the Angus and Perthshire boundaries to the south. This means there are no mountains in the book, but plenty of short hill walks, coast paths and forest trails. A whole day spent pottering a handful of miles is the aesthetic we're going for here.

North East Scotland is also packed with small businesses and independent hideaways, and I was keen to promote as many of these as possible. You'll often find yourself squeezing between towering bookshelves scented with old pages, or chatting to the owner of a mobile coffee van for half an hour as a cabinet of homemade cakes wiggle iced eyebrows at you.

DIV YE KEN ONY DORIC?

More than a thousand years ago, the dominant language spoken in the Cairngorms was Gaelic. This is why many topographic features still reflect their Gaelic origins today. Examples include An Lochan Uaine (the green lochan), Uath Lochans (small hawthorn lochs) and Craig Coillich (the witch's rocky hill).

Separate from Gaelic, Scots is the collective name for a range of dialects spoken across Scotland, each with its own character. The North East dialect, widely known as Doric, is spoken in Moray and Aberdeenshire, as well as further south in Angus. You'll often hear Doric words in conversation here, such as 'I ken' ('I know') and 'blether' (chat). You might also see it written: public toilets are occasionally labelled 'loons' for men and 'quines' for women.

For an illustrated introduction to Doric phrases spoken in the North East, check out the superb *Doric for Beginners* by Karen Barrett-Ayres.

NATURE & THE OUTDOORS

Let me level with you: I'm a humongous nature nerd. And this part of Scotland, with its diverse range of habitats, is a natural feast. You can go beach combing, stargazing, forest bathing, dolphin spotting, or simply soak up the views.

Of all the North East's habitats, my favourite is the ancient Caledonian pinewood. This is named after the Roman word for Scotland meaning 'wooded heights': Caledonia. Once widespread across the country, climate change and human intervention have squeezed its range down to the Highlands alone. It's made up of a diverse blend of tree types including Scots pine, birch, juniper and rowan, whose roots are submerged in heather. Some of the Scots pines we see here today are descended from the first pines that colonised the area thousands of years ago.

The Caledonian pinewood once supported bears, wolves, lynx and wild boar – all of which are now lost. Fortunately, it still provides food and shelter for red squirrels, roe deer, pine martens, woodpeckers and the UK's only endemic bird, the Scottish crossbill. Also found in this ancient woodland is the **crested tit**, which has beautiful bridled facial markings and a punky hairdo. Although tricky to spot when they're foraging high in the trees, if you can recognise their distinctive trilling call, you'll realise there are more of them than you might think.

Rarer in the pinewoods is **twinflower** – named for its pairs of delicate bell-shaped pink flowers. Confined to Scotland and mostly found in the North East, their blooms appear in summer and are only a few inches tall, making them even trickier to find than the trilling 'cresties'. Because twinflower is so scarce, their locations are kept secret, but there's no reason why you can't keep an eye out for any peeping up from under the moss.

Another (mostly) Scottish species is the **Scotch argus**, a small brown butterfly with orange splodges, black spots and white pinpricks at the ends of its wings. In August, scan long grass on forest edges and soggy bogs for these understated beauties.

Pine forests in the Cairngorms are one of the only British strongholds for **capercaillie**, the largest grouse in the world. The males are unmistakable, with glossy black bodies, yellow bills and bright red

◀ **1** Bottlenose dolphin. **2** Crested tit. **3** Scotch argus. **4** Twinflower. **5** Capercaillie.

eyebrows; females have subtler brown plumage. In spring, males attempt to win mates by fanning their huge tails as they make whistling and clicking sounds. Habitat loss wiped them out in Scotland in 1785 and birds were reintroduced from Sweden during the 19th century. Sadly, numbers are still dangerously low and they now face extinction a second time. Consider yourself extremely lucky if you see one – even if they weren't so scarce, capercaillie stay deep in the forest and typically avoid people. Keep to the paths and follow guidance during the breeding season to avoid disturbance.

Some of the more dated leaflets and websites about this area will tell you to look out for **Scottish wildcats** too. Britain's last remaining native felid is technically still here, but like the capercaillie they teeter on the brink of extinction and you're more likely to spot a Pictish beastie (page 16).

You will, however, have much greater chances of seeing **bottlenose dolphins**. The Moray Firth bottlenoses are the largest and most northerly in the world, growing up to 13ft long. They can be seen from Moray and Aberdeenshire coastlines at any time of year, although sightings are most numerous from May to September. Particularly good spots to watch from land are Torry Battery in Aberdeen (page 298) and the end of the peninsula at Burghead (page 152).

Minke whales pop up every now and then, but they're not as acrobatic as dolphins so you usually need a spotting scope to see them. In late summer and early autumn, you might be lucky enough to see a **basking shark**. The second largest living fish in the world, they feed solely on microscopic plankton. You can sometimes watch them from land as they cruise through the shallows, their dorsal fins and tail tips poking above the water. Similar to dolphins, one of the best spots to look for minke whales and basking sharks is Burghead (page 152), with its almost 360° views. A good public Facebook group to check out is 📘 **Caithness & Moray Firth Cetacean Sightings**, where members post sightings of whales, dolphins and special visitors such as basking sharks along the Moray Coast.

CAMPING & DOGS

Wild camping is legal in Scotland but there are guidelines that must be followed. Some places don't allow overnight parking so pay close attention to signs when you arrive; Forestry and Land Scotland sites, for example, are for day visitors only.

Many of the forests, lochs and beaches I've listed in this guide are spectacular places to take your dog. They are usually welcome everywhere, although they should be kept on leads around livestock and ground-nesting birds.

Popular camping areas can get overcrowded during summer – if you arrive and can't see for campervans, move on and find a quieter spot. Never light an open fire during dry spells or in sensitive places such as forests. Finally, this should go without saying but sadly it eludes some folk: take all your rubbish away with you. If you're feeling honourable you could consider picking up any other litter you find too. Please leave these beautiful places as you find them, or better.

ON THE WATER

You haven't really swum until you've dipped your toes in an icy loch or sheltered bay, watching waves at eye level and feeling strands of kelp curl around your ankles. Once you've overcome the initial chill, wild swimming is both relaxing and invigorating. North East Scotland provides ample opportunities for aquatic enthusiasts – hire a paddle board and explore Loch Insh from the loch itself (page 57), or embark on a wildlife-watching tour of the Moray Firth on a high-speed RHIB (page 159).

Always wild swim with others and be aware of potential risks from shifting tides, strong currents or obstacles beneath the surface. Know your limits and have warm, dry clothes ready for when you get out. Also be aware that some lochs in this area have **blue-green algae**, which can cause illness to humans and be fatal to dogs if they swim in or drink water contaminated by it. If this is the case, there should be

KNOW THE CODE BEFORE YOU GO

In Scotland, everyone has the right to walk on most land, as long as they act responsibly. It's up to all of us to respect wild places, wild animals, livestock and other people enjoying the outdoors. This is explained fully in the **Scottish Outdoor Access Code** (outdooraccess-scotland.scot), and you'll see these bullet points on a lot of information boards:

- Take responsibility for your own actions
- Respect the interests of other people
- Care for the environment

a sign warning visitors, but it's best to research the current status of a particular site before entering the water.

A WINDOW TO THE PAST

A significant part of the North East's character comes from the influence of its Neolithic and Pictish history (see below). This ancient period in time is largely imprinted across the landscape in the form of burial cairns, hillforts and stone carvings, with nearly 30,000 sites of historical and archaeological interest in Aberdeenshire alone. Many of these are unmarked and have been reclaimed by nature, adding to the intrigue and requiring deeper investigation into their origins.

Burghead on the Moray Coast is considered a 'Pictish Cult Centre' with its Iron Age fort and unique symbol stones, while nearby Sueno's Stone in Forres depicts a Pictish battle. At 21ft, it's the largest stone of its kind in Britain.

As you'll learn, I'm very fond of stone circles and Aberdeenshire has these in abundance. Erected during the Bronze Age, many of them include a huge horizontal stone called a recumbent, with an upright flanker stone on each side. Usually made from rough granite and always coated in lichen, these recumbent monuments are unique to North East Scotland and thought to be linked to the lunar cycle. Often with

WHO WERE THE PICTS?

The Picts were some of the first inhabitants of northern and eastern Scotland from AD300–900. Their name comes from the Roman word *picti* meaning 'painted people', thought to reflect their practice of tattooing and body painting. They are most famous for the symbols they carved into stone, examples of which can be found all over Moray and Aberdeenshire. Some symbols are repeated across multiple sites, with crescents and Z-shaped rods appearing frequently. Animals featured heavily too – look for salmon, eagles, snakes and an unidentified creature known as a **Pictish beastie**. Some say it resembles a dolphin or elephant, but as the other animal symbols are accurately depicted, it's puzzling why the beastie is so ambiguous.

Along with the true meanings behind their intricate carvings, much of the Picts' origins, language and lifestyle remain a mystery. I'm fascinated by the symbol stones and have listed lots of them in this book. If you want to learn more, I recommend these books: *Pagan Symbols of the Picts* by Stuart McHardy, *The Pictish Guide* by Elizabeth Sutherland and *A Wee Guide to the Picts* by Duncan Jones.

open views to the south, stone circles are arranged to align with the moon's position in the sky during midsummer, with the recumbent and flankers acting like a photo frame. I've featured a handful of the best examples in this guide – while some require a short walk, others are right by the road.

Signs of more recent history are evident in the North East too. Various beaches and forests across the region have motte and bailey castle foundations, World War II pillboxes and other military defences sinking into the sand and dissolving into the trees. These make for excellent historical treasure hunts.

A TASTE OF NORTH EAST SCOTLAND

Baxters soup, Walker's shortbread, Aberdeen Angus beef and Mackie's ice cream all come from the North East, but there's far more to this area than these familiar household names. Because of its varied landscape, local food can come from the sea, rivers or farmland without needing to travel far to the plate. Much of Aberdeenshire's land is assigned to agriculture, including the rearing of hardy **Aberdeen Angus** cattle. This breed is highly regarded across the world for the juicy tenderness of its meat, which comes from its evenly distributed marbling. The region's **seafood** is also internationally recognised, with shellfish, mackerel, herring and a range of other seasonal North Sea varieties landed at the major ports of Fraserburgh and Peterhead. One of Scotland's most famous fish dishes originates from the village of Cullen on the Moray Coast (page 18).

Many restaurants across the North East offer seasonal and organic food and you won't roam far without passing a **farm shop** stocked with fresh fruit and veg, homemade preserves and delicious baked goods. One of my favourites is Finzean Farm Shop (page 269) near Banchory. This old converted farm steading sells locally supplied meat and dairy products, as well as gifts created by local artists and craftspeople. Further west near Ballater, The Cambus O'May Cheese & Milk Hoose Café (page 93) has all the tasty treats you expect in a café and also stocks a selection of Scottish artisan cheeses from Cambus O'May Cheese Company, made using traditional methods and family recipes.

Quite a few small-scale shops provide a **refill** element, which is excellent for reducing packaging and discouraging plastic waste. Bring in your own containers and tot up the amounts of pulses, grains, nuts, spices, shampoo and household items you'd like to buy by weight. Examples of these that are well worth a visit are: The Re:Store Moray in Lossiemouth (page 144), Ethical Gift Shop & Refillery in Huntly (page 251) and Butterfly Effect Zero Waste Café & Refillery near Inverurie (page 244).

There are countless other places to buy local produce and I've highlighted more of my favourite independent cafés, zero-waste refilleries and farm shops at each major stopping point throughout the book.

CULLEN SKINK

Made using smoked haddock and potatoes, this thick, creamy soup is one of Scotland's best-known dishes. It originates from Cullen, Moray, where the Cullen Skink World Championships (⚓ cullenskink.com) take place each year. The event features two competitions: cooking traditional Cullen skink and creating Cullen skink with a twist. Competitors have 30 minutes to make their skink, then the judges blind taste and announce the winners later in the day.

Lynne Watson, owner of Lily's Kitchen Café in Cullen (page 179), won the traditional competition in 2018 and was the runner-up in 2020 and 2023. 'The recipe came from my mum,' she says. 'When we started selling it in the café it went down really well, and customers encouraged us to enter.' I highly recommend visiting Lily's Kitchen for a bowl of this delicious soup, especially on a cold day. Lynne has kindly let me share her winning recipe, which makes six to eight portions.

4½ oz salted butter
1 large onion, finely chopped
35 fluid oz milk (semi or skimmed)

10½ fluid oz double cream
12oz smoked haddock
4lb 4oz potatoes.

Melt butter over a low heat. Add onion and cook until soft – low and slow is best.

While the onion is cooking, peel and chop the potatoes into bite-sized pieces. Wash potatoes thoroughly then cook in water until soft.

Once the onion is cooked, add the milk to the pan, and then add the fish to the milk. Season with salt & pepper and cook on a low heat.

When the fish is cooked, add the drained potatoes and then the cream.

Finish with salt & pepper if needed.

Finally, it wouldn't be a taste of the North East without a dram. The word 'whisky' derives from an anglicised version of the Gaelic for 'water of life': *uisge beatha*. Over time this was shortened to *uisge*, pronounced 'oosh-gae'. The most densely populated place in the world for malt whisky distilleries is Moray Speyside, named after the River Spey. Flavours from this area are less peaty than others and often fruity instead. For example, the Glen Grant's 12-year-old single malt is known for its sweet aroma that combines pear, apple and almond, and its 'apple pie crust' taste. Cardhu's 12-year-old single malt is also smooth and fruity, with golden honey traces and hints of wood-smoke.

"Peer into mash tuns, hear historic tales of illicit smuggling and enjoy a dram in stylish comfort."

Many distilleries around here offer tours, where you can see first-hand how whisky is made. Peer into mash tuns, hear historic tales of illicit smuggling and enjoy a dram in stylish comfort. Glenfiddich is probably the most famous, but instead of including this one I've sought out more obscure examples that offer intriguing insights into the region's whisky heritage. The brown-and-white signs for the **Malt Whisky Trail** (maltwhiskytrail.com), the only one in the world, lead the way to additional distilleries across Speyside, from Glenlivet to Forres. Also in Moray is the fantastic Speyside Cooperage (page 111), the only working cooperage in Britain where visitors can watch whisky casks being made by hand.

GETTING THERE & AROUND

Slow travel is best achieved by ditching the car and using public transport or walking. Due to the remoteness of some of the locations I've featured, relying on buses and trains isn't always easy or even possible. I've consciously tried to group sites of interest close to a town or village, so you can either park and walk or bus hop.

CAR

It takes roughly 2½ hours to reach Aberdeen from Glasgow or Edinburgh, and once you've left the M90 at Perth, that's it for motorways. The **A9** in the far west connects towns listed in chapter one; the **A93** passes through Braemar before branching east to Ballater, Aboyne and Banchory; and

Old Military Road continues north towards Tomintoul. On the far east side, the **A90** follows the coast, looping around Aberdeen and ending in Fraserburgh. In Moray, the main road is the **A96**, which follows the train route through Keith, Elgin and Forres.

Aside from getting stuck behind the occasional tractor, you won't encounter much traffic. There's no need to worry about plummeting into potholes either, as the main roads are mostly flawless. Quieter country roads are often single lane with passing places, however, so watch your speed and be prepared to pull in and wait or reverse for oncoming traffic.

Be aware that Scotland has stricter **drink-driving** limits than England, Wales and Northern Ireland. It's best to avoid alcohol completely if you plan to drive anywhere.

CAR HIRE

Aviemore Car & Van Hire ✆ 01479 811700 ◊ aviemorecarhire.co.uk/home.
Enterprise Car & Van Hire Elgin & Aberdeen ◊ enterprise.co.uk.

TRAINS & BUSES

Trains connect London, Manchester, Leeds and Birmingham to Aviemore and Aberdeen, with a changeover at Edinburgh. Those already in Scotland can reach Aberdeen by train from Glasgow, Dundee and Stirling. A pricey but convenient option if you're travelling from London and southern England is to snooze away the travel time on the **Caledonian Sleeper** (◊ sleeper.scot); the Inverness branch stops at Aviemore.

Each chapter begins with a summary of public transport services in that particular area. Local **train** services are mostly run by Scotrail and cover the perimeter of the North East, providing easy access to most major towns. The Inverness to Aberdeen service connects Forres, Elgin, Keith, Huntly, Insch, Inverurie, Kintore and Dyce, while the Inverness to Perth service stops at Carrbridge, Aviemore, Kingussie, Newtonmore and Dalwhinnie. Another train runs to Aberdeen from Dundee, stopping at Stonehaven. Aside from these, the only trains are the steam-powered **Strathspey Railway** in Aviemore (page 33) and the

---

1 The Moray Coast Path. **2** Cycling in Pennan. **3** Aberdeen Angus cattle grazing.
4 Cullen skink. ▶

Dufftown & Keith Heritage Railway (page 110), both of which are excellent fun.

Megabus (⊘ uk.megabus.com) services connect Aberdeen to numerous destinations across the UK including London, Manchester and Birmingham. The main local bus provider is Stagecoach, and you can find maps and timetables for a range of towns and villages on their website (⊘ stagecoachbus.com).

WALKING & CYCLING

Walkers will find countless options here, from long-distance routes (see below) to simple morning strolls. Throughout the book I've featured several shorter walks that only take a couple of hours but still cover a range of habitats and features of interest. This diversity is one of the region's finest attributes: on the coast in particular you'll often pass woodland, grassland and open country as well as sandy beaches and rocky shores, all offering their own distinctive views and wildlife. Because so many forests are coniferous, fallen pine needles soak up moisture and the ground is rarely boggy. Energetic sea breezes can change the weather quickly, so pack a bit of everything and you'll be covered.

The great thing about outdoor access in Scotland (page 15) is you can walk almost anywhere as long as you're respectful of your surroundings. I find Open Street Map (⊘ openstreetmap.org) helpful as you can zoom right in and see all the hatched footpath lines.

The North East is webbed with long-distance trails that connect many of the towns and villages I've mentioned in this book, although of course you can pick and choose which segments you take on rather than attempting the whole route. I recommend the **Moray Coast Trail** in particular. Beginning inland in Forres, this 44-mile route passes through Findhorn, Burghead and Lossiemouth before finishing in Cullen. It features sandy beaches, unusual rock stacks and dramatic cliffs, but you can sample all of these within just a few miles so, again, there's no need to walk its entirety.

Other long-distance trails include (distances in brackets are for one way):

- Dava Way (Grantown-on-Spey to Forres; 23 miles)
- Deeside Way (Aberdeen to Ballater; 41 miles)

TICKS

Something to be aware of when you're out walking or camping, particularly from March to October, is **ticks**. If they latch on to skin, these spider-like insects can pass on diseases to humans including Lyme disease, but don't panic too much. Most ticks are harmless and if you remove them as soon as you can, they're usually just an inconvenience.

Primarily you should avoid walking through long grass, which is advisable anyway to prevent disturbing any ground-nesting birds. You're also less likely to pick up a tick if you tuck your trousers in your socks. It's a strong look but worth it.

Some chemists and pet shops sell tick removers – an invaluable piece of kit to stick in your rucksack. For more information, check out **NHS Inform** (⊘ nhsinform.scot/illnesses-and-conditions/injuries/skin-injuries/tick-bites).

- Isla Way (Keith to Dufftown; 13 miles)
- Speyside Way (Aviemore to Buckie; 65 miles)

Cyclists will also find lots of variety. National Cycle Routes 1, 7 and 195 cross into the region – for more details on these, visit ⊘ sustrans.org.uk. **Mountain bikers** should check out Laggan Wolftrax (page 69), Moray Monster Trails (page 126) and Tarland Trails (page 260) for routes of varying difficulty. If you'd prefer something more leisurely, many trails along the coast and within nature reserves have flat forest paths or smooth tarmac, perfect for bump-free cycling.

CYCLE HIRE

Backcountry Biking, Aviemore Granish Way, PH22 1UQ ✆ 01479 811829 ⊘ backcountry.scot.

Bike Glenlivet ⅲ assurance.yacht.pass ✆ 07963 217793 ✉ info@bikeglenlivet.co.uk ▮ Glenlivet Mountain Bike Trail Centre.

Bike Station Ballater Station Sq, AB35 5RB ✆ 01339 754004 ⊘ bikestationballater.co.uk ◷ 10.00–16.30 daily.

Bothy Bikes High St, Kingussie PH21 1HZ ✆ 01540 667111 ⊘ bothybikes.co.uk ◷ closed Wed & Sat.

Dufftown & District Community Association ⊘ dufftowncommunity.co.uk/community-type/bikes ✉ hello@dufftowncommunity.co.uk.

Outfit Moray Shore St, Lossiemouth IV31 6PB ✆ 01343 549571 ⊘ outfitmoray.com/bike-hire.

Wee Bike Hub High St, Kingussie PH21 1HX ✆ 01528 544751 ▮ ◷ Mon–Sat.

HOW TO USE THIS BOOK

The book consists of eight regional chapters. As the Cairngorm mountain range naturally divides the National Park in two down the middle, I've separated the populated areas into **East** and **West**. I've divided Moray horizontally, focussing on Speyside in **Central Moray** and giving the frankly glorious **Moray Coast** its own chapter. Aberdeenshire is already split into administrative areas, so I've grouped these into the following four chapters: **The Northeast Coast & Buchan**, **Formartine & The Garioch**, **Marr** and **Aberdeen City & Stonehaven**.

I certainly wouldn't recommend trying to visit all of this in one trip. Each chapter could easily fill a week or more if you're travelling Slow style – an excellent excuse to keep coming back.

OPENING HOURS

I've listed opening times for museums, shops and cafés where they differ from the standard 09.00–17.00. However, as many are run by only a handful of staff, or don't open during low season at all, these times are

TOP FIVE NATURE RESERVES

The following nature sites (listed in chapter order) really resonated with me, either for their natural beauty, historical significance or the fact they require a little rummaging to find.

1. **Muir of Dinnet** Just a few miles outside Ballater, the trails at this diverse nature reserve connect woodland, Loch Kinord, sprinklings of ancient history and a towering granite fish bowl slick with soggy bracken (page 91).

2. **Randolph's Leap** This Site of Special Scientific Interest (SSSI) on the River Findhorn has a sensational gorge, where narrow footpaths ring with the roar of white water below (page 130).

3. **Findhorn Bay** One of the best places in the North East to see both common and grey seals. Depending on the tide, they might be bobbing in the shallows or hauled out on the beach, singing their ghostly song (page 162).

4. **Troup Head** An RSPB clifftop reserve home to thousands of nesting seabirds during summer, including Scotland's largest mainland gannet colony (page 195).

5. **Forvie** Often compared to the Sahara Desert, this coastal reserve north of Aberdeen is most famous for its vast shifting sand dunes (page 220).

often subject to change. On multiple occasions I've staggered back from a hike, looking forward to a slab of cake, only to find café doors locked. If you're desperate to visit somewhere particular, I suggest calling ahead to check the most up-to-date opening hours.

ACCOMMODATION & EATING OUT

Throughout the book, I've given my recommendations for cafés, pubs and restaurants within the corresponding town or village. These range from places to get mid-morning coffee to a proper evening meal after a long day exploring. My student thriftiness has never left me so I always look for good value. I've deliberately searched for spots that offer interesting vegetarian options too. Vegans might struggle in remote areas, but it's slowly getting better. I hope one day it will be as easy to find falafel and tofu here as it is macaroni cheese and steak pies, of which there is no shortage.

Accommodation options are listed under the heading for the area in which they are located: hotels and B&Bs are indicated by 🏠, self-catering by 🏡 and camping by ⛺. Each place has been chosen for its location and the quality of its service and facilities. Further information can be found in the accommodation chapter at the end of the book and also at ⊘ bradtguides.com/nessleeps.

MAPS

At the start of every chapter is a map with numbers corresponding to the numbered headings within that section. Listing postcodes for remote sites usually doesn't help, so in these instances I've provided **what3words** (▦) codes instead. What3words gives every three metre square in the world a unique three-word code to pinpoint its exact location. Download the free app and you can plot your own locations and follow the ones I've suggested on an interactive map. It's handy when trying to describe where a stone cairn is in a 50,000-acre estate, for example.

Interspersed throughout the book are sketch maps outlining walking routes with numbered directions, which should point the way clearly enough without the need for an official map. As this is a hefty chunk of Scotland, you'd need a stack of OS Landranger maps to cover it all. However, if you're looking for that 1:50,000 detail and clarity, the following numbers would be useful: 28 (Elgin & Dufftown), 29 (Banff &

Huntly), 30 (Fraserburgh), 35 (Kingussie & Monadhliath Mountains), 36 (Grantown & Aviemore), 37 (Strathdon & Alford), 38 (Aberdeen), 43 (Braemar & Blair Atholl), 44 (Ballater & Glen Clova) and 45 (Stonehaven & Banchory).

FURTHER READING

I found the following books helpful while researching this guide, and they will provide more information about the places I've covered if you're keen to learn more: *Exploring Badenoch* by John Barton, *The Guide to Mysterious Aberdeen* by Geoff Holder, *Women of Moray* by Susan Bennett et al. and *Moray Coast: From Cullen to Culbin Through Time* by Jenny Main.

FEEDBACK REQUEST

At Bradt Guides we're aware that guidebooks start to go out of date on the day they're published – and that you, our readers, are out there in the field doing research of your own. You'll find out before us when a fine new family-run hotel opens or a favourite restaurant changes hands and goes downhill. So why not tell us about your experiences? Contact us on ✆ 01753 893444 or ✉ info@bradtguides.com. We will forward emails to the author who may post updates on the Bradt website at ⏃ bradtguides.com/updates. Alternatively, you can add a review of the book to Amazon, or share your adventures with us on social:

🗗 BradtGuides & RebeccaOnTheWing ⬛ BradtGuides & rebeccaonthewing
🗗 BradtGuides & beccaonthewing

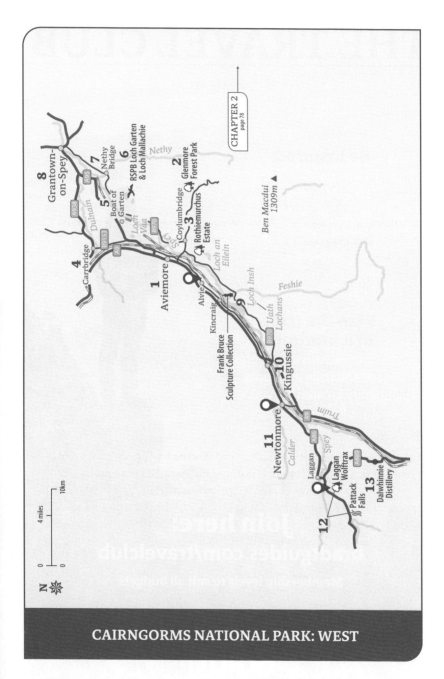

CAIRNGORMS NATIONAL PARK: WEST

1
CAIRNGORMS NATIONAL PARK: WEST

Think of the Cairngorms, and no doubt mountains will come to mind first. You might also think of Scottish writer Nan Shepherd, whose hillwalking memoir *The Living Mountain* chronicles her explorations of Cairngorms wildlife, weather and scenery. Although hulking summits form a large chunk of this multi-faceted national park, with its overlapping layers of river, lochan, pine and peak, you don't need crampons and an ice axe to be fully immersed in the landscape here.

Right by the roadside, stone bridges now as delicate as pie crusts curl over icy water clearer than glass. A ten-minute walk will take you to the banks of lochs where dragonflies stir a near-perfect reflection of the pines beyond. The first snow usually arrives in late autumn; a light dusting that becomes a cotton-wool coat soon after, lingering all year round at the tips of those bulky summits. In summer, weak sunlight flashes on rugs of heather and evergreens that look like model railway decorations from afar.

As you might expect in such a varied environment, the natural world is just as diverse. Rothiemurchus and Abernethy Forests have some of the last remnants of ancient Caledonian pinewood in the country, home to many of Scotland's defining animals. Pine martens (cat-sized ferrets) and capercaillie (huge woodland grouse) are elusive and rarely seen, although the thought that one might be peering down at you from the canopy makes a woodland walk here that bit more exciting. In contrast, red squirrels are frequently spotted bending branches as they forage and fumble, and even if you can't see crested tits, you'll often hear them trilling overhead.

The main town in this western half of the national park is Aviemore, which offers visitors a high street lined with shops and restaurants. It mostly acts as a base for walkers, skiers and mountain climbers heading into the nearby hills, but it also has a forested nature reserve, farm shop, steam railway and miniature stone circle within walking distance. Some 13 miles southwest, the neighbouring towns of Kingussie and Newtonmore harbour a fierce rivalry when it comes to shinty, a Scottish Highland sport similar to field hockey.

Other small towns and villages each have their own uniqueness. In Carrbridge you can watch competitors battle it out to create the most impressive wood carving and the best porridge. Near Boat of Garten, you can embrace your inner Disney princess and hand-feed wild birds close to the loch where ospreys began breeding in Scotland again, nearly four decades after they were hunted to extinction. Spend a whole day ambling around tree-lined lochans or sipping gin infused with botanicals foraged just a short walk from the distillery. It's easy to travel Slow here.

GETTING AROUND

Most of the towns and villages in this chapter make a dot-to-dot along the A9 – the longest road in Scotland – which is joined by the A95 in the northeast and the A86 to the southwest. Veering off the main road takes you to single-lane roads with passing places for navigating oncoming traffic, but these quieter lanes are generally in good condition and have the best scenery. Charge points for electric cars can be found at Grampian Road car park in Aviemore, Boat of Garten Community Hall, the Speyside Centre and Gynack Road car park in Kingussie.

TRAINS
Scotrail services from Inverness stop at Carrbridge, Aviemore, Kingussie, Newtonmore and Dalwhinnie before heading into Perthshire. Trains between Inverness and London's Kings Cross stop at Aviemore and Kingussie. There's also the Strathspey Railway from Aviemore (page 33), which makes the short out-and-back journey to Nethy Bridge via Boat of Garten.

BUSES
From Aviemore, the Stagecoach 37 connects Boat of Garten, Nethy Bridge, Grantown-on-Spey and Carrbridge on its way to Inverness; conveniently, this service also goes to Glenmore and Cairngorm car park. The 39 bus travels south from Aviemore to Kingussie and Newtonmore.

ℹ **TOURIST INFORMATION**

Aviemore iCentre Grampian Rd, PH22 1RH ✆ 01479 810930 ✉ aviemoreTIC@ visitscotland.com

Grantown Museum Burnfield Ave, PH26 3HH ✆ 01479 872478 ✉ dan@ grantownmuseum.co.uk

Caberfeidh Horizons High St, Kingussie PH21 1HR ✆ 01540 661000 ✉ caberfeidh.horizons@gmail.org

Speyside Centre Skye of Curr Rd, Grantown-on-Spey PH26 3PA ✆ 01479 851359 ✉ info@ speysidecentre.com

Aside from Glenmore, most remote locations included in this chapter aren't accessible by bus so you'll need a car or bike to reach them.

CYCLING

National Cycle Route 7 comes in at Carrbridge and travels all the way through the national park, sticking close to the A9. Another popular long-distance route around here is the **Speyside Way**, which connects Aviemore and Grantown-on-Spey before heading into Moray. The 23-mile **Dava Way** starts in Grantown and finishes in Forres on the Moray Coast. Many of the waymarked trails in locations such as Abernethy, Rothiemurchus and Anagach Woods are suitable for cyclists.

🚴 **CYCLE HIRE**

Backcountry Biking Granish Way, Aviemore PH22 1UQ ✆ 01479 811829 ⬦ backcountry. scot. Mountain-bike hire, repair shop, training courses and multi-day bikepacking tours.

Bothy Bikes High St, Kingussie PH21 1HZ ✆ 01540 667111 ⬦ bothybikes.co.uk ⏱ Sun– Tue, Thu & Fri. E-bikes for daily hire, plus repairs and a range of bikes, accessories and clothing for sale.

Wee Bike Hub High St, Kingussie PH21 1HX ✆ 01528 544751 ◼ ⏱ Mon–Sat. Bike hire, repairs and road and mountain bikes and accessories for sale.

WALKING

Because a lot of the more remote locations in this chapter aren't covered by public transport, for day walks it's best to follow circular or out-and-back routes that return to the starting point. Many of the forests and lochs are managed by Forestry and Land Scotland so already have a selection of waymarked routes of varying lengths. I've also given directions for the Wildcat Trail (page 70) – an easy-going walk looping for six miles around Newtonmore and taking in a range of habitats. Shorter highlighted walks include a four-mile incline to Dun da Lamh Pictish fort (page 74) and a three-mile walk through Torr Alvie (page 58), taking in several features of historical interest.

AVIEMORE & AROUND

Aviemore is roughly in the middle of the western half of the Cairngorms National Park and is well-equipped in terms of shops and places to eat, making it a logical place to start your explorations. From here, all sorts of nature, history and local food can be found within an eight-mile radius. Swathes of pine forest flecked with concealed lochans give this area a decidedly green and blue colour scheme, although their waters are muddied by the presence of a villainous earl that prowled here in the 14th century.

1 AVIEMORE

🏠 **Ravenscraig Guest House** (page 316) 🏨 **Aviemore Youth Hostel** (page 317)

Practically everywhere in the Cairngorms is described as sitting at its 'heart' – no matter the size or location – but Aviemore could justify that name because it's so handily located for walks and surrounding villages. While it has some of its own attractions, the town is mainly useful for

THE CUL-DE-SAC STONE CIRCLE

At only 40ft in diameter, this is the smallest of the stone circles I've featured in this book and it made the cut because of its unusual location. It's a Clava cairn, a type of chambered burial cairn found exclusively in the area east of Inverness. Today you can only see the ring of stones that form the outer kerb of the cairn, the largest of which is 3ft tall. The inner kerb is mostly concealed beneath the grass.

According to the weather-worn plaque, it's believed this gathering place was established by farmers around 4,000 years ago. It may contain cremated human remains, suggesting it had significant ceremonial value. Now flanked by houses, it's lost a little of its mystique, but its location makes it easily accessible for a quick visit. To get here from the centre of town, head north along Grampian Road and turn right on to Muirton. After the fire station, take the left turning opposite the health centre and you'll see the stone circle 80yds further down.

hikers stocking up on supplies before heading into the wild – as shown by the outdoor shops lining its main street, Grampian Road. However, there's no denying that the steam railway departing from the station here is a huge draw, especially for impressionable young witches and wizards in the making.

Aviemore may be mostly a practical stop-off point, but I do like the juxtaposition of carrying your shopping out of Tesco beneath the shadow of Craigellachie's bumpy hills, or admiring a centuries-old burial cairn in a residential street. Because so many active, outdoorsy folk spend time here, there's an energetic and bustling feel that's quite infectious. Seeing mountains peeking over the tops of its hotels and shops makes you want to get out there and see it all.

One of Aviemore's highlights is the **Strathspey Railway** (Dalfaber Rd ✐ 01479 810725 ✐ strathspeyrailway.co.uk ☉ Mar–Oct plus Christmas events Nov & Dec w/ends; check website for specific running days). Running beside Scotrail trains at Aviemore Station, this steam locomotive with burgundy carriages looks remarkably like the Hogwarts Express. It follows a section of the 19th-century Highland Railway line, which once connected Perth to Inverness and further north into the Highlands and

"Seeing mountains peeking over the tops of its hotels and shops makes you want to get out there and see it all."

was restored by volunteers in 1978. In just over 45 minutes, it journeys to Broomhill (near Nethy Bridge), via Boat of Garten.

In addition to standard journeys, dining is also available while you trundle along the tracks. Lunch tickets include return travel with soup, sandwiches and hot drinks, while afternoon tea offers finger sandwiches, scones, cakes and a mini bottle of Prosecco. I indulged in this right before Christmas – while slathering clotted cream on scones, I watched the steam billowing in front of snow-covered mountains. Every carriage has a vintage feel, but for a genuine *Harry Potter* experience I suggest treating yourself to first class tickets, where you have your own cosy compartment with sliding doors. Chocolate frogs not included.

Dogs can come onboard for £1 each, although not in first class or dining areas (except assistance dogs). There is no extra charge for bikes, but space is limited so book ahead for this. Conveniently for walkers, the railway line runs parallel to the **Speyside Way**, so it's possible to take the train one way and walk the other, exploring woodland, heathland and the River Spey at an even slower pace.

Craigellachie National Nature Reserve

Parking: Aviemore Youth Hostel, PH22 1PR ⌖ nature.scot

Accessible on foot from Aviemore and bordering the whole west side of town, Craigellachie National Nature Reserve (NNR) contains open glades, lochans, heathland, craggy hills and one of the biggest patches of birch woodland left in Strathspey. Its name comes from the Gaelic *Creag Eileachaidh*, meaning 'crag of the rocky place'. The crag is one of the reserve's key features, occasionally attracting breeding **peregrine falcons**.

There's something to see here no matter the season. Spring is best for woodland flowers, while dragonflies and butterflies are on the wing in summer. Birch trees zing with vibrant autumn colours and fungi emerges in full force as the temperature cools. Winter is quieter, but at this time you can savour white mountains from the viewpoint.

The reserve can be explored on four interlinked, colour-coded trails (see website for details). The half-mile Lochan Trail is the shortest, looping around the western half of Loch Puladdern and back through birch woodland. Herons can be seen here, though its proximity to the A9 means it struggles to feel tranquil. For quieter water views, continue west on either the Buzzard or Woodland trail and you'll reach the more picturesque **reservoir**, where crags and silver birches are reflected in the water.

"Birch trees zing with vibrant autumn colours and fungi emerges in full force as the temperature cools."

The longest route is the 2¾-mile out-and-back **Viewpoint Trail**, which passes a flat, open area with views over Aviemore. A little way up from here is an exposed cairn backed by surrounding hills that are often diluted by mist. Beyond the cairn, Lochan Dubh lies among bunches of heather and rocks covered in zesty green lichen. Watch your step along the last section of this trail – shortly before the cairn, the path consists of whatever cracks you can find between boulders. For those like me who prefer mountains in miniature that only take a couple of hours to leisurely climb, this is a rewarding option.

1 The Strathspey Railway. **2** Craigellachie NNR. **3** Loch an Eilein. **4** Loch Morlich. ▶

The reserve entrance is at the southern end of Aviemore. You can park in the youth hostel car park beside the reserve, but cars mustn't be left here overnight. From this car park, follow a narrow trail on foot away from the main road and into a pocket of woodland. When a caravan park appears on your left, continue uphill to a tubular underpass beneath the A9. The reserve begins on the other side.

¶ FOOD & DRINK

Alvie Forest Food Dalraddy Holiday Park, PH22 1QB 🆚 ☉ check Facebook for times. A small street-food kitchen incorporating seasonal ingredients that have been foraged and reared on the Alvie and Dalraddy Estates. The core menu offers burgers, wraps, loaded fries and dessert of the day, plus daily specials.

The Balavoulin Grampian Rd, PH22 1RL ✐ 01479 812255 ⊘ thebalavoulin.co.uk ☉ daily; hours vary. Don't be put off by any football matches playing on the TV – this bar and restaurant has a relaxed, family-friendly atmosphere. Great food is served every day, sourced from local suppliers like Balliefurth Farm Shop in Nethy Bridge and Pro Fish in Aviemore. There are also seven rooms available as B&B accommodation.

Cairngorm Hotel Grampian Rd, PH22 1PE ✐ 01479 810233 ⊘ cairngorm.com ☉ lunch noon–17.00; dinner from 17.00. Directly opposite the train station, this hotel and restaurant draws the eye with its beige and peach stone walls, sash windows and ornamental cresting. The interior is warmly lit by antler light pieces. Lunch includes light bites and sandwiches, while the dinner menu features a range of classic favourites with intriguing twists. Not a cheap option but excellent for a special meal.

The Old Bridge Inn Dalfaber Rd, PH22 1PU ✐ 01479 811137 ⊘ oldbridgeinn.co.uk ☉ lunch noon–14.15 Thu–Tue; dinner 17.00–20.30 daily. Close to Craigellachie NNR, this rustic pub has candle lighting, exposed beams and heavy wooden tables. It's not the cheapest place to eat, but the menu is small and thoughtfully chosen, with good options for vegetarians and vegans. Dogs are allowed in the lounge area. Booking recommended.

Rowan Tree Country Hotel & Restaurant Loch Alvie PH22 1QB ✐ 01479 810207 ⊘ rowantreehotel.com. Located 2½ miles southwest of Aviemore, this is not the sort of place you'd rock up to in your muddy boots, but if you're looking for some fine dining in countryside surroundings it's a good option. Serves local Scottish produce in both traditional and more modern dishes. Guest rooms and campervan pitches also available.

The Winking Owl Pub & Bar Grampian Rd, PH22 1RH ✐ 01479 812368 ⊘ thewinkingowl.co ☉ from noon Wed–Mon. Known as 'The Winky', this dog-friendly bar serves dishes made with a range of local ingredients, such as seafood from Sutherlands of Portsoy, meat from Balliefurth and beer from the Cairngorm Brewery, just a mile away.

Its claim to fame is that poet Robert Burns breakfasted in the building in 1787, although somehow I don't think he referred to it as The Winky.

2 GLENMORE FOREST PARK

/// essay.accusing.sleepers ⊘ forestryandland.gov.scot

Glenmore is a microcosm of the Cairngorms National Park. Within its boundary are gnarled old pines, lochs bordered by crunchy golden sand and mountains dabbed with snow for most of the year. Many people come through here for longer hikes – the Sugarbowl car park at its southeast edge has routes branching off for various hills and ravines, and Cairngorm Mountain Base Station is situated two miles further down the road.

> "Within its boundary are gnarled old pines, lochs bordered by crunchy golden sand and mountains dabbed with snow."

For more leisurely walks, Glenmore's central hub is its **Visitor Centre** (use the what3words code above to locate). It lies six miles east of Aviemore, beside the road connecting Rothiemurchus and Cairngorm Mountain Car Park. This is a good place to start, with a café and information displays setting the scene and a number of waymarked walking trails beginning from here.

Across the road from the centre is **Loch Morlich**, a blue-grey hollow in the centre of the doughnut-shaped forest. You can explore it from a unique perspective by hiring canoes, kayaks, paddle boards and rowboats by the hour from Loch Morlich Watersports (⊘ lochmorlich. com/hire), at the water's edge. The beach is a picturesque picnic spot but water sports are popular here; both the loch and the adjacent pay and display visitor centre car park can get very busy at the height of summer. Other car parks dotted throughout Glenmore (including several around the loch's perimeter) provide easier access to different parts of the park. Hayfield is attached to a short woodland loop that overlaps with the 3½-mile circular trail around Loch Morlich. Allt Mor car park is a little further south but not as far as the Sugarbowl, and links to one of the more mysterious lochans in the Cairngorms.

Yes, it's pretty famous, but I had to feature **An Lochan Uaine** because it's just magical – and I don't use that word lightly. Its name means 'green loch' in Gaelic and it really is green. Even on an overcast day, it glimmers a dark, almost emerald hue. Spoilsports say this is caused by algae, but the more imaginative believe it's where fairies wash their green clothes.

To get there, follow the blue waymarked **Ryvoan Trail** from the visitor centre. This 3½-mile circular passes ancient trees and murmuring streams and the approach is just as rewarding as the destination. As it's a circular, there are two routes to the lochan, with the path forking just east of the visitor centre. One leads straight on as a flat path suitable for bikes and wheelchairs. The other bears left to follow more interesting but trickier terrain, with narrower paths and a steep stone staircase at the end. I recommend choosing this route for the way out, because descending those rocky steps is a lot easier on the thighs than climbing back up them!

After about 20 minutes along this more uneven path, a steep gully opens up on your right, with sprawling hill views. The trees vary from stumpy spruces to hulking pines. As the path narrows and becomes rockier, pines are joined by silver birches, surrounded by primroses and violets in warmer months. Keep an eye out for coal tits, dunnocks and bullfinches.

At the bottom of the stone steps, cross a short wooden bridge and the lochan appears ahead. Head down a short flight of stone steps and you can perch by the water's edge, watching mallards stirring the green surface.

The return route is a wide, flat gravel path that becomes a compacted earth track running past Glenmore Lodge (a training centre for outdoor courses). This trail is the **Old Logging Way** and if you continue following it past the visitor centre you will reach Aviemore after five miles.

The Stagecoach 37 bus stops outside Glenmore Visitor Centre on its route from Aviemore to Cairngorm Car Park.

3 ROTHIEMURCHUS ESTATE

Owned by the Grant family for 18 generations, the sprawling Rothiemurchus Estate consists of nearly 40 square miles of woodland, mountains, lochs, rivers and glens. The northern part of the estate is the most easily accessed, from several points just south of Aviemore. All forests in the Cairngorms look slightly different and the one at Rothiemurchus is distinctive because of the shape of its trees. Instead of standing uniformly straight like those in Abernethy (page 48), with few branches until halfway up the trunks, the pines here have dozens of limbs, often curled and twisting. Similarly, the birches are furry with lichen and grow in every direction. Many of the trees in this estate are over a hundred years old and some are three times that: this is one of the largest surviving areas of **ancient Caledonian pinewood** left in Europe. With age, the trees here have gained originality in their size, shape and texture.

Sadly, these remaining pockets of ancient forest are a tiny representation of the extensive pinewoods that grew here thousands of years ago. When you're in the Cairngorms, it's easy to think that Scotland is packed with trees, but in fact the percentage of Scottish tree cover trails behind the European average by almost 30%. While that might feel a little doom and gloom, harsh perspectives reinforce the fact that the granny pines of Rothiemurchus must be respected. Some of them stood here when the last Scottish wolves were being hunted to extinction in the 17th century, and it's a privilege to be able to walk beneath them now.

"During a visit in December I was offered a cup of mulled wine – one of the many reasons walking is better than driving!"

Rothiemurchus Estate's famous loch is **Loch an Eilein**. Its name means 'loch of the island' in Gaelic, which is self-explanatory once you see the 14th-century castle stranded in the middle of the water – one of the Wolf of Badenoch's many homes (page 40). Jacobite troops attacked the castle following the Battle of Cromdale in 1690. At that time, it was mainly occupied by women, children and the elderly and they fought valiantly. It's said the Laird's wife, Grizel Mor (Big Grace), made lead musket balls and yelled abuse at the enemy.

Now the castle is a peaceful ruin and you might see goldeneye ducks swimming around it or ospreys flying over in summer. Its glassy surface makes it a popular spot for photographers. A three-mile circular loops all the way round its banks and you can stop for a drink at the tiny **visitor centre** on the northern edge. During a visit in December I was offered a cup of mulled wine – one of the many reasons walking is better than driving!

To get to Loch an Eilein from Aviemore, head south out of town then follow the B970 east, continuing on this road when it turns right just before Rothiemurchus Centre (page 41). There's a small car park on this junction (▥ waggled.condition.tidy ☉ 08.30–17.00), handy for accessing footpaths in the northern part of the forest that eventually reach the loch from the other direction. However, for quicker access, carry on the B970 for one mile then turn left at the

THE WOLF OF BADENOCH

With the nickname and reputation of a *Game of Thrones* villain, the Wolf of Badenoch was the better-known name of Alexander Stewart (born 1343), Earl of Buchan and son of King Robert II. With power came cruelty – Alexander was a tyrant, sacking settlements throughout the Highlands and imprisoning or murdering anyone who got on his nerves. He had a handful of castle strongholds including Ruthven, later the site of Ruthven Barracks (page 64), Drumin (page 101) and Lochindorb, just outside the national park boundary.

Alexander married Euphemia, the Countess of Ross, in 1382. This tactical match increased his wealth and control, but resulted in no children. Euphemia was blamed for this, as Alexander had already fathered some 40 illegitimate children.

By 1389, he had deserted his wife in favour of his favourite mistress, Mariota Mackay. The bishops of Moray and Ross demanded that Alexander return to Euphemia. He agreed, but didn't. Because of her husband's extra-marital relationship with Mariota, Euphemia was heavily backed during divorce proceedings and her marriage was annulled. This was a blow for Alexander, who thus lost his grip on all of Euphemia's lands and wealth. In retaliation, he journeyed east from Lochindorb, sacking the town of Forres on his way to Elgin. There, he burned most of the town and destroyed the Bishop of Moray's seat, Elgin Cathedral.

Any satisfaction Alexander found in this revenge was short-lived. Violence against a church was unforgivable, and he was punished with excommunication. Sources differ on whether he died in 1394 or 1405, depending on how much you believe in ghost stories. Legend has it that, on whichever night he met his maker, he was visited by the Devil and the pair played chess. The following morning, the Wolf was found dead without a mark on his body. He was buried in Dunkeld Cathedral in Perthshire.

brown sign. Another mile later, you'll arrive at the loch's car park (▥ birdcage.betrayed.riskiest).

Unsurprisingly for such a picturesque spot, Loch an Eilein can get busy – nearby **Lochan Mor** promises a much quieter walk. Starting from Loch an Eilein's car park, walk back up the road with the burn on your left. Continue north for half a mile until you reach Milton Cottage. Beside the cottage is a narrow track leading into Rothiemurchus Forest. After the path bends to the right, you'll soon glimpse Lochan Mor between the trees. Also called the **Lily Loch**, after the waterlilies that dot its surface in summer, it's a less-trodden spot where herons prod the reeds and roe deer rustle low-hanging branches. From here you can venture deeper into the forest or loop around the lochan and return the way you came.

ACTIVITIES

Just over a mile southeast of Aviemore, the **Rothiemurchus Centre** (PH22 1QH ⌖ rothiemurchus.net/outdoor-activities-at-aviemore) hosts a range of outdoor activities including quad biking, deer feeding, Highland pony trekking and Hairy Coo Safaris. A working farm produces beef and venison on-site from home-reared Highland cattle and red deer, which can be purchased at the farm shop (see below).

🍴 FOOD & DRINK

Rothiemurchus Farm Shop (⊙ 09.45–16.30 daily in summer; Thu–Mon in winter) is focussed on ethical farming and low food miles. It contains a cheese and deli counter, gift shop, card shop, locally made drinks, honeys, jams, dairy products and homeware. You can also purchase hampers, veg boxes and recipe-meal kits online. Next door to the farm shop is **The Barn** (⊙ same hours), a small cabin café kept toasty by a wood burner. Pop in for filled rolls, soup, stews, homemade specials and hot drinks. Dogs are welcome in a designated section of the café.

CARRBRIDGE TO GRANTOWN-ON-SPEY: THE NORTHWEST CAIRNGORMS

North of Aviemore is a cluster of smaller towns and villages that all have trees in common, whether it's the tiny community woodland within Boat of Garten or the vast expanse of Abernethy Forest south of Nethy Bridge. These forested pockets are visible even from the narrow high streets lined with irregular stone-built houses, looking like beige versions of Mondrian paintings. Grantown-on-Spey is the largest settlement in this section, but even here nature is a big influencer, with sprawling Anagach Woods along its east side and wildlife guided holidays on offer at the bird-themed Grant Arms Hotel.

4 CARRBRIDGE

With the A938 and B9153 forming a T shape through its centre, Carrbridge could be unfairly disregarded as a place just to drive through on your way south to Aviemore. At first glance, it looks like there isn't much here besides a small green and The Croft Café (⌀ 07729 284422 ⓕ). Of the villages in this section, Carrbridge has the most variety for a visitor in autumn in particular, when its yearly competitions for wood

carving and porridge-making draw huge crowds. During the rest of the year, it's a peaceful place to stroll through pine woodland next to the River Dulnain, or hunt for the assortment of wood carvings dotted around the village.

On Main Street is **Carrbridge Artists Studio** (🖉 01479 841247 🖉 carrbridgestudios.com ☉ 11.00–17.00 Tue–Fri, 10.00–14.00 Sat). This workshop and gallery space showcases the work of Jeff Buttress, his wife Alice and daughter Amy. Here you can take your pick of greetings cards, sculptures, bowls, prints and handmade porcelain jewellery. Jeff was working on some ceramic art behind the till when I visited; he sketches and paints directly onto handmade square tiles and frames them in rows like a thumbnail panorama. The finished Raku-fired tiles have a metallic sheen to them – I particularly love the rusty red sunsets.

One of the village's main attractions is the **Old Packhorse Bridge** at its northern end. You get a great view of it from the road bridge on Main Street, but for a closer look, descend a wooden staircase just off this road to a viewing platform. Built in 1717, this is the oldest stone bridge in the Highlands and certainly looks it. It's barely more than a few inches thick between the perfectly even inner edge of the yawning arch and the outer edge, now crumbled and fuzzy with moss.

"It's now no longer a functioning bridge but an intriguing and frequently photographed component of the river landscape."

You'll hear the rush of the treacle-coloured River Dulnain before the bridge is even in sight, but this is a trickle compared to the decimating effects of the **Muckle Spate** of 1829. This catastrophic flood swept through the North East and was regarded as one of the most severe in Britain's history. The bridge's parapets and side walls had already been damaged in the 1700s, and a combination of this and the Muckle Spate has reduced it to its current fragile condition. It's now no longer a functioning bridge but an intriguing and frequently photographed component of the river landscape of Carrbridge.

In the centre of the village, in front of the green, you'll see a miniature version of the Packhorse Bridge that commemorates the original's 300th anniversary. This was Alice and Jeff Buttress's (see above) first major

◀ CARRBRIDGE: **1** Artists Studio on Main Street. **2** An owl carving. **3** Old Packhorse Bridge. **4** The Golden Spurtle World Porridge Making Championships.

collaboration and is one of Carrbridge's most spectacular carvings. Commissioned in 2017, **Bridge 300** is a bench between two wooden pillars, decorated with a roe deer, red squirrel, capercaillie and a swooping osprey on top. Stepping slowly around it, I couldn't find an inch of wood that hadn't been sculpted.

Throughout Carrbridge, there are a number of short, hour-long walking loops through a range of habitats. From the point where you can see the Packhorse Bridge on Main Street, there's a flat, gravel track along the right side of the river that opens into fields. Take this and before long you can cross over the Dulnain via a suspension bridge. Turn left at the sign to the village and follow the track uphill. Once you reach Station Road, you can return to the high street by joining one of the trails through **Glencharrnoch Wood**, managed by the Woodland Trust and dominated by Scots pine. This is a particularly good location for Scottish wood ants – look for large mounds of pine needles beside the footpaths, which form the nests of these red-and-black insects. Next

CARVE CARRBRIDGE

carvecarrbridge.com

On the first Saturday of September, thousands gather in Carrbridge to watch a group of talented wood carvers create beautiful sculptures. As you approach the event field, the drone of the chainsaws grows steadily louder, until eventually you can see sawdust funnelling upwards. It's astonishing how quickly tree stumps take shape – in less than an hour, hooked eagle bills and tufty bear ears already begin to emerge.

The carvers spend four hours on their designs and also do a quick carve in the afternoon, creating a piece in 30 minutes using off-cuts from their main carving. At the end of the day, prizes are awarded and the carvings are auctioned. Many can be seen decorating gardens, fence posts and driveways throughout the village. My favourite is a barn owl beside one of the footpaths in Glencharnoch Wood.

Outside the village hall, across the road from the green, is a carving of an entire tree trunk dedicated to **Tom Jones** (not that one). This Tom Jones was a mountaineer, kayaker and prominent member of Carrbridge's community until he sadly passed away in 2018. His ideas 'gave life to The Gathering', which became Carve Carrbridge. The tree had to be cut down for safety reasons, and village residents decided it should be made into a carving to commemorate Tom's life. It includes a daffodil to represent Wales, where he was born, and a thistle for his adopted country. At the top is an eagle looking towards the field where the competition is held.

to Glencharrnoch Wood is Ellan Wood. Similar in appearance and also with its own trails, it's thought to originate from the Gaelic *ailean* meaning a plain or green.

Carrbridge is busiest in autumn, when it plays host to two unusual annual competitions: **Carve Carrbridge** (see opposite) and the **Golden Spurtle World Porridge Making Championships** (⊘ goldenspurtle. com). For the latter, held in October, competitors gather from all over the world to impress the judges with their version of the classic dish. The event is free to attend, with porridge samples and a marquee of local drinks and gifts on offer.

5 BOAT OF GARTEN

🏠 **The Boat Country Inn & Restaurant** (page 316)

Boat of Garten is a small village five miles southeast of Carrbridge. Most of its visitor appeal comes from its proximity to the ancient pinewoods of Abernethy and the community-driven Milton Loch. It's also known as the **Osprey Village** – after becoming extinct in Britain, the first known pair of these fish-eating raptors to start nesting in Scotland again was recorded at Loch Garten (page 48) in 1954. This loch is three miles away and walkable via a trail starting at the Abernethy NNR car park (▦ bottle.trick.kiosk), just across the River Spey from Boat of Garten. The village is also

"Concealed among the trees further off near the burn, you might also spot Merlin the willow wolf."

one of the stops on the Strathspey Railway (page 33). While here, it's worth popping into **1896 Gallery** (Deshar Rd ⊘ 1896gallery.com) for an array of handmade gifts from Scottish artists and craft makers.

Tucked behind residential streets at the northern end of the village is **Milton Loch Community Woodland** (▦ hounded.overlooks.intention), managed by Boat of Garten Wildlife Group (BoGWiG). Once a rubbish dump, it has been transformed into a community space for walking and watching wildlife, full of mixed trees including lots of silver birch. This small reserve has a short woodland walking trail, pond-dipping station and bird hide overlooking the water. At the reserve's entrance is a 44ft-long boat made of woven willow. This is the **Ark of Caledon**, built by volunteers in 2020. It represents a safe haven for Scottish wildlife, featuring a woven deer's head on its bow. Concealed among the trees further off near the burn, you might also spot Merlin the willow wolf.

'There are lots of small woven creatures around the woodland including robins, swallows and dragonflies for people to find as they explore,' BoGWiG co-chairman Allan Bantick told me. 'The aim of the Ark of Caledon, together with its willow animals, is to highlight the threats that exist to our wildlife and to encourage people to adjust their behaviour to help minimise those threats.'

An interpretive panel beside the Ark tells visitors about the conservation work that's taken place, such as tree planting and installing bird and bat boxes. I love that this small reserve is making such an effort to urge more awareness of our native wildlife.

Next to the Ark, a footpath leads to the loch hide, where you might see little grebes, tufted ducks or perhaps a water rail. Slimmer than a moorhen, these secretive birds have grey and brown plumage, long legs for wading and a skinny red bill. A boardwalk a little way past the hide leads to the pond-dipping platform. To reach Milton Loch from the high street, head north on Spey Avenue and turn left on to Birch Grove. After 300yds, continue straight down a rougher track to a parking area up ahead.

Travelling west out of Boat of Garten and following the A95 south, you'll pass one of the national park's lesser-known lochs. **Loch Vaa** has a satisfyingly winding footpath around the water's edge and through the trees. The rusty red-roofed boathouse on its northwest bank is its most notable feature and the topic of an unsolved mystery. In spring 2020 it was half-submerged as the loch reached its highest ever level, while the year before the waterline barely brushed the building at all. With hardly any rainfall at the time and no streams running in or out of Loch Vaa, it's unknown how the water level fluctuated so dramatically.

"The rusty red-roofed boathouse on its northwest bank is its most notable feature and the topic of an unsolved mystery."

Don't trust Google Maps to get here as the suggested route takes you to a locked gate on the left that leads to a private track. Ignore this and stay on the A95. After half a mile, take a left turning just before a bridge crosses overhead. This is the Laggantygown Cemetery car park

1 Ark of Caledon, Milton Loch Community Woodland. **2** Boat of Garten is known as the Osprey Village with good reason. **3** The author feeding a coal tit at Loch Garten. **4** Abernethy Forest. ▶

(▥ violin.justifies.joys). From here, follow a compacted track up a short hill and then down the other side, where you'll see the western edge of the loch through the trees.

▯ FOOD & DRINK

Anderson's Deshar Rd, PH24 3BN ☏ 01479 831466 🖱 andersonsrestaurant.co.uk. The menu changes each month to reflect seasonal and locally sourced Scottish produce, with a vegan menu also available. During winter, Wednesday night is Pie Night in this cosy, warmly lit spot.

The Boat Country Inn & Restaurant Deshar Rd, PH24 3BH ☏ 01479 831258 🖱 boathotel.co.uk. The décor here is inspired by a rustic hunting lodge, with antler light pieces and wood panelling. Lunch and dinner menus feature classic dishes with modern twists. Dog friendly.

6 RSPB LOCH GARTEN & LOCH MALLACHIE

▥ skimmers.crate.quest; follow brown RSPB signs from Boat of Garten 🖱 rspb.org.uk
☺ reserve year-round; Nature Centre Apr–Sep 10.30–15.30 daily

About equidistant between Boat of Garten and Nethy Bridge is a nature reserve located within the northern reaches of **Abernethy Forest**. Managed by the RSPB, this patch consists of towering pine woodland surrounding two lochs, which when seen on a map form the shape of a high-heeled footprint.

The larger of the pair is Loch Garten – on a still day this paints a perfect replica of the pines and hills across its banks. The smaller one is Loch Mallachie, characterised by rare bog woodland and goldeneye ducks that nest in tree boxes around the reserve. At the **Nature Centre**, accessed via a footpath from Loch Garten's car park, you can peer through binoculars and watch CCTV screens showing what's going on in the reserve during summer – a live feeder cam is also available to watch on the website all year round. A small shop sells gifts, snacks and hot drinks.

"This patch consists of towering pine woodland surrounding two lochs, which when seen on a map form the shape of a high-heeled footprint."

Although a picnic on the lochs' shores will be warmer in summer, I recommend visiting in winter. With the sun reflecting off the water and making the pine sprigs zing with zesty hues, Loch Garten is particularly serene on crisp winter days and you'll be far more likely to have it to

LOCH MONSTERS

Despite their sparkling surfaces and peaceful wooded edges, legends have been told of malevolent forces beneath the surface of these lochs. Loch Mallachie's name comes from the Gaelic *Loch Mallachaidh*, meaning 'Loch of the Curse'. According to legend, a bodach, or evil spirit, once roamed here. Also known as the Old Man of Garten, the spectre was said to appear as a huge white form that gave warnings of impending death with high-pitched screams throughout the night.

As if a shrieking banshee wasn't unnerving enough, other myths tell of a black horse-like creature that lived in the depths of Loch Garten. Only surfacing at night, it was said to prey on children or lambs that strayed too close to the water.

yourself. Winter is also when you can hand-feed wild birds here. When other food is scarce, they swoop down for a much-appreciated peanut on an outstretched palm. At this time, the clearing in front of the Nature Centre thrums with hungry woodland birds. All you need to do is hold out a handful of sunflower hearts or peanuts and wait. Watch them sidle down pine trunks with scratchy hops, then dive down to your palm with wings pinned to their sides until the last possible second. You'll feel a brush of air when they take off, leaving pinprick indents on your fingertips for the briefest of moments. The **coal tits** are the smallest and bravest, though sometimes you'll feel the heavier weight of a great tit on your hand.

To see both lochs, you can join the **Big Pines Trail** from Loch Garten's car park, which runs parallel to the road alongside the larger loch's northern bank to another car park for Loch Mallachie (**///** elevated. glows.sniff), half a mile further on. This footpath passes some of the tallest and oldest trees in Abernethy Forest, and the mossy lumps beside the path are a tell-tale sign that you're walking in ancient woodland. Known as hummocks, these are boulders or tree stumps that have developed a coating of lichen, pine needles and moss. Deadwood is left on the forest floor here, as it provides important shelter and food for insects including **robber flies**. The larvae of these Caledonian pinewood specialists feed on other insects within the deadwood.

Once you reach this second car park, you can follow the 1¾-mile **Two Lochs Trail** down the western side of Loch Garten to the northern bank of Loch Mallachie. This is where you'll see the intriguing patches of bog woodland I mentioned earlier – although some of the trees within these

FOREST BATHING

On one of my visits to Loch Garten I joined Nature and Forest Therapy Guide Cath Wright, who runs forest-therapy business **Highland Quietlife** (⊘ highlandquietlife. co.uk), for a forest bathing session. Forest bathing isn't to be taken literally – rather than a physical bath it's a mindfulness exercise inspired by the Japanese practice of shinrin-yoku. 'One of my key drivers was ensuring that people who needed or could benefit from forest bathing could do so without barriers,' Cath told me. 'I remember a beautiful group of women last summer who were going through their own troubles. As a group, they found healing within the forest and it was quite touching.'

Once the other participants and I had settled at the edge of the loch, Cath led us through a series of exercises to help us connect with our surroundings. We stayed in one patch and concentrated on what our senses were picking up. Closing my eyes helped me notice subtler sensations such as the breeze overhead and the crispy lichen beneath me. By the end of the session I felt noticeably more relaxed.

'There are those who say they already do forest bathing,' Cath said. 'When you delve deeper, they're maybe walking the dog or birdwatching – for these people I love to see the change in attitude. A guide gives gentle instruction, and means you might notice

boggy pools are as old as those on dry land, they're a fraction of the size because the moisture has stunted their growth.

7 NETHY BRIDGE

⌂ **Nethy House Café & Rooms** (page 316)

The village of Nethy Bridge, 3½ miles northeast of Loch Garten, is also known as the Forest Village due to its proximity to vast **Abernethy National Nature Reserve** (NNR), lying along its southern edge. The three-arched bridge that gave the village its name dates to 1810 and was one of many built throughout the UK by Scottish civil engineer Thomas Telford.

Stretching for almost 50 square miles from the River Nethy to the summit of Ben Macdui, Abernethy NNR contains moorland, wetland, mountains and one of the UK's largest remaining areas of ancient Caledonian pinewood. It really does feel older than your average forest. You haven't seen a tall tree until you've visited ancient pinewoods – gaze up and up and it's impossible to make out the top of some of the pines here.

The **Explore Abernethy Visitor Centre** (☉ year-round, weather permitting in winter) on Dell Road is an excellent place to stop things you never normally would, such as bark texture or insects on a bush. During a session they start to see the benefit of someone keeping time for them and gently asking them to direct their attention towards specific things.'

Some people might feel anxious sharing this kind of experience with strangers, but Cath has reassuring advice for beginners. 'Break it down,' she advised. 'Get outside for ten minutes and just be with nature. Focus on sounds around you and don't let your mind wander too far.'

After we all shared our final thoughts, Cath offered us a cup of pine needle tea, which you can easily make yourself.

1. Pick a handful of pine needles. Look for pairs and take green ones, not brown.
2. Immerse the needles in hot water for 25 minutes.
3. The resulting brew contains lots of vitamin C and has a gentle forest taste.

As with all wild foraging, make sure you've identified Scots pine correctly. If you're unsure, ask an expert.

Sipping tea made from the trees we were sitting under was an apt way to ground ourselves again after such a soothing and reflective session. I recommend bringing snacks for an energy boost too, as you'll likely be feeling very chilled out.

before exploring the forest, containing information boards, taxidermy specimens of Abernethy wildlife and interactive games. From here you can follow several waymarked trails through **Dell Woods**, a part of Abernethy Forest that's managed by NatureScot. I recommend the three-mile circular **King's Road Trail**, running beside the chattering River Nethy and through the forest. As well as Scots pines, there are plenty of silver birches covered in tufts of lichen; keep an eye out for tiny fairy houses at the base of their trunks.

Also on this trail, submerged on the west side of Dell Woods, are the remains of a water channel deep enough to stand in. In the 19th century, Abernethy trees were felled for shipbuilding and construction and this water channel diverted water from the Duack Burn to a holding dam, where it powered a sawmill. Other channels dug in the forest were used to float logs down to the River Spey.

Dell Woods is an important site for ground-nesting birds so it's crucial that you stick to the paths and keep dogs on leads from April to August to avoid disturbing them.

Heading north out of Nethy Bridge via the B970, you'll reach **Castle Roy** (▥ dolphins.goose.pocket ⟡ castleroy.org.uk; free entry) after half a mile. Obvious when approaching in either direction, this 12th-century ruin stands propped up on a hill behind Abernethy Old Kirk.

When you head through the castle gate (by which you can park), you'll likely see Murdo the Highland cow. Rejected at birth and subsequently hand-reared, he now lives in the field beside the castle. This simple, four-sided ruin, built some time in the 1100s by the Clan Comyn, has remained mostly unchanged for centuries. There are plenty of gaps to peep out from and a wooden staircase to access a higher viewpoint.

To help preserve the ruins for the future, you can get your own square yard of the castle or grounds in exchange for a donation on the website. Needless to say, this doesn't carry any legal weight, but by stretching the truth slightly you can haughtily inform your friends that you're a laird or lady of a castle. Quite a cool brag.

¶¶ FOOD & DRINK

Balliefurth Farm Shop Station Rd, PH25 3DN ✆ 01479 821245 ⌖ balliefurth.co.uk ⌚ 08:30–16:00 Mon–Sat. A butcher's shop deli serving beef and lamb direct from Balliefurth Farm, two miles away on the road to Grantown-on-Spey. Veggies aren't left out either – take your pick of the meatiest meat-free sausages and burgers I've ever tasted, as well as locally grown vegetables, jams and cheeses.

Nethy House Café & Rooms B970, PH25 3EB ✆ 07963 217793 ⌖ nethyhouse.co.uk. Serves home bakes, rolls, lunches and artisan coffee. Dog-friendly and less than a five-minute walk from Dell Woods. Photography, art and handmade gifts for sale inside.

Speyside Centre Skye of Curr Rd, Dulnain Bridge PH26 3PA ✆ 01479 851359 ⌖ speysidecentre.com. Garden centre and shop 2½ miles northwest of Nethy Bridge. The café serves meals and snacks including clootie dumplings, a traditional steamed Scottish pudding containing dried fruit and spices. Outside is a wildlife-viewing area with trellis-covered benches facing a small garden. As I stepped outside, a red squirrel darted over the stone animals on its way to the peanut feeders.

8 GRANTOWN-ON-SPEY

🏠 **The Grant Arms Hotel** (page 316)

Close to the northern edge of the Cairngorms National Park, Grantown-on-Spey is just far enough from Aviemore to be peaceful even in high season. Once simply called Grantown, 'on Spey' was added to the town's

1 Castle Roy. **2** The Bookmark, Grantown-on-Spey. **3** Grantown Museum. **4** Autumn in Anagach Woods, Grantown-on-Spey. ▶

name in 1898. A narrow, central green called The Square sits across the northeast end of the high street, which has a number of independent outlets. One of these is the small but packed bookshop, **The Bookmark** (⏚ thebookmark.co.uk), where owner Marjory Marshall personally selects every title on the shelves.

During the turbulent time of the Highland Clearances, when lands were emptied and people driven out to make room for sheep farming, Grantown-on-Spey's founder Sir James Grant went to great lengths to support his townspeople. When famine struck in 1782, he personally paid to import grain to prevent them from starving. Over his lifetime he had over 130 miles of road built, connecting Grantown to smaller villages and improving its access. It was this compassion and generosity that earned him the nickname 'The Good Sir James'.

Near The Square, just off Castle Road, is **Grantown Museum** (Burnfield Av, PH26 3HH ✆ 01479 872478 ⏚ grantownmuseum.co.uk ☺ Apr–Oct Wed–Mon). Here you can learn more about Sir James Grant and see a wide collection of photographs and artefacts documenting the town's history. There's a particular emphasis on costumes through the ages, with items such as a beautifully preserved Victorian silk wedding dress on display. This was worn in 1882 by Agnes Helen Gordon when she married Donald MacDougall, a local farmer and Grantown-based shop owner. With video displays and interactive elements, this little dose of local history is accessible for children too.

"Sprawling across the east side of Grantown-on-Spey is one of my favourite locations in the whole of the North East."

One unique element that isn't exhibited in the museum but instead offered for hire to schools and care homes is a trio of Mini Museums containing 20th-century travel essentials, toys and food containers. These were handmade by Suzi Wilson using a vintage leather case, a Sindy caravan and a Walls ice cream tub. You can read more about this on the website, as well as a range of craft fairs, historical dressing-up experiences and live music events that are held at the museum throughout the year.

Sprawling across the east side of Grantown-on-Spey is one of my favourite locations in the whole of the North East. There aren't many forests in the UK where you can lose all sense of human presence, but **Anagach Woods** (▦ bungalows.inversion.smirking) is one of them. At roughly 1,000 acres it's not even that big (Rothiemurchus is seven times the size), but it only takes a short walk before the traffic and bustle of Grantown is replaced by the natural sounds of Scots pinewood.

Anagach Woods was planted in 1766 using young pines from Abernethy, a few of which still stand today. Crested tits and crossbills live in these trees, but an animal that's far easier to see is the red squirrel. A short way along the track from the parking area are some feeders high up on the left. This is a good place to scan the branches for bushy tails. Squirrels shouldn't just eat peanuts, so the feeders are filled with a mix of goodies for a more balanced diet. Still, like children eating around their vegetables, they pick out the peanuts first.

To walk here from The Square, head down the right side of Sylhet Fish & Chips on to Forest Road and continue straight at the crossroads. A small car park with an information board appears after 300yds. From here, turn left into the forest, or you can carry on straight towards the River Spey.

Events held in The Square include the Cairngorms Farmers Market (🇫 ☉ 10.00–15.00 first Sun of month), offering artisan Highland preserves, local gins, recycled oak furniture, handmade gifts, muddy potatoes

"Crested tits and crossbills live in these trees, but an animal that's far easier to see is the red squirrel."

and other locally sourced items. On the last day of the year, Grantown is abuzz with its Hogmanay Street Party (🇫; free entry), complete with hot food and drinks from 10pm and traditional music from 11pm before the midnight fireworks kick off.

Caorunn Gin

Balmenach Rd, Cromdale PH26 3PF ✆ 01479 874933 ⌂ caorunngin.com ☉ 10.00–16.00 Mon–Fri; 18+ only

Caorunn gin (pronounced ka-roon) has been handcrafted in small batches on the same site as Balmenach Whisky Distillery, 4½ miles east of Grantown-on-Spey, since 2009. The word *caorunn* is Gaelic for rowan berry, which is one of eleven botanicals used in the gin. Five of these can be foraged within a ten-minute walk of the distillery. I love a claim to fame and Caorunn has an excellent one: it's the only gin in the world that's distilled in a working copper-berry chamber. This is simply because only one of these particular chambers has ever been made. The copper reacts with the botanicals' fragrances for maximum flavour.

Tours begin at the on-site botanical garden. My guide Gabrielle revealed folklore about each plant used in Caorunn and the different flavours they bring to it. Then we continued to the distilling room – cushions and blankets are a thoughtful touch in this chilly room – where Gabrielle explained the distillation process and gave us a sniff of the raw botanicals.

Next we played dot-to-dot, otherwise known as nosing and tasting. Eleven jars, one for each botanical, were set up on the table, with a paper strip submerged in each one. Our task was to plot on a spiderweb how strong we thought each botanical was. Seeing Gin Master Simon Buley's dot-to-dot at the end was a discovery in just how unsophisticated my nose is.

The tour ended at The Bothy, a bar room with squashy armchairs and forest green walls, where we were served glasses of Caorunn and Walter Gregor's tonic (made in Aberdeenshire). Drivers received a mini bottle to take away and enjoy later.

¶¶ FOOD & DRINK

The Grant Arms Hotel The Square, PH26 3HF ✆ 01479 872526 ⌗ grantarmshotel.com. An elegant and traditional restaurant inside the 'UK's Wildlife Hotel' (page 316), known for its guided nature holidays hosted by celebrity guests. Enjoy three courses of sophisticatedly presented British dishes for £24.95 and Sunday roasts from noon to 14.00. In the Capercaillie Bar, Speyside single malts, Scottish gins and bar lunches are served Monday to Saturday.

KJ's Bothy Bakery 9/2 Achnagonalin Ind Est, PH26 3TA ✆ 01479 788011 f. Tucked away on an industrial estate just outside Grantown, this unexpected take-away bakery is a popular spot for cyclists. It offers coffee, sandwiches, cakes, tray bakes and bread all made fresh on-site using local suppliers. The cake photos on Facebook will make you say 'phwoar'.

The Wee Puffin High St, PH26 3EG ✆ 01479 873377 f. A welcoming, cosy dog-friendly British restaurant with an extensive burger menu, classic favourites and vegetarian options, plus local beers including Cairngorm Brewery. Small and popular so booking ahead is recommended.

BADENOCH: FROM ALVIE TO LAGGAN

⚑ **Dalraddy Holiday Park** (page 317)

Badenoch's name comes from the Gaelic *Bàideanach* meaning 'drowned land'. This refers to the historic flooding of the upper River Spey and

MAKING WAVES IN HIGH SOCIETY

Born in 1749, Lady Jane Maxwell grew up in Edinburgh with her mother and sisters. A highly spirited girl, she supposedly rode down the city's Royal Mile on the back of a pig.

Jane married Alexander, 4th Duke of Gordon, in 1767 and gave birth to their first son just as her husband's mistress, Jane Christie, gave birth to another boy. Both babies were named George, described by the duchess as 'my George and the duke's George'. Not to be outdone, Jane had affairs of her own, including with Henry Dundas, a close friend of British Prime Minister William Pitt. The duchess threw lavish parties and continued to wear tartan after it was banned in 1746 to suppress the Jacobite rebellion.

The duke and duchess's unhappy marriage came to an end in 1805. Jane Christie moved in with the duke at Gordon Castle, Fochabers, and a house called Kinrara was built for the duchess beside the River Spey. She died in London in 1812 and was buried near Kinrara.

the region's landscape in general, which has been shaped by lochs, floodplains and marshes. It consists of several parishes starting with Alvie, five miles from Aviemore, and finishing in Laggan, twenty miles southwest. Around here you can explore concealed lochans, evocative wooden sculptures, waterfalls and Britain's first open-air museum. The largest settlements in Badenoch are Kingussie and Newtonmore. This is Clan Macpherson country, the ancestral heart of a fierce clan that has the Scottish wildcat on its crest. You can learn more about this in Newtonmore, where the Clan Macpherson Museum shares the clan's historic and modern influences.

9 LOCH INSH & AROUND

In the northeast of Badenoch is **Loch Insh**, the result of a glacier melting 10,000 years ago. On a sunny day its surface shimmers, reflecting the clouds from higher vantage points and tree canopies from the water's edge. At its northeast corner is **Insh Church**, a squat white building backed by pine trees and surrounded by lichen-crusted gravestones. Also known as the Chapel of the Swans, it's dedicated to St Adamnan, a disciple of St Columba.

Unlike Loch an Eilein and Loch Morlich (page 37), it's not possible to walk all the way around Loch Insh's perimeter. The spot of most interest is the church, where you can admire the loch and watch for birds. Mostly it's used as the base for **Loch Insh Outdoor Centre** ($\lozenge$ lochinsh.

Through Torr Alvie

✾ OS Explorer map OL57; start at Dalraddy Holiday Park, just off the B9152 🚶 finger. vowed.fines; ♥ NH8584108286; 3¼ miles; moderate.

In the crofting hamlet of Alvie, a steep-sided ridge known as the **Torr of Alvie** rises high above the Spey, through pine and juniper woodland. The ridge itself is fantastic, but it also contains points of historical intrigue: nearby Kinrara Estate is linked to Alexander, 4th Duke of Gordon, his wife Jane (page 57) and their son George, the 5th and final Duke of Gordon. This is an out-and-back trail but there's plenty to look at both ways. If you're peckish after your walk, look out for **Alvie Forest Food** (page 36) within the holiday park itself.

1 From Dalraddy Holiday Park, walk back towards the road and turn right down a track signed Kinrara, just beside the turning for the holiday park. A short distance down this track, around the first bend, the Speyside Way cuts across the path – ignore this and continue straight on.

2 After 100yds, a field opens up to your left. It's not possible to see from the path, but near here is Croftgowan Pictish Cemetery, described as the largest known Pictish barrow cemetery. An archaeological dig here in 2021 revealed preserved human remains in round barrows, dating back to somewhere between the 5th and 7th centuries. Although the skeleton had gone, its outline was imprinted in the ground at the time. As the path bends away from this field, the main track continues but a narrower path on the left climbs up into the trees. Take this left fork and follow it to the edge of a field. Bear left, sticking close to the fence around the field's edge. On the far side, head through a metal gate.

com), which offers a range of land-based and aquatic activities such as kayaking and sailing. Day tickets are available from April to October for visitors to hire equipment for a range of water-based activities. From December to March, winter mini-tickets permit a three-hour session trying four different activities: archery, pedal karting, tubing (similar to sledging) and ice skating.

To get to Loch Insh, head southeast through the village of Kincraig, six miles southwest of Aviemore. Cross over the River Spey on a single-lane bridge and follow the road for another 200yds before reaching a parking bay opposite a footpath down to the loch. A little further down the road, a narrow track curves around the steep bank and up to another parking area in front of Insh Church's cemetery.

3 At the next fork, bear left and carry on through the woods before breaking above the treeline.

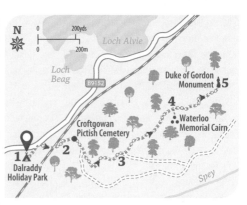

4 After roughly three quarters of a mile, look for a subtle, lightly trodden trail on the right. Follow this up a brief rocky slope to the Waterloo Memorial Cairn, which looks like a stone igloo on the hillside. It was built in 1815 by George, 5th Duke of Gordon, in honour of two close friends who died at Waterloo. It clearly wasn't intended to be a sad place – behind the door it's said there's a miniature wine-cellar, used during the duke's shooting parties. However, a key for the door hasn't been found, so nobody knows exactly what remains inside now. Return to the main path and turn right to continue uphill.

5 Before long the Duke of Gordon Monument appears through a gap in the trees, with views in every direction. There are inscriptions in English, Latin and Gaelic listing the 5th Duke's military titles and the date of his death, 28 May 1836. When you're ready, retrace the outward route back to Dalraddy Holiday Park.

Something close by that's well worth visiting but tucked away out of sight is the **Frank Bruce Sculpture Collection** (page 60). Less than a mile east of Loch Insh Outdoor Centre via the B970, this outdoor exhibition combines intricate wood carvings with a peaceful forest setting.

Uath Lochans

Forestry & Land Scotland ⫽ slip.overpower.photo

🖉 forestryandland.gov.scot/visit/uath-lochans

When the sun's shining in a cloudless sky, this place doesn't look real. Insects make ripples like invisible fingertips tracing across the water, and light reflecting off the surface sparkles on tree trunks. It's often so

FRANK BRUCE SCULPTURE COLLECTION

/// worm.intensely.grace ⟁ frank-bruce.org.uk; free entry

Close to Loch Insh is a rustic art exhibition slowly rotting away. The Frank Bruce Sculpture Collection is a series of wood and stone carvings on the western edge of Inve23 and Inshriach National Nature Reserve, which contains ancient pinewood, mountains and heather moorland. Connecting each sculpture like a treasure map is a mile-long footpath, suitable for buggies and wheelchairs.

The sculptures don't contrast with the landscape but rather belong within it, making the discovery of each wooden face or cupped hand more surprising. Some are carved into the twisted chopped boughs of trees too broad to loop your arms around. Each sculpture has a plaque alluding to its meaning: the central theme of the series is Scottish culture, exploring landscape, conscience and conflict. With their evocative expressions, the peering wooden faces remind me of the comedy and tragedy theatre masks.

Frank Bruce was a self-taught sculptor who settled in Aviemore with his family in the 1960s. Art created from wood inevitably has a limited lifespan and Frank wanted his work to age and decay as part of the natural cycle of life. This was linked to his scepticism of commercial art – he insisted that his work should always be free and accessible. These sculptures were originally positioned 80 miles north, on Aberdeenshire's coast, but many were made using pines from nearby Inshriach Forest, so it's fitting that they were returned here in 2007.

This trail is an innovative addition to the Cairngorms National Park that I'd recommend to anyone searching for something unexpected. As each one is made from natural materials, I wondered how easy they would be to find, and some are certainly trickier than others. You might not like them all – some are unsettling to look at and read about – but there's no denying that they make you stop and think.

quiet you can hear the thrum of chaffinch wings. In spring you might see goldeneye ducks and greylag geese stirring the lochans, while summer is the time for dragonflies and damselflies. Some of the mammoth trees have hanging canopies big enough to stand under and roots the size of dinosaur feet.

There are four lochans here, looking like a blue pawprint on a map. Their name (pronounced 'wah' lochans) means the 'small hawthorn lochs' in Gaelic. To get here from Loch Insh Outdoor Centre, turn right on to the B970 and, after half a mile, fork left down a no through road. Another mile further on, you'll see a Forestry Commission sign for the lochans on the right.

White waymarks lead around a 1½-mile trail threading between the smaller lochans and around the biggest one, taking in woodland, heather moorland and patches of bog via a boardwalk. There's also a red waymarked 2½-mile trail that climbs a rock-bobbled slope to **Farleitter Crag**. From this vantage point, you can gaze over the lochans, the Spey Valley and trees wrapped over the feet of the Glen Feshie hills. In spring the pines echo with the drumming of woodpeckers, amplified in the quiet. As it climbs, the path narrows to single file, and before long you'll see Loch Insh to the north.

This is a circular so you can continue following the red waymarked posts to loop away from the lochans and return to the start point. It's a perfectly nice return route, but you're hemmed in on both sides by trees so views are more restricted. Also, as the forest switches from native Scots pine to Sitka spruce, you're less likely to hear birdsong than if you return via the outward route.

Invereshie & Inshriach National Nature Reserve

/// relegate.cups.burst

On the western flank of the Cairngorm plateau, 3½ miles southeast of Loch Insh, is a nature reserve containing some 14 square miles of pine woodland, moorland, alpine heathland and mountains, with golden eagles for satellites. Scottish rarities such as crossbills, red squirrels and crested tits are all found here. Sprays of heather are at their brightest from July to September, adding violet hues to the forest greens.

"As more of a forest sprite than a mountain goat myself, I found the reserve particularly good for a short stroll."

Many people come here for Sgòr Gaoith – a mountain meaning 'windy peak' in Gaelic – so the only established path runs in a straight line from the car park towards the summit. At 3,668ft, this certainly is a blustery peak and shouldn't be attempted without proper clothing, equipment and navigational skills.

As more of a forest sprite than a mountain goat myself, I found the reserve particularly good for a short stroll because just 30 minutes on the established trail enables you to see the landscape change from woodland to shrubby clearings to distant hills.

However, for scenic views you only need to walk for a few minutes away from the road. One of the first sounds you'll hear is the whisper

of the Allt Ruadh (Red Burn), a tributary of the River Feshie. For the first mile or so, this burn runs parallel to the main track, and there are plenty of spots for perching on its banks and watching the rapids churn up white froth. Grey wagtails often appear, fluttering from rock to rock. During one of my visits, I watched one swoop to the top of a Scots pine and start singing, its voice so loud I could hear it above the water.

If you're approaching from Loch Insh, head east on the B970. After crossing the River Feshie and rounding a U-bend, turn right at the sign for Glen Feshie Hostel. After one mile down this single-lane road, pass over a cattle grid close to the Cairngorm Gliding Club and continue for another 1½ miles until you reach a small gravel car park on the left. If this is full, there's another one half a mile further down.

10 KINGUSSIE

Seven miles southwest of Loch Insh is Kingussie, a small town with grey stone buildings lining its high street. Its Gaelic name, *Ceann a' Ghiuthsaich*, means 'head of the pinewoods', but today you'll most likely encounter birch and juniper while walking around town. Although there are some wilder spots, for me Kingussie's appeal comes from the cosy cafés and bookshops either side of the A86, which splits it down the middle.

En route to Kingussie from the north, you'll pass a lay-by beside **Glebe Ponds** (▥ static.eternity.rapport), half a mile from the centre of town. In spring, this spot is covered in daffodils, and at any time of year the A9's grumbling is stifled by the conversations of mallards and greylag geese. It takes less than five minutes to follow the boardwalk across a stream and back around. With plenty of benches, it's a peaceful picnic spot.

Kingussie itself lies beside the River Spey and is cut in half by the **Gynack Burn**. The short but sweet Gynack Mill Trail runs for one mile in a squished figure of eight across the burn. To begin, walk north on Gynack Road with the burn on your right. About 350yds up, a trail sign points right down a wooden staircase to a bridge across the Gynack. The path becomes a gravel track bordered by silver birches. After a brief steep section away from the water, emerge on to Ardbroilach Road. Follow

---

◀ **1** Uath Lochans. **2** Crested tits can be spotted at Inshriach National Nature Reserve.
3 Frank Bruce Sculpture Collection. **4** Loch Insh.

trail signs left and shortly you'll see the burn again. Cross another bridge over it to return to Gynack Road, which leads back towards town.

Kingussie's high street has a number of independent shops worth a browse. At number 14, The Bookshop (☉ Mon–Sat) is a secondhand warren of wonders, run by community charity **Caberfeidh Horizons** (⊘ caberfeidhhorizons.com) that also has a charity clothes shop next door and a community hub across the road. There are three rooms of fiction, non-fiction and poetry – I was particularly smitten by the entire room dedicated to Scottish interest and left with an armful of books instead of the one I'd gone in for. Further east along the high street, at number 26, is **Grassroots** (◆ Grassroots General Store ☉ Tue–Sat), selling garden materials, food for wildlife, gifts (look out for the 'animal of the week' highlights on their Facebook page), package-free wholefoods and seasonal items such as homemade Christmas wreaths.

Continuing up from Grassroots you'll come to the wonderful **Minerva's Emporium** (◆ ☉ Mon–Sat), selling yarn, stationery, sheet music and a vibrant display of books. Younger bookworms can crawl through a wardrobe portal into the children's section on the other side. Community is key here, with sessions such as the Speyside Spinning Group and their spinning wheels meeting twice a month.

From here, a right turn on to Duke Street will bring you to **Iona Gallery** (⊘ theionagallery.co.uk ☉ 13.00–17.00 Mon–Sat), which exhibits the work of local crafters and hosts events and workshops throughout the year. Run by the Society of Badenoch and Strathspey Artists, this is the only public art gallery in the Cairngorms National Park.

On a grassy hill overlooking Kingussie are the ruined **Ruthven Barracks** (▥ unroll.driftwood.ruins; free entry), an impressive sight as you leave town via the B970. There was a structure on this mound as far back as the 13th century – the Comyn family built a castle here, made from timber and earth, as their chief seat in Badenoch. In 1306 the Lord of Badenoch, John Comyn, was slain by Robert the Bruce in a church in Dumfries, sparking a civil war that brought an end to the Comyn family. Alexander Stewart, also known as the 'Wolf of Badenoch' (page 40), took ownership of the castle in 1371.

By the end of the 16th century, the Earl of Huntly had rebuilt the castle in stone, but a century later it was burnt down by Jacobite commander Viscount 'Bonnie' Dundee. A garrison was built in the 1700s to police the area more effectively, but succumbed to a Jacobite siege and now stands in ruin. Like many ruined sites, there are plenty of cubby holes to peer into, including several you need to bend double to access. Signs on the walls tell of how up to ten soldiers were lodged in a single room and how much of their ration was required for half a pint of rum.

¶¶ FOOD & DRINK

The Sugarbowl Café & Gifts High St, PH21 1HR ℰ 01540 661641 ⊘ thesugarbowl.co.uk. This place has an inviting wall of gifts worth a browse after warming up with a delicious soup. The décor is vibrant, with blocks of colour complementing the crafty feel of the place.

11 NEWTONMORE & AROUND

🏠 **Glentruim Lodge** (page 317)

The next village along the A86 from Kingussie is Newtonmore, three miles southwest. Similarly, most of its amenities are located on this central road, lined with a mix of the same old stone buildings as Kingussie and some newer frontages providing flashes of colour.

Newtonmore is perhaps best known for Scottish wildcats. Although you're very unlikely to get a sighting of this critically endangered cat here anymore, its emblem appears in the Clan Macpherson crest (see below) and is still an important part of Newtonmore's character. As you walk around, you'll likely spot colourful cat statues peering through windows

'TOUCH NOT THE CAT BUT A GLOVE'

This is the motto used by the **Clan Macpherson**, referring to Scottish wildcats. Here the word 'but', or 'bot' as it's sometimes written, means 'without'. It acts as a warning not to approach a wildcat with its claws extended from its 'glove' or paw. The inference is that, like the wildcat, the Clan Macpherson is not to be messed with. (Some interpret the motto to mean that you shouldn't handle a wildcat without wearing a glove yourself, but I reckon touching a wildcat is unwise in any case if you'd rather keep your fingers.)

Described as the 'guardians of the heart of the Scottish Highlands', the historic Clan Macpherson patrolled established routes across Badenoch and Speyside trodden by drovers, soldiers and pilgrims. Having settled in Lochaber in the West Highlands in the 9th century, the Macphersons later defeated the Clan Comyn in battle and took over their lands in Badenoch. Over time, they demonstrated impressive military prowess, earning themselves a fierce reputation to match the wildcat representing them. Modern-day members of the clan still meet today at their annual Gathering, where a huge family photo is taken in front of the Clan Macpherson Museum (page 68).

or perched up in trees. This is the **Wildcat Experience**, a famous treasure hunt around the village. In the **Wildcat Centre** (⌂ wildcatcentre.org ☺ Mon–Sat), next to the village hall, you can buy an assortment of wildcat-themed gifts as well as a £10 Wildcat Experience track pack. This contains a map for plotting over 130 cat statues hidden throughout Newtonmore. Track packs are also available in the post office and The Wild Flour Café.

There are a number of different walks around Newtonmore, ranging from the six-mile **Wildcat Trail** (page 70) to a five-minute stroll around **Loch Imrich** (▨ brilliant.clashing.pelting). This small loch isn't well-signposted from the road but can be easily reached at the northeast side of town, 100yds past the Co-op. Pass through a wooden gate and follow a soft earth track down to the water. Keep your eyes peeled as there are a couple of painted wildcats to find here.

Once you've had your fill of wildcats, there are two **museums** that sit like bookends at either end of town, and a couple of decent places to grab a bite to eat. The only official place for visitors to leave their **cars** in Newtonmore is a small parking area just off Main Street on Glen Road, opposite the village hall.

Highland Folk Museum

Kingussie Rd, PH20 1AY ⌂ highlifehighland.com/highlandfolkmuseum ☺ Apr–Oct; free entry

This extraordinary place was the first open-air museum in Britain and spreads for a mile from end to end; you'll see it on the left just before you enter Newtonmore from the north. Its key focus is domestic and rural life, showcasing how people in the Highlands lived, worked and shopped from the 1700s to the 1950s. Set out like a village of time capsules, a gravel path connects more than 35 historical buildings, from the Glenlivet Post Office to Knockbain School and a clockmaker's workshop. The 18th-century Highland Township was used as a location for the first series of *Outlander*.

The attention to detail here is incredible. Each interior is like a film set, with hundreds of items specifically chosen to evoke the scene, including

---

1 Dun da Lamh Fort. **2** Highland Folk Museum. **3** Exhibits at the Clan Macpherson Museum. **4** The Wildcat Trail at Newtonmore. **5** Ruthven Barracks, Kingussie. **6** Dalwhinnie Distillery. ▶

spectacles, magazines, umbrellas and even decades-old calendars. It's like the occupants suddenly rushed out, leaving their belongings where they were last used. The wonderful staff wear historical clothes and host events, demonstrations and re-enactments throughout the season.

This is a completely visual insight into times gone by. There's very little to read – everything is in situ which is such an engaging way for both adults and children to see what shops, houses and farm buildings once looked like. Even the road signs and post boxes are vintage. Many visitors are drawn to the Highland Cottage with its photogenic thatched roof. As well as looking the part, it also smells authentic, with smoke drifting up the chimney. My favourite building is the schoolhouse with its original desks and cast-iron range. It's now presented in a 1930s' setup with a timetable written on the blackboard and a nature table of skulls, feathers and nests.

The story of the museum begins with Dr Isabel F Grant, a pioneer of British folk life studies and the author of *Highland Folk Ways*. Dr Grant was inspired by the open-air museum movement in Scandinavia and in 1943 she bought an old hunting lodge and three acres of land in Kingussie. The Highland Folk Museum opened the following year, containing her collection in what she called 'Am Fasgadh' (The Shelter) – a safe place for her artifacts. Land in Newtonmore was bought in the 1980s and the new museum was officially opened to the public in 1996.

"It's like the occupants suddenly rushed out, leaving their belongings where they were last used."

At the far end of the site is a private collection and research facility with the same Gaelic name, *Am Fasgadh*. Although this isn't open to the public, it's possible to arrange a guided tour in advance (✆ 01349 781650 for enquiries and bookings).

Clan Macpherson Museum

Main St, PH20 1DE ⊘ clanmacphersonmuseum.org.uk ⊙ Apr–Oct Wed–Mon; free entry

Formally opened in 1952, this small but packed museum is dedicated to the Clan Macpherson (page 65) and has exhibited relics and artefacts from the family for more than 50 years. Displays are set out chronologically, with plaques, maps and portraits beginning in the 14th century and passing through the Civil War, Jacobite Uprising and Queen Victoria to present-day clan gatherings. With a fair bit to read, it's not the most child-friendly museum, although a cosy alcove called Cluny's Cave has a table for younger visitors to do some colouring.

Other aspects of village life are featured too, including shinty matches. Each year, rival teams from Newtonmore and Kingussie play for the Sir Tommy Macpherson Memorial Trophy. Sir Tommy was one of the most highly decorated British soldiers of World War II. After D-Day, he drove behind enemy lines in a stolen German car and told the commanding officer there were 20,000 troops waiting to attack. This wasn't true, but the Germans believed the ruse and surrendered. By doing this, Sir Tommy successfully intercepted 23,000 Wehrmacht soldiers. This is just one of the intriguing local stories told here.

¶¶ FOOD & DRINK

The Glen Hotel Main St, PH20 1DD ✆ 01540 673203 ⌂ theglenhotel.co.uk. Comfortable, informal dining serving 'good honest pub grub'. You can choose to eat in the lounge bar or dining room.

The Wild Flour Main St, PH20 1DA ✆ 01540 670975 ⬛ ◷ Tue–Sun. Vines and flowers have been painted on to the mirror and art for sale covers the walls of this café. Choose a spot at the front or head up the steps to a back room overlooking a rockery garden. The lunch menu features soup, sandwiches and baked potatoes, including some creative vegetarian options. A popular spot and for good reason.

12 LAGGAN WOLFTRAX & PATTACK FALLS

▥ year.today.hiker ⌂ visit/laggan-wolftrax ◷ 10.00–17.00 Wed–Sun

With over 20 miles of trails threading through pine forest, graded from easy to extreme, Laggan Wolftrax offers some of the most diverse mountain bike routes in North East Scotland. A centre was opened in 2015 to provide a permanent base for bikers, equipped with electric car charge points, toilets, showers, a bike shop and a café serving hot drinks, soup and cakes.

There are waymarked walking trails here too. One heads north to **Dun da Lamh**, a Pictish fort positioned on a hill overlooking woodland and the River Spey (page 74).

About 2½ miles southwest along the A86 from Laggan Wolftrax is Druim an Aird car park (*▥* headboard.backs.mango). From here, it's less than a minute's walk to **Pattack Falls**. This small, concealed gorge pinches the River Pattack as it cascades between boulders towards the road. From the car park, either continue straight on a flat footpath or

The Wildcat Trail

❄ OS Explorer map OL56; start at Calder Bridge: 🎥 camcorder.climbing.lined
📍 NN7059798715; 6¼ miles, following wildcat waymarks; easy – watch your step along the steep gorge section.

- -

Running all the way around Newtonmore, this superb circular walk passes woodland, a gorge, open country, mountains and rivers. Aside from one short steep section, the entire route is flat so is suitable for families. You can branch off and return to the village at any point if you don't fancy walking it all in one go. A trail brochure can be bought from the Wildcat Centre (page 66), although its estimate of 2½–3 hours is a vast underestimate; it took me four hours to complete, stopping every now and then for photos. It's not possible to leave cars at the start point at Calder Bridge – your best option is to use the car park in Glen Road, three quarters of a mile away on the A86, and walk down.

1 Head through the metal gate beside the blue bench at Calder Bridge. Almost immediately after this, walk through another small gate before turning right to follow the bank of the River Calder.

2 Shortly, you'll pass Banchor Cemetery on the right. This is the location of an early Christian cell dedicated to St Bride. She is associated with oystercatchers, a common wading bird in the North East.

3 The path climbs steeply then turns sharply back on itself, leading above the Calder gorge – take care of the steep drop towards the river on one side. After passing through another gate, the path climbs again on to more hilly terrain. Beside the path is an information plaque about the mountains of Glen Banchor, which you will now be able to see in front of you.

4 When you reach Glen Road, turn right and walk along the tarmac. You can either continue down this road, following it round to the left and over a cattle grid, or follow the next wildcat post left for a brief diversion through Milton Wood, which will bring you out further down Glen Road.

5 Follow the trail at the next left turn, signposted with a worn brown sign for Upper Knock and a fresher, blue sign for Golden Acre. Head up the vehicle track between a couple of houses and through a gate into an open field. Livestock are kept here so keep dogs under close control.

6 Follow the vehicle track around the base of the hill on your right through a stand of birches. You'll shortly see a sign pointing right to a viewpoint over Newtonmore, which is worth a look. You might have to duck under low-hanging branches. Once you're ready, return to the vehicle track and turn right towards another gate. There might be pigs on the loose this time so again, keep your dogs close.

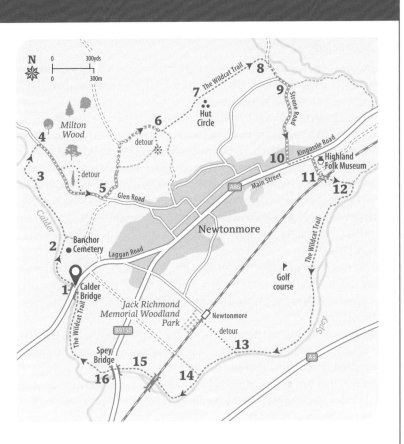

7 After several more kissing gates there's another detour to the right to a hut circle. This small clearing shows the foundations of Pictish dwellings belonging to those who lived and farmed on these uplands thousands of years ago. Carry on straight after this. The fields on your left are a good place to spot lapwings wheeling in the air or foraging on the ground at any time of year.

8 After leaving this patch of birch trees behind, turn right on to a vehicle track heading gently downhill.

9 Pass through two gates, turn slightly left and then right to join Strone Road. At the end, you'll emerge back on to Main Street.

10 Turn left and continue on the pavement until you see a sign for the Highland Folk Museum up ahead. Just as the road begins to bend by the sign, there's a wooden post with the Wildcat ▶

The Wildcat Trail (continued)

◀ Trail symbol on the right-hand side of the road. Carefully cross over and walk south down this single-track lane.

11 Carry on past the museum gates – there's no access to the museum here and you must enter via reception further down the road if you plan to visit. Follow the mud track round a bend, over the railway bridge and through a metal gate.

12 The path narrows to a wiggly pedestrian track between the fence and the burn. Ignoring the wide fence with a tiny concrete bridge, pass between a stand of tall silver birches until the path veers right over a larger boarded footbridge. Now you'll have the golf course on your right and the river on your left. There are stepping stones and other small bridges for when the river rises. This area is a Site of Special Scientific Interest (SSSI) with plenty of wildlife using the river including herons, wagtails and sandpipers. Hugging the pebbly bank of the River Spey, this part of the trail continues around the entire golf course, passing through open grassland humming with birdsong. Once you're out of the trees, enjoy fantastic views of mountains straight ahead.

13 At the edge of the golf course there are two gates. Beside the first one, a path branches right back to Newtonmore. Follow this for a short loop through Jack Richmond Memorial Woodland Park. Wheelchair-friendly, this tennis court-sized shady patch of trees has a couple of picnic tables.

14 Back on the Wildcat Trail, pass through the second gate and follow the edge of an open field. At the other end, the path follows the curve of the river, bending right to a gate in the corner. After passing through this, walk under the railway bridge.

15 Follow the track through a row of trees beside the river, crossing two more gates. Up ahead is the arched Spey Road Bridge. Walk under here and you'll be at the point where the River Calder joins the Spey.

16 After another gate, pass through a patch of newly planted alder. The path threads up and emerges on to the A86 at the Calder Bridge starting point.

branch left up a jaunty stone staircase, the sound of the falls already clear on the air. A few steps later, the falls open up below. White water churns over hulking rocks and stumpy crags on either side. Squat trees and heather grow directly out of the rock, livening up the grey with splashes of green. Another flight of flattened boulders leads down to a lookout point.

There are a few different trails to choose from in this patch. Turning left up a slight hill away from the falls takes you through a dense patch of pine woodland, where shrubs burst with buds in spring. Once you break on to a vehicle track, turn right and follow signs to **Druim an Aird ruins**. When the track forks, bear left to carry on passing under the yellow overhead cables. After the fourth signpost for the ruins (not including the one at the car park), you'll reach the edge of a field. Turn left so the fence is on your right. About 300ft further up is an interpretive plaque about a township that used to be in this spot. Now it's reduced to knee-high walls of ruined stone, looking particularly wild as they disappear into the long grass.

FOOD & DRINK

Caoldair Coffee and Craft Shop 🏔 highly.quietly.chip 🖉 01528 544231 📘 Set out as a steading with several doors along one stone building, serving hot drinks and lots of tempting cakes and bakes. Cards, candles, knitted clothing, jewellery and other locally made gifts are also available.

13 DALWHINNIE DISTILLERY

Dalwhinnie PH19 1AA 🖉 01540 672219 🖉 malts.com/en-row/distilleries/dalwhinnie

Dalwhinnie is a small hamlet at the southwest edge of the national park, pressed against the River Truim. Its name in Gaelic means 'meeting place', which might seem odd given its remote location between the Cairngorm and Monadhliath mountain ranges. However, this was once a well-trodden crossroads for cattle drovers making their way north to south. Today, Dalwhinnie lies close to where the A889 joins the A9, and it also has a train station, so its name continues to ring true.

The main site of interest for visitors to Dalwhinnie is its distillery – both the highest and coldest working distillery in Scotland. It was built here because of its close proximity to the railway, which

"My guide points out snow guards on the roof and a tree that's been blown so fiercely that it now grows at a diagonal angle."

brought in supplies before lorries took over the job. Dalwhinnie is one of the more striking distilleries – the smart white building has a smoky grey roof and two ventilators with the concave-shaped eaves seen in East Asian pagoda-style architecture and lots of other whisky distilleries. On arrival, you'll see the visitor centre beside the distillery itself, and there's also a covered bar area under a tarpaulin, where you can admire cloud-capped mountains while sipping a drink.

Black Wood & Dun da Lamh Fort

✳ OS Landranger map 35; start: Laggan Wolftrax Centre 🔲 year.today.hiker;
4¼ miles; moderate.

This out-and-back route leads away from Laggan Wolftrax and up into the hills on a gentle incline. At the top of hilly Black Craig is the **Pictish fort** of Dun da Lamh, where chaffinches call in the pines and bees buzz in the heather in summer. All that remains visible of the fort now are sections of laid stone

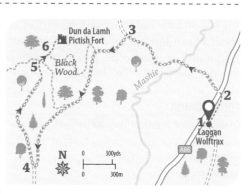

disappearing into mossy banks. It's a fantastic vantage point, offering views south over lumpy hills and northwest to a wide swelling of the River Spey, its surface changing colour as clouds shift overhead.

1 Walk northeast away from Laggan Wolftrax Centre towards the far corner of the car park, where the purple waymarked Dun da Lamh trail begins.

2 In 200yds, the path bends left and reaches the road. Cross over and head down a vehicle track.

3 Half a mile later, a small wooden sign for Hilltop/Fort appears on the left. Follow this through a wide gate and you'll emerge into an open clearing with a bank of towering trees on your right and hills further back to your left. As the path begins to climb, the forest closes in on both sides briefly before opening out again.

4 After climbing steadily for a while, the path hairpins to the right. The forest above you is Black Wood. Continue on this uphill track for half a mile. Once you're back under the trees, the vehicle track narrows to a footpath and steepens, but this sharper incline only lasts a few minutes before levelling out.

5 Straight ahead you'll see a picnic table and an interpretive plaque. Next to this, a wooden post points right to the fort.

6 The path enters a brief clearing scattered with deadwood, then climbs a steep bank beside a rocky outcrop covered in heather. This is trickier terrain to walk on, with chips of rock and roots underfoot. At the top you'll reach the fort site. Once you've had your fill of the view, return via the outward route.

A 45-minute tour guides visitors through the process of making Dalwhinnie's 15-year-old single malt, nicknamed 'the gentle spirit'. Start by learning about the fresh mineral water sourced from Lochan na Doire-uaine and finish with a nosing and tasting of three different drams, each paired with its own handmade chocolate truffle.

There are numerous whisky tours to choose from in this part of Scotland and I always look for something special. Dalwhinnie is one of the most remote distilleries in the Cairngorms, and wilderness is what the region is known for. It's fully exposed to the elements; my guide points out snow guards on the roof and a tree that's been blown so fiercely that it now grows at a diagonal angle. It's Dalwhinnie's isolation that makes it unique, but the truffles were a welcome bonus too.

CASTLE ROY TRUST
www.castleroy.org.uk

Murd... ...ucket List!

Castle Roy offers all ability access, a
quiet picnic spot, and stunning views
of the Cairngorm Mountains...

Let your imagination run free!

Castle Roy, Nethy Bridge, PH25 3ED

Forest Bathing Walks in the Cairngorms National Park

Forest Bathing or Shinrin-yoku, is the
practice of immersing yourself in
nature to enhance health and wellbeing.

Sessions suitable for all abilities and
ages - private and group sessions
available all year round.

www.highlandquietlife.co.uk

The award-winning Slow Travel series from Bradt Guides

Over 20 regional guides across Britain.
See the full list at bradtguides.com/slowtravel.

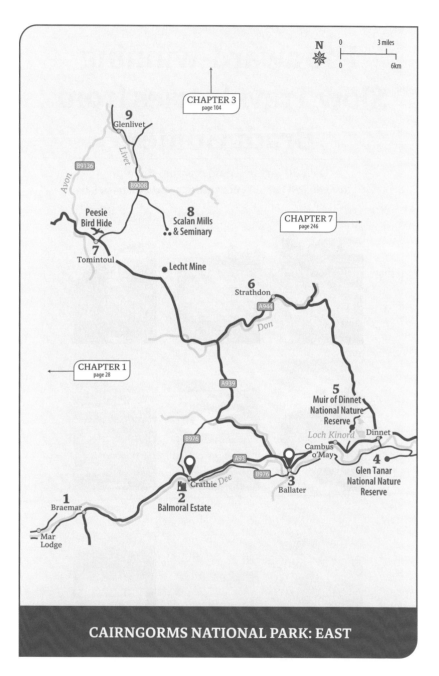

N

| 0 | | 3 miles |
| 0 | | 6km |

CHAPTER 3
page 104

9 Glenlivet

Avon

Livet

B9136

B9008

Peesie
Bird Hide

8 Scalan Mills
& Seminary

CHAPTER 7
page 246

7 Tomintoul

Lecht Mine

6 Strathdon

A944

Don

CHAPTER 1
page 28

A939

5 Muir of Dinnet
National Nature
Reserve

Loch Kinord **Dinnet**

Cambus
o'May

B976

A93

B976

3 Ballater

4 Glen Tanar
National Nature
Reserve

2 Crathie *Dee*

Balmoral Estate

1 Braemar

Mar
Lodge

CAIRNGORMS NATIONAL PARK: EAST

2
CAIRNGORMS NATIONAL PARK: EAST

Separated from the western half of the Cairngorms National Park by the Grampian Mountains, the eastern half is mostly more secluded, with larger expanses of moorland between its few settlements. It extends from Glenlivet Estate in the north to Braemar in the south and Dinnet in the east. Outside of the populated hubs of Tomintoul, Braemar and Ballater, it'll mostly just be you, sheep and the occasional buzzard. Many places of interest around here are located within Royal Deeside – a region overlapping the River Dee as it flows east across the national park towards Aberdeen.

A link to royalty is what draws many visitors to this side of the Cairngorms: the royal family's Balmoral Estate lies between Braemar and Ballater. If this is something that interests you, look out for the Victoria Heritage Trail signs with Queen Victoria's silhouette on them, which point out places she was particularly fond of visiting. Rather than include Balmoral Castle, which unsurprisingly gets a lot of attention, I've rummaged around for some quirkier locations, such as ancient hut circles, a roadside stone that rings like a bell and a miniature jungle inside a towering granite bowl.

Thirty miles north of Balmoral is Glenlivet Estate, offering a generous selection of historical curios: crumbling bridges, a secret seminary, a Slow-moving distillery, smugglers' trails and an iron-ore mine in the middle of nowhere. Many of these are linked by waymarked paths that cross woodland, moorland and rivers. This area also has official Dark Sky sites, making it a great place for stargazing or – if you're lucky – seeing the northern lights.

Everything feels more remote on this side of the national park. There's only one main road connecting its top and bottom halves and even that is compressed on both sides by heather and hills. This is arguably the book's best example of genuine Scottish seclusion.

GETTING AROUND

Because of the mountains in the middle of the Cairngorms National Park, getting from the west side to the east requires a trip north or south, depending on where you are. From Grantown-on-Spey, you can travel north on the A95 and back south on the B9008 to reach Glenlivet. If you're way down in Dalwhinnie, you'll have to dip south into Perthshire and pass through Pitlochry in order to head back north on the A93 towards Braemar.

Luckily, this latter route is a visual treat, taking you over the Cairnwell Pass. At 2,199ft, this is Britain's highest public road and part of the **SnowRoads** (⌀ snowroads.com). A 90-mile route starting in Blairgowrie (Perth), the SnowRoads cover most of the main roads in this chapter. If approaching from the southern end, you'll be welcomed to the Cairngorms with an alpine climb on unblemished tarmac, dotted with laybys named things like 'Devil's Elbow Viewpoint'. Utilise these pull-over spots – it's a chance to savour the majesty of the mountains without leaving your car.

"Utilise these pull-over spots – it's a chance to savour the majesty of the mountains without leaving your car."

The SnowRoads lead through Braemar, Ballater and Tomintoul before continuing to its final stop at Grantown-on-Spey. It's a stunning drive but, as the name suggests, not one to be messed with in severe weather. If you do visit in winter, check the forecast in advance and follow any travel warnings (visit ⌀ traffic.gov.scot for live updates) before starting your journey.

Many other roads in this area are single lane with passing places, but this is part of what makes it special. Slow is the aim of our game, after all. Petrol stations can be scarce, so I recommend filling up in villages such as Ballater before setting off on long trips.

BUSES

If you swear by public transport, I'm sorry to say the eastern half of the Cairngorms National Park makes life a challenge, as there are no trains at all. The Stagecoach 201 bus from Aberdeen connects Dinnet, Ballater, Crathie and Braemar, but Glenlivet Estate is another story. The 364 from Grantown-on-Spey can get you to Tomintoul on Wednesdays at 10.35 and 13.25, or there's the 365 from Keith to Tomintoul on Tuesdays, Thursdays and Fridays at 16.30. But that's all, folks. Your best bet for

i TOURIST INFORMATION

Ballater iCentre Station Sq, AB35 5QB ✆ 01339 755306 ✉ ballater@visitscotland.com
Crathie Information Centre The Car Park, Crathie AB35 5UL ✆ 01339 742414
✉ crathie@visitscotland.com
Tomintoul & Glenlivet Discovery Centre The Square, AB37 9ET ✆ 01807 580760
✉ discovery@tgdt.org.uk

exploring Glenlivet is a car rental, but even then you'll have to go to Aviemore (page 20) to pick one up.

WALKING & CYCLING

Whether you prefer striding or strolling, there's a trail to suit here. Maps and waymarks are particularly plentiful in Glenlivet Estate, making navigation along established trails nice and easy. The terrain will depend on where you decide to go; Balmoral Estate has undulating but compacted earth tracks, while attractions catered to visitors such as Muir of Dinnet National Nature Reserve have even trails suitable for wheelchairs and buggies. Many villages have produced excellent walking leaflets, often available on map boards or in tourist information centres. As well as describing colour-coded trails, they also provide overviews of the history, wildlife and landscape of each village.

Cyclists interested in long-distance routes might consider joining parts of National Route 195. Beginning in Aberdeen, this extends west into the national park, loosely following the A93 before finishing 41 miles later in Ballater. Because of all the country lanes, especially around Glenlivet, road cycling is a great way to travel while sticking to smooth surfaces.

CYCLE HIRE

Bike Glenlivet ⧉ assurance.yacht.pass ✆ 07963 217793 ⬛ Glenlivet Mountain Bike Trail Centre. In the middle of a forest and accessible by a gravel track that doesn't register on Google Maps – best seen on satellite view. As well as hiring bikes, you can also cycle on-site trails and refuel at the café. Check Facebook for events.
Bike Station Ballater Station Sq, AB35 5RB ✆ 01339 754004 ⬦ bikestationballater.co.uk. Hire prices start from £25 per day for mountain bikes and £40 per day for electric mountain bikes. Helmets, locks and tool kits included for all models.

BRAEMAR TO DINNET

Encompassing the villages of Braemar and Ballater, this is the most populated part of the eastern Cairngorms, and also offers the most variety in terms of shopping and eating out. That said, you'll still find plenty of wilderness in and around these two settlements, with regularly alternating pockets of pine woodland, rivers and lochs inside quiet glens. From the south, access to this half of the national park is via the Cairnwell Pass on the A93, which takes you on an impressive tour through the mountains (page 80).

1 BRAEMAR

🏠 **Cranford Guest House** (page 317)

Best-known for the annual **Braemar Gathering**, arguably the most famous Highland Games, Braemar sits in the centre of the national park, closer to the Grampian Mountains than anywhere else in this chapter. Its grandest building is the centrally located Fife Arms Hotel, with its large stone wall frontage, bay windows and terracotta-coloured gable ornaments. Other, more modest, buildings are constructed of the same large stone blocks and many have sash windows, giving them a cottage feel. The River Dee loops around Braemar to the north, while Clunie Water dissects it through the middle. A good spot to admire this narrower water channel is via the bridge beside the war memorial on Old Military Road.

The **Braemar Highland Games Centre** (Broombank Tce, AB35 5YX ⚭ highlandgamescentre.org ☉ Jul–Oct 10.00–16.00 Sat & Sun), just west of the village centre, has an exhibition about Highland Gatherings throughout Scotland. Displays include 19th-century letters from the Braemar Highland Society, bagpipes played at previous games and programmes going back some 50 years. The earliest record of a modern Gathering here is from 1832, when the Braemar Highland Society awarded cash prizes to competitors for the first time. Queen Victoria first attended in 1848, by which point the event was already well-established, and members of the royal family have attended every year

---

1 A walk up Creag Choinnich gives lovely views over Braemar. **2** Braemar Gathering annual Highland Games. **3** Balmoral. **4** Ballater's pretty station is now a tourist information centre. **5** A Balmoral Memorial Cairn. ▶

VISITABERDEENSHIRE

VISITABERDEENSHIRE

VISITABERDEENSHIRE

IMAGE COURTESY OF THE BRAEMAR GATHERING ANNUAL

ANGUS REID/S

Balmoral memorial cairns

❋ OS Explorer map OL53; start at Crathie car park ▦ nicer.tummy.daffodils;
📍 NO2639994956; 6 miles; easy.

- -

Parking in Crathie for the day demands a hefty £5, so this long walk connecting most of the Balmoral Cairns justifies the price of the privilege. With no way markers, I recommend following this specific route, which includes what3words codes for each cairn so you can see where they are.

1 From the car park, follow a minor road just left of the post office. After 500yds, turn right at the T-junction and continue to a suspension bridge over the Dee. Cross and turn right on to the B976, then left at the next junction, signposted for Lochnagar Distillery. After a brief hill, turn right to cross a tiny road bridge, then immediately turn left up a private road.

2 Opposite a stone fountain memorial is a sign for Prince Albert's Cairn, pointing left up a narrower footpath. Follow this and pass through a metal gate. Around the bend you'll see Princess Beatrice's cairn (▦ object.party.landowner) ahead.

3 At the top of this uphill path is the biggest and most famous cairn: Prince Albert's (▦ purely. wells.inversion). Standing to the left of it with Balmoral's dense forest spread out below you, head left to join a footpath meandering southwest through the trees.

4 After bending downhill, the path joins a vehicle track. Turn right and follow it to a fork, with a signpost to Crathie Car Park pointing right. Head left through a wooden gate.

5 Carry on for half a mile, ignoring the first side path branching right. Take the second one further up, just as a white building appears through the trees ahead.

6 After a quarter of a mile, turn right, steeply uphill. Princess Alice's cairn (▦ collision.wound. rooks) emerges in 300yds. After this, continue along the path, following it around until you arrive at a T-junction.

7 Turn right, heading uphill, then left at the next T-junction. After 150yds, step off the main track and take a trodden path that branches left into the trees to Prince Arthur's cairn (▦ walled. gagging.compiler). Carry on past the cairn, bending right until you rejoin the main trail.

8 Stay straight at the next T-junction, past a sign for Balmoral Estate walks. Shortly after, a detour to the left takes you to Prince Leopold's cairn (▦ windpipe.year.showrooms). Retrace your steps to the junction with the estate sign. Now turn left and then left again as another path joins from the right.

9 Climb into the open and the Purchase Cairn (▦ carting.corrosive.research) appears, commemorating when the estate was bought for Queen Victoria in 1852. When you've finished admiring the vast bird's-eye view of the estate here, continue following the path.

10 After 200yds you'll reach Princess Louise's cairn (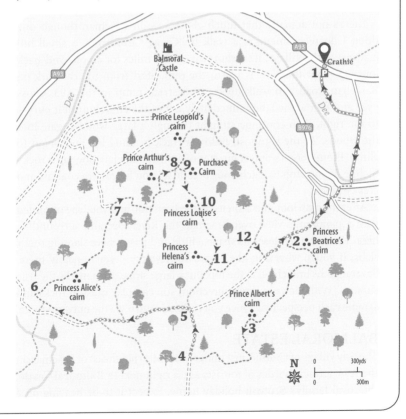 caves.appear.tastier) on a grassy knoll. Follow a detour track branching right for a closer look, before returning to the main path and following it for another 500yds.

11 Look for rough rocky steps branching right for a short detour to Princess Helena's cairn (flatten.distilled.sleeps). Afterwards, return to the main path and bear left at the fork, crossing a footbridge over a dry gorge.

12 Turn right at the next junction and climb a gradual hill, passing a cottage on the left. At the end of this path, turn sharply left and head through a wooden gate to join a vehicle track. The Prince Albert Cairn sign you followed near the start appears again, now on the right. Retrace your steps to the car park.

since. While here, look up at the impressive octagonal ceiling window, which has a central aperture that gives it the appearance of a huge wheel. In each of the spaces between the 'spokes' are portraits of men in formal Highland dress, painted by Kenneth Macleay in 1870.

On Balnellan Road, just off the main road that runs through the centre of Braemar, you'll find the fragmented remains of **Kindrochit Castle**, believed to date back to the 14th-century reign of King Robert II, son of Robert the Bruce. In one area, excavations have revealed a large number of bones belonging to sheep, deer, salmon and even eagles and otters, making this a likely location for the larder or kitchen. Sir Malcolm Drummond, the king's brother-in-law, added a tower that reputedly made Kindrochit Scotland's sixth largest castle. Today, it's reduced to crumbled walls and looks rather maze-like with footpaths running between shoulder-height stone dividers, thickly fringed in grass.

There's not actually that much else to see in Braemar, though one thing I do recommend is a walk up **Creag Choinnich**, a small hill just east of the village. It's a short hike – 1½ miles for an out-and-back journey – but the view is worth the puff. Start from the car park on Balnellan Road and walk up the pedestrian ramp to the A93. Cross over and follow the lane immediately left of the church until it curves to the right, then continue straight through a large wooden gate into the woods. At the signpost, follow a track heading left and begin to climb. From here it's only a quarter of a mile, but a fair slog, up a rocky incline. If you stop to catch your breath, all you'll hear are coal tits and creaky pines.

After the path loops back on itself, the trees thin and you'll be rewarded with a panoramic view over Braemar, the River Dee and surrounding hills. The path then loses its shape a little and passes over slanting rocky slabs. If you're wheezing like I was, don't worry – you're nearly there. Several paths branch off at the top, but a large stone cairn marks the true summit. With views in every direction, you can play musical rocks and sample each perspective. Once you're done, return via the outward route.

2 BALMORAL ESTATE

The tiny village of Crathie, just under nine miles northeast of Braemar on the A93, attracts hordes of tourists as it's right next to **Balmoral Castle**, the royal family's Scottish holiday home. Expect it to be heaving on a midsummer's afternoon, though you can escape the crush by arriving in the morning for a thoroughly enjoyable stomp through Balmoral Estate before anyone else shows up. The pine forest here is impressive by itself, but it has the added bonus of a treasure hunt (page 84). You might have heard of the 40ft-high stone pyramid erected among the trees in memory of Prince Albert, made from uniform grey blocks that taper to a fine point, but also hidden in the forest are smaller cairns commemorating each of his and Queen Victoria's children. These are conical stone structures made from lichen-crusted boulders and chips of smaller rock stuffed into the gaps.

3 BALLATER

🏠 **Ballater Hostel** (page 317) ⛺ **Howe of Torbeg** (page 317)

Eight miles east of Crathie is Ballater, an attractive village of old stone buildings. Two small greens are separated by Glenmuick Church, and around this central square you'll find a number of independent shops and restaurants, including the George Strachan deli (⌀ georgestrachanltd. co.uk) with its old-fashioned forest green frontage. The village is hemmed in on three sides by a pair of steep, forested hills and a loop of the River Dee, which all have their own established footpaths. I've highlighted two of these in a guided walk (page 88).

"The village is hemmed in on three sides by a pair of steep, forested hills and a loop of the River Dee."

Highland Games have been held in Monaltrie Park, at the north end of Ballater, every August since 1889. One of the more gruelling events is the hill race, where competitors run up and down the steep nearby hill of Craig Coillich. Ballater Hostel has a league table of the fastest times – during my stay the record was 13 minutes 24 seconds.

The restored white- and peppermint-coloured building next to the visitor car park in Station Square, now a tourist iCentre (page 81) and library, was once – as the signs still attest – Ballater Station. This refers to the Deeside Railway line, which was extended to Ballater in 1866 and ceased running in 1966. The long-distance **Deeside Way** starts in Ballater and loosely follows this old railway line to Aberdeen.

Along central Bridge Street you'll find a range of tightly packed giftshops. My favourite is **Deeside Books** (⌀ deesidebooks.com) – it doesn't look big from the outside but there are roughly 10,000 books in here, so it's definitely worth a rummage.

Two loops around Ballater

✻ OS Landranger map 4; start: Bridge Square, Ballater ◫ beams.couriers.earth;
♥ NO37146 95655; 4 miles; moderate.

This route climbs through Pannanich Woods up to Craig Coillich ('the witch's rocky hill' in Gaelic) then follows a river path beside the Dee. The terrain is mainly even, although it's a steep uphill slog to Craig Coillich. Take your pick of motivations – the view from the top perhaps, or something tempting from Shorty's ice-cream parlour (page 90).

1 From the small green at Bridge Square, cross the road bridge over the Dee. At the T-junction, a couple of paths into Pannanich Woods appear ahead. Cross the B976 and take the left footpath to begin climbing. After the first bend, the path splits into three – take the middle route up a steep rooty bank.

2 When the trail breaks on to a wider gravel track, cross over and continue up a narrow winding trail into more trees – this is the thigh-burner section. Keep left when another trail cuts across from the right and carry on to the highest point, Craig Coillich (1,302ft), marked by a stone cairn. Walk past it on the same path, now curving downhill. When another track crosses in front of you, turn right on to it. This follows a bumpy but downward sloping track along a corridor between pines, with views of distant hills.

3 Bend right again and the now wide vehicle track leads downhill to a T-junction. Cut straight across to a narrow footpath in the bracken beside a wooden post marked 'Mackenzie Memorial Walk'. This enters a pocket of birch woodland, contrasting with the pines encountered earlier. In 100yds, the path presses up against a pool on the right.

4 When an established gravel footpath comes in from the left, bear right to join it. The **Mackenzie Memorial** appears after another 100yds – a pink stone structure with a pyramid-topped wall in the centre and shallow steps leading to a wide oval platform. Beneath a stag's head crest is an inscription in memory of Sir Allan Russell Mackenzie (1850–1906). The Mackenzies were well-loved in Ballater and it's said they gave venison to poorer people during hard winters.

5 Some 150yds past the memorial, take a path forking left, leading downhill to the B976 you crossed near the start. Return over the road bridge.

Many visitors flock to Ballater for Loch Muick, a popular upland loch 11 miles south in Balmoral Estate. However, I recommend staying in the village for a walk – there are a number of options that don't require a car to reach and offer a broader range of habitats. The route above includes pine woodland, shingle riverbanks and wildflower-rich grassland.

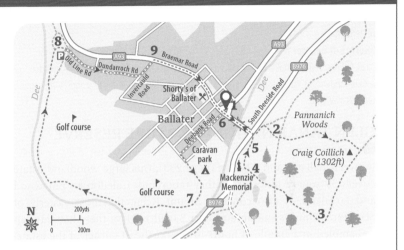

6 Opposite the green at Bridge Square, take the side street on the left, Deebank Road, and walk to the end. Turn left, following a green sign for Riverside Walk, and take a narrow gravel footpath to the right of the caravan park. Follow it round to the right, passing patches of honeysuckle that thrum with bees in summer.

7 The river appears on the left, but the path leans away from it, hemmed on both sides by broom, beech and birch. You'll emerge by the river again 500yds further on, at a shingle bank. Look out for dippers – as their name suggests, these river-dwelling birds dip almost constantly. Follow this footpath in a big U shape, keeping close to the water.

8 When you arrive in a gravel car park, bear right out of it and continue straight to Old Line Road. At the crossroads, keep straight again down a footpath with a stone wall running down the left side. This joins Dundarroch Road. At the end, turn left on to Invercauld Road to reach Braemar Road.

9 Turn right to walk back through Ballater to the start point, or stop for that ice cream on the way.

FOOD & DRINK

Clachan Grill Bridge Sq, AB35 5QP ☏ 01339 755999 🖱 clachangrill.com ⏱ 12.00–20.00 Thu–Sun. Within a converted steading close to the River Dee, serving modernised Scottish classics with locally sourced ingredients such as meat from Neil Menzies Butchers in Braemar and produce from the deli down the road (page 87). Dogs welcome in the bar area.

Lochnagar Indian Brasserie Church Sq, AB35 5NE ✆ 01339 755611 ⬠ lochnagarindian.
co.uk ⊙ 12.00–14.00 & 17.00–23.00 daily. Fresh and light Indian cuisine, offering both
popular classics and original dishes using traditional recipes passed down from generation
to generation.

Shorty's of Ballater Bridge St, AB35 5QP ✆ 01339 756215 ⬠ shortysicecreamparlour.
co.uk ⊙ noon–18.00 daily. Ideally placed on the green. Choose from dough rings, gelato
cookie sandwiches, sundaes, waffles and smoothies as well as a variety of scoops, with vegan
options available.

4 GLEN TANAR NATIONAL NATURE RESERVE

/// safest.gems.thank

Between Ballater and Aboyne (page 263), this large woodland estate
covers 39 square miles of heather moorland, Caledonian pinewood
and farmland. It also contains Mount Keen, the most easterly of
Scotland's Munros (mountains over 3,000ft). All of these habitats can
be sampled in a couple of hours in the northeast corner of the estate,
where you'll find a visitor centre, toilets and several short circular
walking trails. The two-mile Knockie Trail passes pine woodland in
one direction and the Water of Tanar, another river en route to the
Dee, in the other. A range of trees line the riverbanks including silver
birch, pine and beech. Halfway round this trail is **Knockie Viewpoint**,
an excellent spot for taking in the sweeping hills. In 1843, a hoard
of Bronze Age bracelets, axe heads and cups were unearthed from a
hole in the ground here – why they were stashed together remains
a mystery.

Close to **Braeloine Visitor Centre**, a small building beside the car
park offering a condensed history of the estate, is the small **Chapel of
St Lesmo**. Named after a Christian hermit who lived here over 1,200
years ago, the chapel is simply built with rough-cut stone and a tiled
roof. During the 17th and 18th centuries it was an inn offering food and
shelter to cattle drovers; it now hosts local weddings.

The estate's appearance is largely down to Thomas Coats, known as
Lord Glentanar. Much of Deeside's timber was felled during World
War II, but Coats ensured that the most ancient trees were spared. He
introduced continental woodland management strategies and mixed
young and old trees together to create a more natural habitat. Coats's
daughter, Jean Bruce, inherited the estate in 1971 and established it as
a National Nature Reserve, protecting the glen's landscape and wildlife.

5 MUIR OF DINNET NATIONAL NATURE RESERVE

🏠 **Loch Kinord Hotel** (page 317)

AB34 5NB 🌐 hothouse.rods.spindles 🧭 nature.scot

This is one of my favourite spots in the book because it combines wildlife, geology, woodland scenery and history in one small area. Located 5¾ miles northeast of Ballater, the reserve has a selection of trails, all offering something different. In the pine woodland you might see red squirrels or roe deer, while the long grass in the open meadow flickers with the hasty retreats of mice. **Loch Kinord**, inhabited by mute swans, greylag geese and goldeneye ducks, has several islands including one that once held a castle before it burned down in the 17th century. Now the loch is overcome by waterlilies, their white flowers clearly visible even from its far side. Flat paths of gravel or grass link all of these habitats together.

I must start with **The Vat**, the reserve's most spectacular feature, which is accessed via a waymarked trail of less than a mile starting from the car park. When the path ends beside a narrow rocky crevice, carefully step across the rocks, duck beneath a giant rock slab and emerge into what feels like a granite fishbowl. Across this small clearing, a skinny waterfall gushes down slick boulders. Icy water seeps between a cluster of smaller rocks, across the grit of the clearing, and out through the stepping stones you just walked across. Either side are hulking giants of granite as tall as houses, with bracken and birch saplings stuffed in the cracks. The sharp rustle of the waterfall blends with the deeper mumble of the stream beneath.

A morning visit is better – you're more likely to have the place to yourself and at this time the sun streams through the gap in the bowl, making the rock glisten. Forgive me for being dramatic but honestly, with its shaggy foliage and dripping boulders, The Vat wouldn't look out of place in a sticky jungle. If there was ever a place to meditate, this is it.

Elsewhere on the reserve are pockets of history spanning thousands of years. The 2½-mile **Little Ord Trail** links up a 9th-century **Pictish stone cross** and the remains of **thatched huts** some 2,000 years old – now marked by circles of boulders half-hidden in grass. With access to reeds for thatching, stone and turf for walls, and bracken and heather for bedding, this land was ideal for hut building. On the opposite side of the trail are the crumbled fragments of abandoned farming cottages, home to the community of Old Kinord in the 1840s. Of its 22 inhabitants, the

youngest worker was Elizabeth Eggo, an 11-year-old servant of one of the farmers. Now the ruins are home to lapwings, rabbits and a flurry of butterflies and moths.

I happily filled four hours ambling along the Vat and Little Ord trails without even completing the whole circuit of Loch Kinord. The small **Visitor Centre** here is staff dependent so may not be open even in summer. If it is, you'll find wall displays about the wildlife, landscape and history of the reserve and a nature table of skulls, nests and snake skins.

FOOD & DRINK

Cambus O'May Cheese & Milk Hoose Café AB35 5SD ✆ 01339 753113 ⬛. This small roadside café between Ballater and Muir of Dinnet serves toasties, ice cream, homemade quiche of the day and fresh cakes and bakes. You can also purchase a selection of locally made and handcrafted cheeses from Cambus O'May Cheese Company here.

MOVING NORTH THROUGH THE HILLS

Heading north from Ballater, you'll follow the A939 as it bends with the River Gairn then passes over it across the steeply arched Gairnshiel Bridge. On the other side, Old Military Road leads through a brief section studded with pines before breaking into the open, where you'll be surrounded by heather moorland in every direction. Despite its seclusion, the road is wonderfully smooth.

Half a mile past the bridge is a worthwhile diversion: turn in and park just past an unused stone bridge to the left of the road (▥ skewing. initiates.coveted). A narrow, indented path in the grass leads away from the bridge, up a tiny hill. Over the crest is a slanting boulder with a flat edge and deep lines across its front face. Although it looks no different from any other rock, it's actually a geological marvel. If you tap it with a stone, it makes a dull clanging sound like a bell. Try other parts of the boulder and you'll hear different pitches. Rocks like this are described as **Ringing Stones**, although explanations for why they ring are still largely speculative. I love this one because it's easy to reach, yet countless people drive past without even knowing it's there.

◀ **1** Muir of Dinnet NNR. **2** The Vat – Muir of Dinnet's most striking feature. **3** Glen Tanar NNR.

Once you've had your fill of hitting rocks, this is a peaceful spot to stop among the heather and watch buzzards mewling overhead before setting off again.

6 STRATHDON

Named after its location across the River Don, Strathdon lies roughly equidistant between Ballater and Glenlivet. Consisting almost solely of houses and a Spar convenience store, it's perhaps most famous for the Lonach Highland Gathering held here each August. Regarded as 'Scotland's friendliest games', it includes a march from the Lonach Highlanders, a group of non-military men belonging to the Lonach Highland and Friendly Society. As is tradition for most Highland Games, the day also features field events, pipe music and Highland dancing.

In a field beside the A944, just before the road bends east through Strathdon, is a large mound that looks like it's had its top chopped off by some unruly giant. This is the **Doune of Invernochty**, which has supported a range of structures such as a Pictish fort, a 12th-century motte and bailey castle, and a church. During World War II, it was used as a Royal Observer Corps Observation Post.

Almost directly across the road is a small free car park (excavated. mourner.fame), ideally positioned for a closer look at the Doune before heading off on a proper ramble along the **Bunzeach Trail.** Though it has the odd vehicle track, most of this 4¼-mile circular is a stomp through woodland devoid of footprints. In summer it's a particular treat as the grass brushes your waist and butterflies flicker in every direction. I love a walk that doesn't feel like it's walked very often.

From the car park, walk away from the Doune and cross a footbridge over the Don. Head uphill to reach **Upper Donside Parish Church** with its delicate spire and miniature turrets. After this, turn left at the T-junction. The Bunzeach Trail continues up a grassy track to the right of the tarmac road, through a wide metal gate. For the first stretch it stays in the open, bordering the forest to the right with fields below to the left.

After trees appear on both sides, the path climbs gently to another junction. The walk can be extended straight on towards Coulick Hill, but turn right to keep on the main Bunzeach Trail. Now the path is much grassier, especially in summer, but there are faint vehicle treads for easier walking. You'll pass through classic Cairngorms pines with their trunks tinged orange. Look out for dragonflies perched on the gorse in warm weather.

Eventually the path meets another T-junction. From here the route gets more complicated, but there are now blue waymarkers to guide you. Turn right then take another right at the next blue post. After rounding a bend to the right, look for two posts close together on the left. Follow them downhill into the open and bear right to run parallel to a minor road. Shortly after, the path curves back uphill then left into a shaded plantation.

Pass through two metal gates. After the second one, the path turns sharply to the right. Before that though, it's worth turning left for a bonus view of the church and mountains behind. Once you're done, return to the gate and continue straight on to the vehicle track you came up at the start. Turn left and follow it back to the church.

GLENLIVET ESTATE

Glenlivet Estate has a jumble of ruined castles, forests, rivers, ancient bridges, distilleries and isolated historical oddities. There's a good mix of habitats in its hushed landscape, with the chance to amble along rivers, heather-lined hedgerows and woodland edges in just a short distance. Whisky springs to mind too – The Glenlivet distillery stands in a remote valley, which was the perfect location during the era of illicit distilling.

Located at the northern boundary of the national park, 14 miles east of Grantown-on-Spey, the estate's 90 square miles of farmland, woodland and moorland are well signposted; boards containing local information and walking trails of varying lengths are at every major parking place. Within the estate boundary are the Cromdale Hills to the northwest and the Ladder Hills to the southeast.

The only substantial village in Glenlivet Estate is Tomintoul, on the south side, and this is where you'll find most people. In most cases, it'll just be you and the wilderness. Seeing as there are so few built-up areas, this part of the national park is an excellent place for stargazing, and was awarded International Dark Sky status in 2018. Check out the public Facebook group Cairngorms Astronomy Group (🈳) to find out about local sightings and events throughout the year.

If you're approaching from Strathdon, you'll pass the **Lecht Mine** (🈳 mull.fewer.forum) first, lying just off the A939 as it bends west towards Tomintoul. In the 1730s this was a site for digging iron ore, from where it was then carried 20 miles on horseback to Nethy Bridge. The only remaining building is a crushing mill that looks like a plain grey house, half a mile from the car park. The track to it runs parallel to a burn threading in the opposite direction, looking especially lovely if the heather's in bloom. At the turn of the 19th century, when illegal stills were hidden in these remote hills, this was one of the paths used to smuggle whisky.

7 TOMINTOUL

🏠 **Argyle House** (page 317)

Tomintoul lies east of the River Avon, which begins beside Cairngorm Mountain as Loch Avon and eventually joins the Spey near Ballindalloch Castle (page 115). This village is sometimes described as the highest in the Scottish Highlands, although measurements of it vary from 1,131ft to 1,160ft. A mere 29ft might seem frivolous at these heights, but Dalwhinnie, 50 miles southwest, is a close contender at 1,151ft. I'm not fussed either way: Tomintoul is undoubtedly quite high up and a lovely place to visit.

"The estate's latitude and dark night skies make it one of the best places in the UK to see the northern lights."

Main Street has some weathered old stone houses and within the central square you'll find a restaurant, post office and **Tomintoul & Glenlivet Discovery Centre** (☉ Mar–Oct 10.00–13.00 & 14.00–17.00 daily; page 81). As well as leaflets, walk maps and other tourist information, this has a stylish museum showcasing Tomintoul's geology, wildlife, sport, agriculture and history, including the age of illicit whisky stills. It's all in one large room but displays cover the walls and free-standing pillars. Rocks and minerals, flint arrowheads, clothes, shoes, coins, farming machinery and even 1930s skis add to the experience. Many of these items were found in or near Tomintoul, like the smart men's coat with mother of pearl buttons that was discovered stuffed between the rafters of a house in 2003. There's also a den for little ones to crawl into and a virtual reality display at the front of the museum, where you can explore an illicit still.

Beside the museum room is a small **exhibition** celebrating Glenlivet's Dark Sky Park. The estate's latitude and dark night skies make it one of the best places in the UK to see the northern lights. In Scottish

A FIELD OF PEESIES

Just outside Tomintoul, beside the A939 as you approach from the east, is **Peesie Bird Hide** (*///* stumpy.verge.poetry). This cosy wooden building overlooking marshy grassland is easily walkable from the village, yet far enough away to be completely silent. Information boards fixed around the interior and star constellations on the ceiling give the hide dual purpose for birdwatchers and stargazers. Known as the Field of Hope, this spot is one of Glenlivet's **Dark Sky Discovery Sites**, offering good chances of seeing the northern lights on a clear winter's night.

Unlike in some other hides, the Peesie has windows on every side because birds can be seen from any angle. The area is a stronghold for breeding waders, and it's thanks to traditional farming practices that species such as curlew, redshank and lapwing – known locally as 'whap', 'feltifare' and 'peesie' – are thriving here, unlike in some other parts of Britain. Lapwing chicks in particular need open, damp ground with lots of insects. Tricky birds to find on the ground, they're often seen wheeling around in the air, beating wings shaped like tennis rackets.

Grassland is a more challenging habitat to spot birds in than lochs or estuaries, but that makes the eventual glimpse of its green iridescence and comma-shaped crest even more rewarding.

Gaelic folklore, they are known as 'na fir-chlis', meaning 'the nimble men'. The exhibition walls are covered floor to ceiling in planets and the green smudges of aurora, lit by moody blue lighting and annotated with Gaelic names. Learn about *A' Ghealach* (the moon), *An Corg* (Mars), *An Rìbhinn* (Venus) and more. The exhibition also features a section on Tomnaverie Stone Circle (page 260) and other ancient sites throughout Scotland.

Glenmulliach Forest

/// insisting.flicked.zipped

Spoilt as we are with so many forests in the Cairngorms, this is perhaps not the most promising one at first glance. However, Glenmulliach – 2¼ miles southeast of Tomintoul – offers a unique perspective not always possible when surrounded by towering pines. With a little uphill effort, you can rise above the trees to a viewpoint dominated by overlapping hills and snow-dusted peaks. A simple out-and-back 1½-mile **Viewpoint Trail** starts from the car park and leads you up a moderate incline through the forest. Begin beside a winding burn, which acts as a constant companion up the hill. Once you reach the viewpoint, pad across a stepping stone in the stream to a plaque pointing out surrounding landmarks such as the Cromdale Hills, blushing purple with heather in summer, and Cairngorm Mountain, imposing even from over 15 miles away. Here you're surrounded by short evergreens, either standing alone or with mismatched partners.

An alternative to returning the way you came is to take a slight detour via the **Nature Trail**, which heads roughly parallel to the Viewpoint Trail but higher up. This is more enjoyable terrain to walk on, with trees pressing in on both sides. Halfway along is a wooden hide so small you'll have to duck under the doorway to get in. With a thatched roof and logs criss-crossing at each corner, this rustic hidey-hole is complete with fold-up windows – perfect for scanning the opposite hillside for roe deer. Elsewhere on this trail are information plaques about wildlife you might be able to spot, including less conventional nature finds such as the great black slug.

ⓘ FOOD & DRINK

The Clockhouse Restaurant The Square, AB37 9ET ✆ 01807 580378
⊘ clockhouserestaurant.com ⊙ Apr–Oct. Classic Highland cuisine including haggis, venison and salmon. As well as lunch and dinner, you can drop in for home bakes, tea, coffee, local ales and malt whiskies.

8 SCALAN MILLS & SEMINARY

This is one of Glenlivet Estate's most charming and concealed historical spots, eight miles east of Tomintoul. Young priests were taught in secret here when Catholicism was outlawed in Scotland in the 18th century. Naturally, it had to be well-hidden, and Scalan is isolated in the middle of heather-coated hills and farmland bordered by mossy stone walls. It's unlikely you'll hear anything except a disgruntled curlew or distant sheep.

Any sign of people comes from Scalan itself, consisting of several stone farm buildings within a fenced enclosure. There are also two mills, once used by the farming community that lived and worked in this valley. Farming endured here from the late 17th century until as recently as 2003; the last family, the Mathesons, left after 150 years. Despite sitting so closely together, the North and South mills (built in the 1870s and 1900s respectively) were fed by separate burns and used by different tenants.

Similar to – although much smaller than – Newtonmore's Highland Folk Museum (page 66), Scalan has been left largely as it once was, allowing visitors to wander between the buildings and imagine what it would have been like centuries ago when grain was processed and priests were trained. There are boards dotted around and it's very visitor friendly, but preserved in a way that maintains the site's historical identity. Scalan provides a special insight into both the farming life of the past and of a Catholic refuge – whether you're religious or not, it's an ideal place for quiet contemplation.

The secret seminary was set up in 1716 by Bishop James Gordon and ran for 83 years. When it was in use, local residents kept an eye out and raised the alarm if they saw the authorities nearby. Letters were often intercepted, so code words were used including 'labourer' instead of 'priest' and 'the shop' instead of Scalan's name. Even today, the old seminary is significant for Roman Catholics as a place to commemorate a time when their faith was persecuted. The Scalan Association, that looks after the site, hosts a summer pilgrimage here each year, with hundreds of attendees from all over the world.

Visitors can explore inside the seminary building for free. Head through low doorways, across stone floors and beneath beamed ceilings to see where the bishop slept and the boys studied. The house has two storeys and its rooms are largely empty except for stone fireplaces and simple wooden tables. Thanks to its stone walls, it's cool even on a hot summer day.

A subtle brown sign on the B9008 for 'Scalan' – 4¾ miles northeast of Tomintoul just before the hamlet of Knockandhu – is the only clue that the seminary is here. Follow this sign right, down an unnamed single-lane road, through 3¼ miles of farmland. After passing buildings for a Chivas Brothers distillery and Highland Spring water, the road quality deteriorates, but you're almost there – branch right at the next

"Scalan is isolated in the middle of heather-coated hills and farmland bordered by mossy stone walls."

fork and down this track you'll arrive in the free Carrachs car park (headset.trustees.suits). This is another of Glenlivet's designated Dark Sky Sites, where it's possible to get fantastic views of the stars and Milky Way. From here, it's a half-mile walk through the glen to the seminary, following a flat path.

9 GLENLIVET

At the northern edge of Glenlivet Estate is a tangle of B roads also known as Glenlivet, which isn't quite a village but has a medical centre, primary school and its biggest draw: The Glenlivet Distillery (page 102). One of the most eye-catching features is the **Old Bridge of Livet** (▦ panoramic.boxer.hostels), a crumbling structure similar to the Old Packhorse Bridge in Carrbridge (page 43). There's space for a couple of cars just off the road, and a short staircase leads down to a viewing platform on the bank of the River Livet.

Peering out from its camouflage of saplings and shrubs, this bridge originally had three arches, but one was swept away in the Muckle Spate of 1829 (page 43); its two remaining arches now sport a shaggy fringe of grass. The clearing beside the bridge has a couple of benches and makes for a great picnic spot. Stop for a while and watch the peaty, golden water of the Livet flow under this fragile archway that's slowly dissolving into nature. As with all ancient monuments, please don't climb on it.

One mile west of the bridge is the ruin of **Drumin Castle** (▦ flaked. bloom.dices). It sits at the northern edge of the Cairngorms National Park, close to the point where the rivers Livet and Avon converge. With only two walls remaining, this tower house is thought to have been constructed around the early 1370s.

Depending on the time of year, Drumin Castle may be partially or completely concealed behind trees, but the open parking area beneath it has signs leading the way. The quickest route is via a path climbing uphill with a mix of shallow steps and pine needle-packed earth. At the top, look back for a panorama of open fields, rushing river and distant hills flanked by silver birches that glow purple in winter. The path forks, leading left to the castle and right to a walled garden. Currently the garden contains a small regiment of saplings, but one day it'll hopefully be a vibrant orchard of colour.

Down the left fork to the castle, head through a narrow alley between a stone wall and a private farmhouse garden next door. The first feature that draws the eye is a semi-circular cavern with moss cloaking its rocky edge. The ruin is very fragile, so it's best to admire it from ground level. Jackdaws have made the place their own and swirl overhead.

◄ **1** Upper Donside Parish Church. **2** Lecht Mine. **3** Peesie Bird Hide. **4** Old Bridge of Livet. **5** The Glenlivet Distillery.

It's possible to see Drumin on the 3½-mile **George Smith Trail**, the easiest of three routes through the wild Livet landscape. These **smugglers trails** enable you to walk in the footsteps of the region's historic whisky smugglers. A map of the routes can be picked up from The Glenlivet Distillery's visitor centre (see below), though note that the other two trails are graded as strenuous and advised for experienced walkers only.

The easy-going George Smith loop is named after the distillery's founder. It follows narrow grassy pathways across farmland, coniferous woodland and the River Livet, passing Drumin Castle before circling back. Close to one of the footbridges, there's a particularly pretty section where the trees dip their branches in the water. To begin, turn left out of the distillery car park, following the road until fields appear on both sides. Pass through a pedestrian gate on the left – from here you can follow trail waymarkers.

The distillery car park is also where you need to leave your car to visit the ruin of **Blairfindy Castle** (⊞ haircuts.pulse.accented), half a mile southeast. Tall, narrow and crumbled at the top with a couple of chimneys sticking into the sky, the castle is now occupied by wildlife – bird boxes and bat roosts have been fitted to provide suitable habitat. Duck under the stone doorway, only shoulder height on me, to see the interior: the walls are a combination of irregular slabs of grey and beige rock and smaller chips of flint-like rock, all filled in with cement.

Blairfindy Castle was constructed in the 16th century by John Gordon of Cluny, designed to look robust. Despite having stood in ruins for nearly three centuries after supposedly being burnt during the Battle of Culloden, it still looks strong today. Some of the missing stone sections have been filled in with standard house bricks, looking noticeably uniform beside the randomly slotted slabs of the original building.

The Glenlivet Distillery

AB37 9DB ☏ 01340 821720 ⊘ theglenlivet.com

Visitors are greeted at this distillery, tucked away in the northern end of Glenlivet Estate, with a cosy fireplace and plush armchairs in a luxurious reception area and shop. Golden colours, exposed brick and touches of copper all set the scene for a stylish tour and reflect the honey hues of The Glenlivet's whiskies, which burst with fruit and spice flavours.

Considering The Glenlivet is one of the world's best-selling Scottish whiskies, I was impressed by how local produce and sustainability

A TALE OF TWO PISTOLS

The Glenlivet has been in almost constant operation since 1824, and its remote location in the Livet Valley made it ideal for founder George Smith to start distilling illegally. Despite being concealed from customs officers, word still got out, and even King George IV requested a dram during a visit to Scotland.

Shortly after that, George Smith rode to Elgin to get his licence and he became the first legal distiller in the Livet Valley. This didn't sit well with illegal distillers and smugglers in the area, and they threatened to burn his distillery to the ground. George carried a pair of flintlock pistols on his belt for ten years, though he only fired warning shots to ne'er-do-wells twice. They're now on display in the distillery's visitor centre (see opposite).

Fighting to protect The Glenlivet continued as its popularity and reputation grew, with other distilleries adding the name to their own in imitation. After George's death in 1871, his son John battled hard in court to protect the name. Eventually, in 1884, he signed an indenture giving him the rights to it. By simply including 'The', he ensured there was only one true Glenlivet whisky.

remain firmly implanted in the company's principles. During the Original Distillery Tour (1½ hours), visitors learn how the barley is locally grown, the oak casks come from Isla Cooperage in Keith and the water is sourced from a well five minutes up the hill – the same water used by founder George Smith in the 19th century (see above).

Through informative videos, you're introduced to Sandrine and Ronald, who ensure that the distillery is as sustainable as possible. This includes turning byproduct into cattle feed or renewable energy, returning 96% of the used water back to the environment, and making all their electricity 100% zero carbon. You discover all of this while standing in an indoor field, where real barley lines a winding path lit by yellow fairy lights. I love that sustainability is such a key part of the visitor experience here.

Your guide explains the distilling process while you're standing inside a converted washback – the enormous circular containers where yeast is added. The warehouse has a satisfying display of rows of bottles showing how the whisky gets darker and richer in colour as it matures in the cask. You'll also see how much evaporates over time: this unavoidable part of the process is known as the 'angel's share'. Tours finish with three drams in the tasting room, at a horseshoe-shaped counter curled around a display column of bottles.

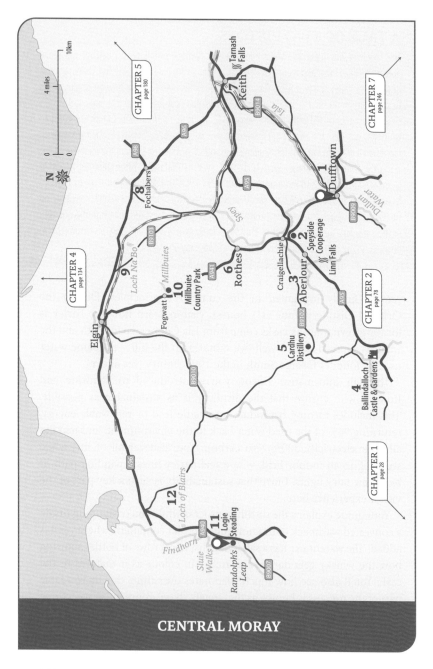

CENTRAL MORAY

3
CENTRAL MORAY

When plotted on a map, the sites within this chapter seem arranged in isolated bundles. Between them are empty windows where no text is printed on the map, marked instead by hills with Gaelic names and neighbourhoods of mountain hares and red grouse rather than people. If the Cairngorms National Park is defined mostly by its extensive coverage of pine woodland and purple hills, this part of Moray's landscape has a particular abundance of freshwater features. These range from miniature waterfalls sidling down rocky crevices to forest lochs as steady as mirrors.

Linked to the watery theme is the River Spey, the fastest and one of the longest rivers in Scotland. Wiggling through the eastern half of Moray in an area called Speyside, it supports one of the region's key exports: whisky. Throughout Speyside, you'll find a string of distilleries all offering their own unique take on whisky, including at Dufftown, Aberlour and Rothes. If you fancy sampling a bit of everything, then several of these sites are linked up by the **Malt Whisky Trail** (⊘ maltwhiskytrail.com).

While many people come to Moray for whisky, there's plenty more on offer for Slow explorers. Walking in particular is excellent: woodland strolls are punctuated by the whisper of unseen burns, building momentum beneath narrow footbridges and drooping canopies before surging over waterfalls into shuddering pools below. The most dramatic example of this can be seen at Randolph's Leap near Logie Steading, where a frenzied section of the River Findhorn whips itself into white froth as it churns through a spectacular gorge. Millbuies, Loch Na Bo and Loch of Blairs are more composed, their surfaces disturbed only by ducks and herons.

On rainy days, you can peruse an entire church full of antiques and artefacts in Fochabers Folk Museum, clamber the tightly winding staircase of Ballindalloch Castle, or admire the lesser-known but wonderfully detailed Pictish stones at Inveravon Church. The largest settlement is Keith, where the A95 and A96 converge. As well as secluded woodland and one of Moray's secret waterfalls, this historic town honours tradition and has won awards for its dedication to preserving the Scots language.

For the purposes of this chapter, I've defined Central Moray as everything north of Glenlivet and south of Forres, which you'll find in the East Cairngorms (page 79) and Moray Coast (page 135) chapters respectively.

GETTING AROUND

From the Cairngorms National Park, the main routes into Moray are the A940 to Forres and the A95, which heads northeast from Grantown-on-Spey through Aberlour and on to Keith. On the far eastern side, the A96 to Keith runs from Elgin to Aberdeen.

TRAINS & BUSES

Scotrail services from Inverness to Aberdeen stop at Keith every couple of hours. The Keith & Dufftown Railway (page 110), also known as The Whisky Line, is a unique seasonal route (☉ Apr–Oct) offering vintage train lovers a more leisurely way to travel the 11-mile journey between these two towns.

The Stagecoach 10 **bus** service stops at Keith and Fochabers on its way from Aberdeen to Inverness, while the 36 runs from Dufftown to Elgin and stops at Aberlour and Rothes. This makes accessing the Dufftown end of The Whisky Line, Speyside Cooperage and The Glen Grant Distillery easy.

WALKING & CYCLING

Keep an eye on village map boards for local **walks**. Easy-going routes through a mix of woodland and open countryside can be found in Dufftown, Rothes and Aberlour. These are made more intriguing by elements such as waterfalls, ruined castles and a fairy village. The trails follow mostly flat terrain and are rarely busy because they're not immediately obvious when you first arrive.

For those wanting to really stretch their legs, the **Isla Way** walking route links Dufftown and Keith via a 13-mile countryside path. The trail follows the route of The Whisky Line (page 110), so if you don't fancy taking on the whole thing you can travel part of it by train and walk the rest. This is the best option for wheelchair users, as only the middle section of the Isla Way (Loch Park to Drummuir) is suitable for wheelchairs. After Drummuir, the trail mostly follows public roads and isn't always signposted.

> **ⓘ TOURIST INFORMATION**
>
> **Rothes Visitor Centre** New St, Rothes AB38 7BJ ℰ 01340 831474
> ◊ rothesvisitorcentre.scot

Mountain bikers might consider a trip to **Moray Monster Trails** (◊ forestryandland.gov.scot/visit/moray-monster-trails) just outside Fochabers, where a range of abilities can be tested on undulating tracks through the forest.

⛟ CYCLE HIRE

Dufftown & District Community Association ◊ dufftowncommunity.co.uk/community-type/bikes. Volunteer-run charity offering a bike-hire scheme by the day (10.00–17.00) or longer, including electric adult and non-electric children's bikes. Book all year round on the website and collect from the bike shed in Dufftown's Tininver Park (**Ⅲ** signified.embraced. overlaid). Customers are provided with a helmet, lock, puncture-repair kit, pump and route map. An electric car is also available to hire from here.

THE DISTILLERY ZONE

Whisky is a key component in the following section and so I've named it as such. The zone in question covers Dufftown to the southeast, Cardhu Distillery to the west and Rothes to the north, forming a squat triangle over the River Spey and the point at which the A95 and A941 converge.

You're spoilt for choice when it comes to distilleries in Moray – as I was while researching. The most famous is arguably Glenfiddich in Dufftown, but in the spirit of finding more obscure locations, I've highlighted two lesser-known distilleries that both offer something special. If you're not a whisky drinker you needn't skip ahead! There's plenty more to see here, including a stately home with dazzling gardens, Pictish stones and a heritage railway.

1 DUFFTOWN

🏠 Dunvegan B&B (page 317) **The Milking Sheds** (page 318)

Dufftown is quiet and unassuming at first glance, but it's known as the malt whisky capital of the world and has six working distilleries to prove it. The town is arranged like an upside down 'T', with old stone

Fairy Village including Mortlach Church

❀ OS Explorer map 424 or Landranger map 28; start: Dufftown Clock Tower, ⏣ staging. frown.refrain; ♥ NJ3237239957; 2¾ miles; easy.

- -

This easy-going circular loops through a secluded wooded glen containing a number of points of interest, including historic Mortlach Church and a fairy village, plus ample picnic spots. Halfway around, the path joins a stream and passes over a few footbridges: look out for waterfalls and intriguing rock formations along this section.

1 From Dufftown Clock Tower, head south down Church Street. Past the community centre, the road dips gently downhill beside a mossy stone wall. Several footpaths branch left but continue straight until the end, where it meets an unnamed road.

2 Turn slightly right on to this and directly ahead you'll see Mortlach Church. A gate on the northern side commemorates the Battle of Mortlach, which occurred nearby in AD1010. From the road you can't appreciate how far back the grounds go, but beyond lies a cemetery on three different levels. Past the church, take the left fork sloping downhill. Shortly before the driveway for Dufftown Distillery that you can see up ahead, ignore another footpath sign and carry on straight.

3 Follow the road uphill, past the driveway to the distillery. When it levels out, pass some warehouses on the right and walk under a minimum height barrier to a country lane between fields.

4 After half a mile, the path dips downhill and a grassy trail branches left. Take this trail and follow it beneath an avenue of trees into an open clearing beside the narrow Dullan Water. At the end of the clearing, cross a wooden footbridge.

5 On the other side, the path forks. The first branch, passing over a much smaller footbridge, leads to the Giant's Cradle. This hollow in the rock is large enough for a family to sit in, cupped on all sides with the stream passing beneath. Back on the main path, continue uphill, taking care of rocks and roots underfoot. A second detour, this time to the right, leads to the Fairy Village – this collection of tiny decorative houses dotted around a small clearing was funded by one person and has more added to it every year. There are also picnic benches and a child's gazebo with a doll's house inside. Return to the path and descend some compacted

brick buildings lining the A941 and B9009 that meet at a perpendicular angle at the southern end, beside a **clock tower**. Made from grey and peach granite, this three-storey structure has a clock on its four faces, overhanging mini turrets at each corner and a bellcote in the centre.

mud steps. After crossing over three short sections of boardwalk the path climbs, becoming rockier.

6 The path bends to the left beside Linen Apron Waterfall – a glistening slick of mossy black rock – and now undulates, climbing higher until the stream is screened by coppiced trees. Various tributaries pass beneath you before the path levels off back at the water's edge, now still and smooth.

7 After a quarter of a mile, you'll reach a weir. Keep following the footpath and pass the other side of Dufftown Distillery, then the turning you could have chosen after passing Mortlach Church.

8 Carry on straight between two of the church's cemeteries, keeping the burn on your left. At the end of the vehicle track, join the single lane road at Mortlach Distillery and continue northeast until you reach the A941. Turn left and follow the road back to the clock tower start point.

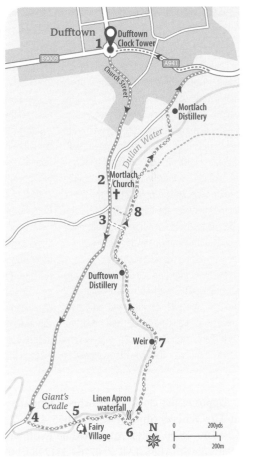

It was built in 1839 and once used as a jail, but has been closed for some years. Dufftown & District Community Association purchased the tower in 2020 and have plans to restore the building to give it new purpose for the community.

THE MOST NORTHERLY HERITAGE RAILWAY IN BRITAIN

AB55 4BA ✆ 01340 821181 🖥 keith-dufftown-railway.co.uk ⊙ Apr–Oct 3 trips daily Fri–Sun

The most unique way to travel from Dufftown to Keith is via The Whisky Line: a jolly green, two-carriage locomotive with narrow doors that swing open to reveal rows of retro padded seats and worn leather travel cases stowed in the overhead racks. Buy a tiny card ticket stub from either station, their walls decorated with vintage signs and photos – all adding to the feeling that you've drifted back in time. Most people ride for the whole journey between the two towns, but it's also possible to disembark for a short walk in the woods at Drummuir, halfway along the route, before catching the next train.

Whichever direction you make the 11-mile journey, you'll spend 40 minutes chugging through Speyside country and snatching glimpses of Balvenie Castle (see opposite), Loch Park, Drummuir Wood and several whisky distilleries. The River Isla accompanies the train for most of the route too. Look out for roe deer poking their heads out of the long grass – the train guard will likely have to clap their hands out the window to shoo them off the tracks.

Both Keith and Dufftown stations have a miniature museum containing memorabilia from 1862 to 1991, when the railway was fully operational. Keith also has a small shop with cold drinks and train-themed books for sale, while Dufftown has the **Sidings Café** (⊙ Mar–Nov 10.00–16.00 Tue–Sun), serving light lunches, home bakes, drinks and ice cream inside an old railway carriage. For an additional extra, it's also possible to tuck into an afternoon tea during your journey: finger sandwiches, scones, cupcakes, the works. For this, you'll need to depart from Dufftown as all the treats are made in the Sidings Café.

Opposite the clock tower, whisky fans can browse over 600 varieties at **The Whisky Shop** (Fife St, AB55 4AL 🖥 whiskyshopdufftown.com ⊙ 10.00–18.00 daily). Another shop worth visiting is **Collectors' Cabin** (Balvenie St, AB55 4AB ✆ 07763 331228 ⊙ 09.30–17.00 Mon–Wed, Fri & Sat), 100yds north of the clock tower. Run by owner David Hanson and receptionist Bertie the cat, it sells gemstones, fossils and antiquities. Next door is sister shop **Singing Bowls with Good Vibrations** (🖥 goodvibrations.vistaprintdigital.com), which has a large table covered in copper-coloured bowls of different shapes and sizes. 'Singing bowls are amazing,' David told me. 'We use hand-beaten bowls from Nepal and Tibet. The vibrations spread through the body and agitate the water molecules. This is good for circulation, relaxing muscles and removing toxins.'

David believes he's now got the largest collection of singing bowls that visitors can study and buy in the north of Scotland. He passed me a bowl and invited me to hold it flat on one hand, slowly but firmly running a mallet around the edge. After a few moments the bowl began to hum, increasing in volume as I pressed more firmly. You can have a go yourself at one of the free workshops, held during school holidays and on most weekends.

David also offers relaxation experiences with pebbles collected from Hopeman (page 149). The stones are heated then placed on the skin to warm the body. On sunny days, it's possible to have treatments outside in the garden, with birdsong adding to the sensory experience.

Lurking behind a bank of trees at the northern edge of Dufftown, just past Glenfiddich Distillery, is **Balvenie Castle** ($\mathring{\partial}$ historicenvironment. scot/visit-a-place/places/balvenie-castle $\odot$ Apr–Sep 09.30–17.30 daily). Although its roof and top edges are missing, it's still largely intact, its high stone walls studded with narrow windows. A wide arched gatehouse leads into the centre of the castle. This was once the home of the Comyn Earls of Buchan, notorious rivals of King Robert the Bruce. Perched high and overlooking the glen, it would have been quite the imposing fortress.

¶ FOOD & DRINK

The Coffee Pot Balvenie St, AB55 4AB $\mathscr{D}$ 01340 820246 ⨍ The Coffee Pot-Dufftown. Bought in 2022 by Chloe Campbell when she was only 19 years old, having previously worked there as a waitress. Serves soup of the day, light lunches, scones and a selection of wonderfully creative cakes such as Mars Bar crispies, Kinder blondies and Drumstick Squashie millionaires.

The Dufftown Glassworks Conval St, AB55 4AE $\mathscr{D}$ 01340 821534 ⨍ $\odot$ Mon, Tue & Thu–Sat. Small, cosy tea room opposite the clock tower, serving paninis, toasted sandwiches and homemade cakes and bakes. Beside the till is a wall of Scottish greetings cards, arts and crafts, jewellery and prints.

2 SPEYSIDE COOPERAGE

Dufftown Road, Craigellachie AB38 9RS $\mathring{\partial}$ speysidecooperage.co.uk $\odot$ tours 09.00–15.00 daily; café 09.00–16.00 daily

There are plenty of whisky distilleries in Moray, but Speyside Cooperage is the only place in the UK where you can watch casks, the wooden containers where whisky is matured, being made. One of the first things you see as you arrive are hundreds of these barrels, stacked up like giant Toblerone pyramids beyond the car park.

The hourly **Acorn to Cask** tour shows visitors how the casks are made, beginning with a 4D sensory experience in a small cinema room. As you watch the casks being steamed, dry ice appears at your feet, and when they're put into the furnace the room glows red. After that immersive taste, you don high vis and goggles and watch the working coopers from a viewing gallery. Even from up here the sights, sounds and smells of the workshop are overwhelming.

"There are no chemicals, nails or glues involved – reeds are used to seal the casks, which are made from oak."

A single cooper works on a cask from start to finish, expertly shaping, charring and wheeling it along the floor from station to station. There are no chemicals, nails or glues involved – reeds are used to seal the casks, which are made from oak. This is the only wood suitable, as it prevents leakage while still allowing the whisky inside to breathe. A cask can return to the cooperage for inspection and repair for as long as 60 years before being recycled into furniture.

The visitor centre opened in 1992, but the art of coopering has been taking place here since 1947. This is the UK's largest independent cooperage – those wanting to learn the trade can join a four-year cooper apprenticeship programme using traditional methods and tools. Annually, almost 150,000 oak casks are made and repaired here for distilleries in Speyside, as well as the rest of Scotland and internationally. A small shop stocks locally sourced Scottish gifts and a selection of cask-themed items unique to the cooperage. There's also a barrel-themed café offering sandwiches, soups and cakes, including gluten-free options and Fairtrade coffee.

3 ABERLOUR

ᐱ **Hideaway Under the Stars** (page 318)

Two miles southwest of Speyside Cooperage on the A95, Aberlour is a small village with a Gaelic name that means 'the mouth of the chattering burn'. This refers to the Burn of Aberlour that flows into the much larger River Spey on the village's northwest side. Its wide high street is lined by

1 Balvenie Castle. 2 Linn Falls, Aberlour. 3 Singing Bowls with Good Vibrations, Dufftown. 4 Dufftown's Fairy Village. ▶

CROWN COPYRIGHT HES

LIAM MCBRIDE

REBECCA GIBSON

REBECCA GIBSON

rough stone houses with white sash windows characteristic of the area. Most activity is found in Charlestown at the southern end. The Speyside Way (page 23) threads through here too.

Aberlour is perhaps best-known as the home of **Walker's Shortbread**, and you'll pass the factory on your way in from the north. The red tartan tins are world famous and the delicious biscuits are made with a recipe that hasn't changed since 1898. You can visit the original bakery shop in the high street (AB38 9PD ⊘ walkersshortbread.com ⊙ Mon–Sat).

One of the town's most scenic spots is **Linn Falls**, a miniature woodland waterfall on the Burn of Aberlour. To get there, head southeast on Queen's Road, away from the high street. At the junction to Allachie Drive, after a quarter of a mile, cut on to a narrow grass footpath on the left, signposted 'Fairy Knowe'. When this forks, bear right at another sign to Fairy Knowe. You might feel like you're wandering down a private drive but it's just a narrow avenue. Continue on to a grassy track and pass around a gate.

"At the bottom you'll reach the falls: a photogenic double cascade emptying into a pool that soon becomes the burn again."

The path climbs into a patch of woodland and forks again. Ignore the gate on the left and curve right downhill, descending some rough, rocky steps. Turn right again to put the burn on your left. At the bottom you'll reach the falls: a photogenic double cascade emptying into a pool that soon becomes the burn again. The amber water contrasts with the pale boulders submerged in the shallows.

Once you've taken in the views, continue beside the now subdued burn, which picks up speed again as it topples over a weir. Turn right immediately after the electricity substation in the corner of the sheep field, passing an old cottage behind the wall on the left. This leads to Mary Avenue. At the crossroads, turn left to return to High Street.

¶ FOOD & DRINK

The Gather'n AB38 9QB ✆ 01340 881749 ⓕ. Dog-friendly café combined with 3 Bags Wool yarn shop. Cosy seating and a simple menu including soup, wraps, sandwiches and salads. The vegetarian all-day breakfast is excellent.

The Mash Tun AB38 9QP ✆ 01340 881771 ⊘ mashtun-aberlour.com. Whisky bar and restaurant serving fairly upmarket dishes, with whisky-themed accommodation upstairs. Tables are limited so booking recommended.

4 BALLINDALLOCH CASTLE & GARDENS

AB37 9AX ♪ 01807 500205 ◇ ballindallochcastle.co.uk ⊙ Apr–Sep 10.00–17.00 Sun–Thu

Known as 'the pearl of the north', Ballindalloch is a handsome, ivy-fuzzed castle eight miles southwest of Aberlour. Its **grounds** provide even more charm, featuring a walled garden, rockery, grass labyrinth, pond, model railway and several walking trails extending to a porter's lodge along the River Avon. You could easily spend two hours exploring everything. This is one of the few castles in Scotland still inhabited by its original family, the Macpherson-Grants. Since it was built in 1546, an impressive 23 generations have lived here.

Elsewhere on the estate is a working farm, home to the world's oldest herd of Aberdeen Angus cattle in continuous existence. A more recent venture is Ballindalloch Distillery, situated in a restored 19th-century farm building. Production started in 2014 with the first bottles released in 2023.

One of the highlights of the castle's interior is the **watch tower**, up a narrow and tightly winding stone staircase. When you want to come down, you have to ring the bell and call 'Gardy-loo!' to anyone about to ascend. This phrase dates back to the 16th century when chamber pots were emptied out the window. The French 'gardez l'eau' ('watch out for the water') was used as a warning to prevent a nasty surprise below.

I found my favourite part of the castle right at the end. Displayed on two small shelves are dozens of Victorian silver pin cushions in the

INVERAVON PICTISH STONES

▥ dolls.blackbird.probing ▮

On your way to Ballindalloch Castle from Aberlour, it's worth veering off the A95 to visit Inveravon Church. A small, white building with slim stained-glass windows, it's most notable for the four high-quality Pictish stones sheltered in a porch on its right-hand side. The largest clearly shows an eagle carving and the others have a mix of mirror, comb and crescent symbols. Mounted in a small alcove in the wall, the fourth stone was unfortunately broken when made into a building block, but it clearly shows the head of a Pictish beastie.

Strangely, Inveravon Church isn't widely promoted for its Pictish carvings but these are some of the most clearly defined examples I've seen. Even better, they were all unearthed in and around this churchyard from the early 19th- to the mid-20th centuries, so haven't been squirreled miles away.

shapes of animals. The collection includes rhinos, tortoises, hares, swans and penguins, each with a tiny pad of velvet for the pins.

5 CARDHU DISTILLERY

AB38 7RY ✆ 01479 874635 ⟢ malts.com/en-row/distilleries/cardhu ☉ Mar–Oct 10.00–17.00 daily; Nov–Feb Tue–Sat

With so many whisky distilleries to choose from in Moray Speyside, Cardhu appealed to me because it was the first distillery to be pioneered by women and is still run under female leadership today. I joined the **Flavour Journey** tour, intrigued by the 'highly immersive' website description, and was greeted on arrival by the distillery's three Highland cows, peering at me through their shaggy hair.

"Helen and Elizabeth were notably headstrong, refusing buy offers and maintaining their family values and quality control."

The tour begins in a beautiful story room with long sofas, where visitors watch an animation to learn the history of the distillery. With stencil silhouettes onscreen and swaying barley projected on the walls, it's told in such an entertaining way that it feels like a fairy tale rather than real history. Cardhu started life in founder Helen Cumming's kitchen during the days of illegal distilling in the 19th century. When the authorities came knocking, she dowsed herself in flour as a ruse and snuck out the back to raise a red flag and warn her neighbours. This symbol is reflected today on Cardhu bottles and in the gold statue of Helen holding a flag in the distillery grounds.

After the video, the tour continues into the distillery. The warehouse is an original building dating from 1884, and has a commemorative plaque with EC printed on it for Elizabeth Cumming. This was Helen's daughter-in-law, who took over the business as it grew in the 1800s. Helen and Elizabeth were notably headstrong, refusing buy offers and maintaining their family values and quality control. As a result, they transformed a kitchen venture into a hugely successful business that's still thriving today.

You don't have to be a whisky drinker to enjoy this interactive tour: by the end, even I could smell the difference between fruity blends and smokier, peaty aromas. Finish by sampling three different Cardhu malts in the glitzy Tasting Kitchen. If you're driving, you'll get a non-alcoholic cocktail and your trio of mini drams to take home.

Everything at Cardhu is coordinated in bold shades of red, black and gold, and there's so much attention to detail: cut grass, orchard fruits and malt in glass aroma jars; a rainbow flavour wheel; copperware in the kitchen reflecting the copper stills of the distillery; and tiny models showing what's happening on a larger scale. It really is a journey from barley, water and yeast to whisky.

6 ROTHES

Rothes is a small town beside the River Spey, nine miles northeast of Cardhu. Its name has several possible origins – either *Rauis*, Irish for 'red water' and acknowledging the burn flowing through it, or the Gaelic *Rathuish*, meaning 'bending of the river'. Either way, water has shaped its history and it suffered huge losses during the 1829 flood – three bridges and 80 acres of farmland were decimated as water levels rose. Nowadays it's a town many would simply drive through, but stop a while and you'll be rewarded with a secluded walk through jumbled woodland and a ruin in danger of being forgotten.

As you head north along the A941, the main route through Rothes, your eye will inevitably be drawn to a copper pot still in the car park of the Station Hotel. This alludes to Forsyths, the coppersmith and still-making factory that has operated in Rothes since the mid-19th century. It's now owned by the fourth generation of Forsyths.

At the end of New Street is **Rothes Visitor Centre** (page 107). Volunteer-run and referred to simply as 'The Cottage' by Rothes residents, the centre contains information about local attractions and cards, clothes and gifts made by local artists and crafters.

"You'll be rewarded with a secluded walk through jumbled woodland and a ruin in danger of being forgotten."

Perhaps the most tranquil way to spend half a day in Rothes is by stretching your legs on the **Dounie Footpath**, a three-mile circular starting from the town centre and taking in the Burn of Rothes and a hushed woodland glen. Turn on to Burnside Street, down the side of the police station, and in a quarter of a mile you'll reach Glenrothes Distillery. Ignore a footbridge to the left signposted for the castle and continue through the distillery buildings. Past the main part of the distillery, turn left over a second footbridge, this time signposted for the Dounie. The path bends to the right, following the stream. After a brief spell under the shade of the trees, emerge into an open glen.

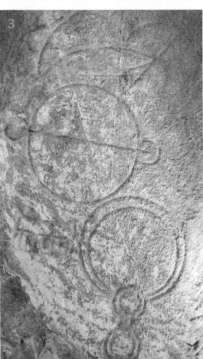

A mile later, the path turns left into a forest plantation. The burn fades out, replaced by hesitant birdsong. Pass down a short flight of earth steps into a deep dell flanked by jagged boulders dripping with dew and steeply slotted Sitka spruce.

Shortly afterwards, the path climbs to a small clearing high on the bank. Turn left at the next two T-junctions, now following a vehicle track. When the path levels off you'll pass a golf course; at the end, bear right on to a tarmac lane leading back to Rothes.

Before the lane reaches the road, there's a left turning for **Rothes Castle**, visible ahead through the trees. Only one wall now remains of the ruin, but it still looks impressive mounted on a hill overlooking the town. The exact origins aren't clear, but it's believed to have been founded circa AD1200 by Peter de Pollok, who was ordered by William I to build a structure that enabled him to patrol this part of the valley. After several attacks in the 17th century, the decision was made to demolish the rest of the castle, although why this single wall has endured remains a mystery.

The Glen Grant Distillery & Gardens

AB38 7BS ☎ 01340 832118 ⚲ glengrant.com ☉ Apr–Oct daily; Nov–Mar Mon–Sat

The Glen Grant Distillery was founded in 1840 by brothers John and James Grant. What sets this distillery apart from others is its extensive grounds – easily the most spectacular feature here – and you can access them as part of the tour ticket price. From the visitor centre, follow a gravel footpath beside the Back Burn into the **Victorian Gardens**, established in 1886. There are ponds, curving lawns, apple orchards, water features and sprays of colour from azalea flowerbeds in spring and summer. Near the end is the Dram Pavilion, built by James Grant – this dinky wooden hut, complete with mossy roof and antler light fixture, is a great place to perch and peek out at the grounds.

Beside the pavilion, the path splits. One trail loops back to the main path via two short bridges, while the other follows a gorge, passing low through a shady ravine and zigzagging over the water. The barriers either side of the bridges and paths are made from roughly cut branches, giving the route a jungle feel. You'll soon reach a tiny wooden gazebo;

◀ **1** Ballindalloch Castle & Gardens. **2** Cardhu Distillery. **3** A Pictish carving at Inveravon Church. **4** The Glen Grant Distillery. **5** The gardens at the Glen Grant Distillery.

inside is a Whisky Safe that once belonged to another James Grant, the nephew of co-founder John, for storing whisky bottles. This is visible as a square metal door embedded in the rock. At the far end of this loop, the path turns up a steep flight of woodchip stairs and returns to the pavilion.

Unusually, two different water sources are used to make whisky here: the burn and a spring. The distillery has eight stills arranged in working pairs; alcohol vapours rise to the top then pass through a purifier. This feature, unique to The Glen Grant, ensures that only the purest vapours pass into the condenser.

You can learn about the site's history on a one-hour tour, finishing with a dram of both the 10-year-old and Arboralis, which has a dried fruit taste. During summer, these might be served outside on the terrace, where you can perch on barrel-shaped seats overlooking the courtyard. There's also a small café serving hot drinks and snacks.

KEITH, FOCHABERS & AROUND

You can arrive in the town of Keith on board a heritage train that's trundled through Moray's peaceful valleys (page 110). Once here, a bit of exploring on foot will reveal a 17th-century bridge hunched demurely beside the busy A96, and shady wooded dells splashed by waterfalls. Nearby Fochabers has its own forest trails, lifting you up onto pine-stacked hills for a glimpse of the coast. I've highlighted a couple of lochs dotted around these two settlements that require a little effort to find, but this makes their discovery even more rewarding.

7 KEITH

Regarded as the eastern gateway to Moray Speyside, Keith lies 11 miles east of Rothes. It's the largest settlement in this chapter, dissected down the middle by the narrow River Isla and with the more populated eastern half arranged in a uniform grid layout. For a town, it doesn't offer a huge amount for visitors, but a couple of subtle footpaths lead to rewarding wild spots just outside the centre.

In 2014, Keith was the first to win the official status of **Scots Toun** – an award launched by the Scots Language Centre to recognise communities that promote the use of Scots language. Judging criteria for this award include how visible Scots is in a community, with particular emphasis on young people, and how available the language is to learn. Keith was awarded the status based on its application of Doric in schools and daily life throughout the town.

A perfect example of Keith community can be found at **Keith Kilt & Textile Centre** (Mid St, AB55 5BJ ✐ 01542 886846 ⊘ kiltsandtextiles. org ⊙ noon–16.00 Tue–Thu), on the town's high street. At the front is a gift shop selling a selection of locally made crafts, while at the back is a work room where a range of craft courses are available, such as needle felting and teddy bear making.

The main event is a kilt-making course; after making their first kilt, students have the opportunity to progress to the SQA-approved Customised Traditional Handcraft Kilt Making Skills Award, unique to the Centre. Most of the kilt-making process here is done entirely by hand. The precision and attention to detail required for such a complex garment is astonishing, and I asked the Centre's chairwoman Linda Gorn how long it takes to make a kilt from scratch. 'If it's properly hand-stitched by somebody qualified and experienced, maybe 30 to 40 hours,' she said. 'Taking eight metres of tartan to fit a person is truly magical and a huge skill.'

The Centre's mill is based in Keith and they buy almost all their tartan from House of Edgar in Perth. Sourcing locally is important to Linda, who has received an MBE for services to the economy of Banffshire, but insists it's a group effort. 'There's no point saying it's all my work because you can't do it without the students and customers. We're a social enterprise with charitable status – it's a whole team.'

"These days, its only traffic comes from pedestrians passing over from Regent Street to the adjacent cemetery."

Even if you're just visiting Keith, you can still get stuck into some crafting and join one of the Centre's day courses (⊙ 10.00–16.00). One of these is needle felting, where students make their own felt brooch in the morning and design a felt landscape in the afternoon. Bookings for all courses can be made on the website.

If you walk north up Mid Street from the Kilt Centre, you'll meet the A96. Turning left here brings you towards the River Isla, where you can see the **Auld Brig**. Built in 1609, this single-arched stone bridge was once used for packhorses. These days, its only traffic comes from pedestrians passing over from Regent Street to the adjacent cemetery.

Keith is well placed for a number of nearby explorations. There's a tranquil 3½-mile circular through **Dunnyduff Wood**, reached by walking for a mile down Bridge Street (which soon turns into Edindiach Road). When the road forks, branch right up to a gravel parking lay-by for Dunnyduff (⊞ represent.glossed.glue) – a handy option if you don't feel like walking from Keith.

From here, follow the footpath and take the first right turn up a slightly steeper hill with compacted mud steps and roots across the ground. This leads to mixed woodland with birches, rowans, oaks,

THE FISHWIVES PATH

Keith sits at one end of the 13-mile Fishwives Path to Buckie on the Moray Coast. Generally regarded as a moderately challenging route, it reveals the astonishing journey that women in fishing communities throughout Moray undertook to sell their catches during the 19th century.

Before harbours were built and windlasses (or winches) were introduced, women helped drag boats ashore. They also baited lines, repaired nets, gutted fish and carried men to their boats to prevent their clothes getting wet before they left. At home, they knitted clothes including ganseys, a kind of woollen jumper – each family had its own unique knitting pattern, so a fisherman could be identified by his gansey alone. On top of all this, women managed the family finances, performed household chores and took care of the children.

A lot of women worked as gutters and packers and followed the herring shoals along the coast. With cloots (scraps of cloth) tied around their fingers to prevent chafing and cutting, they worked in teams of three – two gutted and graded the fish while the third packed them in ice-filled barrels. This work was monitored by a Fisheries Officer and if any poor packing was observed, the entire barrel would be emptied.

Once the fish was processed, it needed to be sold. Women walked for miles on rough tracks, with baskets containing as much as 60lbs of fish strapped to their backs. They exchanged the fish for potatoes, vegetables, butter, cheese and eggs. When the railway was built in 1885 they were able to travel by train, but fish baskets were still carried on foot from Buckie to Keith until well into the 20th century. During the peak of the 'Herring Boom' in 1913, it's believed that around 6,000 women followed herring around the British coastline, and 2½ million barrels were processed.

You can take the same journey as these tenacious women by following the waymarkers on the Fishwives Path, but be aware that some of the route incorporates main roads with no pavements, and care should be taken. A leaflet detailing the trail and its history can be found on the Scottish Outdoor Access Network website (⊘ soan.org.uk).

beeches and spruces. Carry on straight at the crossroads, following the gravel path as it curves around the trees. At the next fork, turn right – this leads to the **Falls of Tarnash**, whose whispers grow louder as you walk downhill. Approaching the edge of the trees, the path bends sharply down to the right, now parallel to the Burn of Tarnash below. A small green footbridge appears shortly after. Follow the path as it gently slaloms down and cross the bridge to see the falls in a shady dell to the right. The water surges between two walls in the rock, gathering in a pool before funnelling back into the burn.

Afterwards, retrace your steps over the green bridge and continue straight on the other side with the burn on your left, away from the staircase you just came down. Break out of the woods and cross another bridge, heading up a gentle hill to a junction, and follow signs pointing left to Keith Square. The path returns into the trees to press against the Den Burn on the left, before coming close to, but high over, the A96. At the next fork, bear right to follow the higher track. The path bends left, passing impressive beech trees with skirted roots. After emerging on to Old Den Road, turn right and follow it to the A96 back into Keith.

A mile further along the single-lane road from the lay-by for Dunnyduff Wood is a Forestry and Land Scotland site called **Balloch,** named Meikle Balloch Hill on Google Maps (▥ cheeks.protester. cooked ⌾ forestryandland.gov.scot/visit/balloch). From the car park, two colour-coded trails lead off on rugged walks threading through patches of heather, Scots pine and silver birches – they both require a bit of an uphill slog. The shorter of the two, the blue waymarked Herricks Walk (2¼ miles), heads steeply into the forest and out on to the Meikle Balloch Hill, initially passing through an avenue of pines on both sides. The trees become so dense that the forest falls into near darkness before emerging into an open area of heathland. This looks particularly impressive with low-lying mist, casting a harsh contrast between white air and dark trees prodding the skyline.

¶ FOOD & DRINK

Boogie Woogie Regent Sq, AB55 5DX ✆ 01542 888077 ⌾ boogiewoogieshop.com
🕓 10.00–16.30 daily. Finalist at the Scottish Café Awards 2022, Boogie Woogie offers locally sourced ingredients from suppliers including Spey Fruit Elgin and AJ Jamieson Butcher in Fochabers. Take your pick of breakfasts, hot filled rolls, omelettes and sweet treats. Hot food served until 14.00. Upstairs is a small boutique of ladies' clothes and accessories.

Square Roots Café Mid St, AB55 5AF ✆ 01542 488540 ⏷ squarerootscafe.co.uk
🕐 11.00–16.00 Wed–Mon. Conveniently located beside Reidhaven Square car park, Square Roots Café is run by two local farmers and crofters, offering traditional farmhouse cooking and passed-down family recipes. As well as hot filled rolls and waffles for breakfast and grilled sandwiches and salads for lunch, it also has an extensive alcohol menu featuring Scottish beer, cider, gin, vodka, rum and whisky.

8 FOCHABERS

🏠 **Duke Cottage** (page 317)

Eight miles northwest of Keith is the village of Fochabers. Its streets are arranged in a similar grid format and here they meet at a central green, split in half by the high street. Surrounding this green are stone-brick houses, a church with a central spire and four-pillared portico, a large fountain and several bays for visitor parking. From this point, you can either wander northwest to reach the River Spey and adjacent Speyside Way walking route, or southeast for a selection of shops and restaurants.

My favourite place to visit here is **Fochabers Folk Museum** (High St, IV32 7DU 🕐 summer Thu–Sun 13.00–16.00; free entry). Housed within Pringle Memorial Church, the museum was opened in 1984 by the Christie family, who also own a nearby garden centre, to house their collection of horse-drawn gigs. More items were added over time and the museum now resembles an antique shop, with narrow walk spaces between items in cabinets and on the floor. The ground level is stacked with farming

"Warm light streams through the large church windows, giving the museum an even greater historical feel."

tools, a shop's worth of old food containers, historic photos of Fochabers, badges from Fochabers Curling Club and more. At the back is a separate room dedicated to 20th-century fashion, as well as a corner set up to look like a classroom, complete with wooden desks and leather-bound books. An assortment of gigs, bakers' carts, penny-farthings and spinning wheels are clustered together upstairs. Warm light streams through the large church windows, giving the museum an even greater historical feel. I've never seen so much packed into one space, and really you need to visit more than once to appreciate everything on display.

◀ **1** Loch Na Bo. **2** Fochabers Folk Museum. **3** Highland Games at Gordon Castle. **4** Auld Brig.

Half a mile northwest from the museum is the turning for **Gordon Castle** (⊘ gordoncastle.co.uk). Originating as a 15th-century fortress, it was transformed into a grand mansion (some say a Scottish Versailles) by Alexander, 4th Duke of Gordon, in the late 1700s. Now a wedding and corporate venue, each May an excellent **Highland Games** is hosted here (see castle website for details). I've spent merry afternoons eating scandalously good donut balls from **Popseys** (**f**) while watching Highland dancing competitions, field events and dog training displays. The atmosphere is wonderful, with whole-hearted cheers for the furthest caber toss. Even more special, a huge pipe band marches in procession between the events, the pipes so loud they thrum in your chest.

Half a mile northeast on the A98 from Fochabers is **Winding Walks** (**▥** abstracts.pens.lightly ⊘ forestryandland.gov.scot/visit/winding-walks), an undulating Forestry & Land Scotland site with opportunities to walk waymarked paths and mountain bike on Moray Monster Trails. When you arrive the car park might appear busy, especially during summer, but once you've joined one of the trails the trees soon muffle any other sound.

Stroll on the yellow trail through 19th-century woodland to **Peeps Viewpoint**, or search for **Longhowe Loch** on the green trail. My

BAXTERS SOUP

I don't believe it actually 'has to be Heinz' where soup is concerned. I much prefer Baxters, and Fochabers is where this Scottish brand was born. In 1868, George Baxter opened a small grocery shop in Fochabers with his wife Margaret, who made jams using local fruits. Their son William and his wife Ethel took on the mantle in 1916 and built the company's first factory. William cycled to markets all over Scotland to sell Ethel's jams and also canned fruit – it's said he wore out six bikes during his first year doing so.

Business blossomed and in 1929 Ethel started making soup using venison from Upper Speyside, resulting in the now famous 'Royal Game' flavour. By 1952, Aberdeenshire cook and artist Ena Robertson had joined the mix, marrying William and Ethel's son Gordon and creating other famous Baxters soups including cock-a-leekie and Scotch broth.

After decades at the helm, Gordon stepped down as head of the company in 1992 and his daughter Audrey took over. Manufacturing now also takes place in the US, Poland and Australia, and Baxters has become an international name. However, its history remains deep-rooted in family and Audrey insists that Fochabers will always be its spiritual home.

favourite is the blue three-mile Monument Trail, which passes the loch then climbs up into secluded Whiteash Hill Wood. At the top is a **pyramid cairn** commemorating Frances Harriet, Duchess of Richmond and Gordon (1824–1887). Married to Charles Gordon-Lennox, Duke of Gordon, the duchess split her time between Gordon Castle and estates in Sussex. From this vantage point, you can peek northwest over the trees towards Lossiemouth and, on a clear day, across the Moray Firth to Helmsdale in Sutherland. Also along this blue trail is **Ranald's Grave**, referring to the chief of a gang who robbed travellers on the road from Aberdeen to Inverness. Ranald was executed and buried on this spot, although it's unclear exactly when. His burial is marked by a heap of pale stones.

"From this vantage point, you can peek northwest over the trees towards Lossiemouth and, on a clear day, across the Moray Firth."

Personal Development and Breathwork Coach Jen Price of **Mindful Routes** (⊘ mindfulroutes.co.uk 🔲 mindful.routes) often takes on the Moray Monster Trails at Winding Walks. 'I love riding my bike off-road in North East Scotland for the varied terrain we have here,' she told me. 'The woodland bike trails at Fochabers are particularly stunning in autumn as the seasons change, with a wonderful viewpoint overlooking the mouth of the River Spey.' Jen offers guided mountain-bike rides and mindful adventure weekends and retreats in a variety of locations across Moray.

FOOD & DRINK

The Quaich Café High St, IV32 7DH ✐ 01343 820981 🇫 ⊙ Tue–Sun. This dog-friendly café has a cosy vibe with waxy tablecloths and wall decorations that include guitars and a mounted Highland cow head sculpture made from kindling. Serves comfort food such as pancakes, paninis and baked potatoes.

9 LOCH NA BO

/// parkland.overused.sprouted

Six miles west of Fochabers is the artificial and inconspicuous Loch Na Bo. This is a peaceful walking spot (cycling is not permitted and dogs should be kept on leads), with two circular trails around the loch, one fitting inside the other. The longer, three-mile trail marked in yellow passes through Loch Na Bo Wood. Narrow and squeezed by branches at times, the path threads around oaks, beeches, pines and a corridor of silver birch saplings.

The two trails converge at the northern end of the loch and on a sunny day the view through dangling birch branches is glorious. Tufted ducks and little grebes cruise across the water and on the loch's eastern side you can see Loch Na Bo House, a large self-catering property (⊘ lochnabo. com). Although it's naturally occurring, the loch is contaminated with green algae (page 15) that's harmful to people and dogs if ingested, so it's not a safe swimming spot.

10 MILLBUIES COUNTRY PARK

/// desktop.hedgehog.rummage ⊙ 08.30–dusk

Eight miles west of Fochabers is the snake-shaped loch at Millbuies. It's used commercially for fishing, but wildlife can be seen here too including herons and the occasional red squirrel. In summer it's a good spot to watch butterflies and there's a sprinkling of wood anemone among the tree roots – this white-flowered plant is an indicator of ancient woodland.

From the car park, a footpath leads along an earthy bank to the loch. You can walk all the way around, a distance of 1¾ miles, or cross over halfway via a footbridge. The path dips frequently, sometimes pressed against the water's edge and at other times climbing high above it. There's a nice range of flora levels with Scots pine, gorse and low-lying heather all muscling in.

"In summer it's a good spot to watch butterflies and there's a sprinkling of wood anemone among the tree roots."

Rhododendron is currently being removed at this site. It was introduced to the UK in the 18th century and has since spread rapidly. As well as outcompeting native plants for light, it also alters soil conditions, affecting earthworms, birds and other plants. After rhododendron has been cleared from certain sections of Millbuies, it's hoped that native flowering species will be introduced to increase biodiversity.

ALONG THE RIVER FINDHORN

One of the longest rivers in Scotland, the Findhorn crosses this chapter area on the far western side. It begins in the Monadhliath Mountains, a range lying west of the Cairngorms, and flows northeast for 62 miles before reaching the sea at Findhorn Bay (page 159). The section near Logie Steading passes through jagged rocky gorges accessible on foot. Follow winding ridge paths here that are backed by trees on one side and peer down at the river on the other – depending on where you're standing, the water can either be flat calm or crashing. There aren't many locations in the North East where you can get such an elevated vantage point over a major river, making this section a diverse and dramatic one.

11 LOGIE STEADING

⚓ **Ace Adventures** (page 318)

/// impulse.segmented.thuds ⌂ logie.co.uk/steading

Built in the 1920s as a model farm, Logie Steading now houses a heritage centre, café and a selection of independent retailers within sandstone buildings arranged around a sun-trapped courtyard. It sits within the Logie Estate, seven miles south of Forres on the A940. As you turn into the driveway you'll likely pass a herd of aptly named Longhorn cattle, once bred for draught as well as milk and beef. Shopping aside, many people come to Logie Steading for its proximity to Randolph's Leap (page 130), a formidable section of the River Findhorn that is just a short walk away.

"You'll likely pass a herd of aptly named Longhorn cattle, once bred for draught as well as milk and beef."

Two miles north is a quieter section of the river known as **Sluie Walks**. Only a short distance downstream from Randolph's Leap, it's topographically very similar but offers denser woodland and an even higher vantage point over the river. To get here from Logie Steading, return to the B9007 and turn left then left again on to the A940. After 1½ miles, look for a discreet brown sign on the right for Sluie Walks, pointing to the driveway on the left. Turn right at the fork to reach the parking area (*///* bangle.enacted.scrambles).

12 LOCH OF BLAIRS

/// putty.merchant.electrode ⌂ blairsloch.com

Five miles north of Logie Steading is another waterside walk at the far more serene and inconspicuous Loch of Blairs. Tucked behind a screen of trees, it's a well-kept secret so don't tell anyone. I find this route particularly satisfying because you can walk a 1½-mile lollipop

River Findhorn to Randolph's Leap

✳ OS Landranger map 27; start: Logie Steading; ♥ NJ0066550492; 2½ miles; moderate.

In the dappled shade of twisted oaks and beeches, this dramatic trail skims the edge of a steep rocky gorge over the River Findhorn, which transitions from glassy pools to churning rapids. The geological formations and ancient semi-natural woodland make this area a Site of Special Scientific Interest (SSSI).

Randolph's Leap refers to a specific section on this river walk, where the two banks are closest together. In the 14th century, Thomas Randolph, Earl of Moray, lived on the other side of the river from Logie Steading, while Sir Alexander Comyn and his six sons lived on this side. Traditionally they held the title of ranger of the Forest of Darnaway but Randolph told them to keep out. Alastair, Alexander's eldest son, rallied his men together and attacked Randolph. After an ambush, Alastair and three other men leapt back over to their side of the river, so it should really be called Comyn's Leap instead.

1 From the driveway into Logie Steading, take the grass track to the right of the children's play area. After 200yds, follow a blue marker to the left.

2 Bear right down a gentle hill. The path bends back on itself, zigzagging a couple of times at a steeper angle before reaching a viewpoint over one of the calmer sections of the river. Turn left and walk upstream, keeping close to the water. In 500yds, the River Findhorn converges with the River Divie and the path curves left. After another 350yds, it joins the B9007.

3 At the road, turn right and cross Divie Bridge, continuing a short distance down the road to the first track on your right. This takes you to the water's edge before looping back up to the road about 100yds further along.

4 Almost immediately, descend a set of steps right, back off the road again, beside an interpretive plaque for Randolph's Leap. Stay straight downhill when the path forks, keeping an eye out for dippers on the rocks below. About 200yds down is a squat stone commemorating the

shape up to the loch and then all the way around it. A viewpoint jetty snakes into the middle of the water at the southern end, and there's also the option of stopping at one of several wildlife hides dotted around its circumference.

The paths at Loch of Blairs are in the shadow of towering Scots pines and in late August to early September the forest floor shimmers with ling heather. Sheltered within this dense ground cover you'll hear invisible wrens grumbling to anyone who'll listen, and you might spot a buzzard floods of 1829. After three days and nights of rain, the water level here rose by a staggering 50ft. It's scary to think about, especially when you see how high up the stone is.

5 Just beyond the flood stone, bear left, taking care of the sheer drop into the gorge on one side. Keep straight ahead when another path forks left. Some 150yds later is a viewpoint high above the river. This is close to its narrowest stretch, where Alastair supposedly made his leap.

6 Near the viewpoint, a set of steep steps leads down to a viewing platform closer to the water. If you like, take this brief detour to watch the river churn from a different vantage point, then return up the steps to carry on the same path. Turn left, passing a second flood stone. Keep left and follow the path back up to the B9007. Walk beside the road to the bridge then retrace the rest of the outward route.

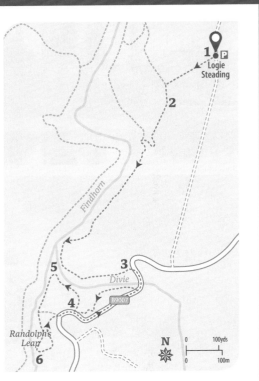

gliding through gaps in the canopy. Visit in autumn for impressive fly agarics (the red and white-spotted fairy toadstools) that often sprout up overnight.

Keep your eyes up as well as down because I've seen crossbills here before. These finches have the lower mandible of their bill hooked upwards beside the upper one, an adaptation that comes in handy for tweezing conifer seeds. Their call sounds like rubber soles squeaking on a polished floor and you might see them zooming overhead. Males

1

2

3

are a flashy blood orange colour while females have similar plumage to a greenfinch.

When cartographer John Thomson published a map of this area in 1830, there was no sign of a loch here. It did appear in the first Ordnance Survey maps in 1872, putting its creation somewhere between these two dates. Later, the loch was used as a trout fishery by local anglers, but after boat hire stopped it became a place for walkers and wildlife. About halfway around the circular walk, you'll find the old fishing bothy. It fell into disrepair but was restored by volunteers and equipped with basic amenities. Now it's available to hire by the hour or day for classes, meetings or just to window watch – see website for details.

Loch of Blairs isn't signposted but it's simple to find once you know. From Logie Steading, head north on the A940 for nearly five miles then turn right at the signs for Rafford and Dallas Du Historic Distillery. Less than half a mile down this single-lane forested road, you'll reach the car park on the right.

◀ **1** Loch of Blairs. **2** Randolph's Leap. **3** River Findhorn.

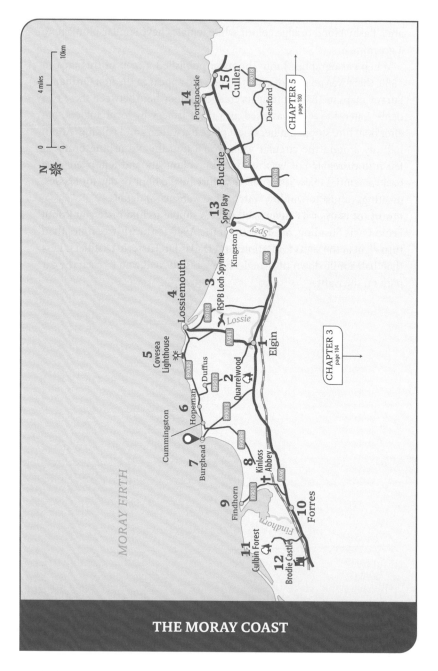

THE MORAY COAST

4
THE MORAY COAST

The Moray Coast is an ideal place to lean into the Slow concept: local traditions, heritage, natural history and landscape are all fundamental to the essence of the area. It faces the **Moray Firth**, a triangular section of the North Sea that tapers to a point at Inverness. This is said to be one of Europe's best spots for bottlenose dolphins – with luck and calm conditions you don't even need a boat to watch these huge mammals tumbling around and performing acrobatic feats. Even better, they can be seen at any time of year.

Aside from occasional banks of pebbles and shingle, most notably at Spey Bay, the beaches here usually consist of fine sand, perfect for padding barefoot. Tidal range can be vast, so the shallows might be either a few feet or several hundred yards away. Low tide has its advantages, as reflected sunsets gleam on damp sand and wading birds pinball between puddles.

Unsurprisingly for a coastal region, the fishing industry has had – and still has – a huge influence on life here. This is perhaps best seen in villages like **Cullen**, where Cullen skink, a thick fish soup, continues to be celebrated with an annual competition. Elsewhere are ancient ruins, Pictish stones and magic wells that can still be admired in situ.

This is a land of 'oldests' and 'largests'. **Culbin Forest**, on Moray's western boundary, stands on one of Britain's largest sand dune systems – the setting for vicious sandstorms that inundated local villages in the 17th century. In the main city of **Elgin**, you can visit Scotland's largest gravestone and oldest independent museum – the latter is home to a replica of Moray's very own prehistoric reptile, *Elginia mirabilis*, which was munching leaves here 250 million years ago. Further west, **Findhorn Ecovillage** is one of the biggest intentional communities in Britain and a champion of Slow living.

Along this coast you'll find communities with shared stories and treasured traditions, but the area's relaxed, welcoming nature means visitors and newcomers alike slot in smoothly. Whether you're walking on tarmac, sand or pine needles, almost everyone you pass will say hello.

GETTING AROUND

The main road is the A96, which stays inland, connecting Inverness and Aberdeen via Forres and Elgin. The A98 from Fochabers links the coastal towns of Portknockie and Cullen. Villages on the west side of the coast – Findhorn, Burghead, Hopeman and Lossiemouth – are well-connected by quiet B roads. Both these and the main roads are generally in great condition and noticeably lacking in potholes. There can be the occasional queue in and out of Elgin during weekday commutes but, like much of the North East, congestion is rare. Brown-and-white signs point out stops on the **Malt Whisky Trail** (page 19).

TRAINS & BUSES

A **Scotrail** service runs regularly throughout the day from Inverness to Aberdeen via Forres and Elgin. Historically there was once an extensive rail network throughout Moray; some of the old tracks are partially grown over but still visible in sites such as Roseisle Forest, providing an intriguing insight into times gone by.

Despite the area's rural nature, many towns and villages are easy to access on Stagecoach **buses**, though you nearly always have to start from Elgin. From this city's bus station you can get the 31 to Findhorn and Forres, the 32 to Duffus, Hopeman and Burghead, the 33A/33C to Lossiemouth, the 10 to Aberdeen and Inverness and the 35 to Aberdeen via Portknockie and Cullen.

Detailed public transport timetables can be found on **Traveline Scotland** (⏴ 0871 200 22 33 ⏴ travelinescotland.com).

WALKING & CYCLING

You can encounter woodland, farmland, rivers, heathland, coastal cliffs and beaches in less than half a day in this part of Moray. Watch the land transform as you walk: each of these habitats has its own wildlife, from red squirrels and stonechats to kingfishers, fulmars and seals.

Coastal forests are perfect for rainy days, as the dense pine canopy provides good cover. Also, the bed of needles beneath your feet means

---

i TOURIST INFORMATION

Elgin Library Cooper Park, IV30 1HS ⏴ 01343 562608 ✉ visitorinfo@moray.gov.uk.

the ground is rarely muddy. If you visit during summer, don't be fooled by a cool sea breeze – I've walked sunlit coast paths for hours, blissfully unaware I was being barbecued.

The **Moray Walking & Outdoor Festival** (morraywalkoutdoorfest. co.uk) is a week of guided walks that takes place annually in various locations across the region and is great for Slow exploration. Offering a range of easy strolls and demanding hikes covering nature, history and local heritage, there's something for every ability.

Cyclists can enjoy bump-free riding on long stretches of flat trails. The **Moray Coastal Cycle Route** spans 29 miles of beaches, craggy cliffs and farmland from Burghead to Cullen, with lots of cafés along the way to rest your legs. Part of National Cycle Route 1 covers the Moray Coast from Forres to Cullen via Elgin, connecting many of the towns mentioned in this chapter. A 13-mile circular route called the **Elgin Experience** starts in Cooper Park (page 140) and loops west out of the city before dipping south and returning through New Elgin.

The Moray Way (morayways.org.uk) features local trails and information on all things walking and cycling.

CYCLE HIRE

Outfit Moray Shore St, Lossiemouth IV31 6PB 01343 549571 outfitmoray.com/bike-hire. Mountain, urban and electric bikes are all available to hire here. Helmet, gloves, lights and repair kit included.

ELGIN & AROUND

The Moray Coast's main hub is the city of Elgin. Less than ten miles from seaside villages such as Lossiemouth and Burghead, it provides a handy base for venturing north to the coast and south to Moray Speyside (page 105). It also offers its own spots of nature and history, with a river walk set back from thrumming roads and a towering monument of the Duke of Gordon, perched candle-like on a hill overlooking the whole city. Blended with these older aspects are contrasting modern additions such as a chic tea room and a number of independent gift shops.

Lying across the A96, Elgin is the only place on the Moray Coast with any noticeable traffic, but even during weekday commutes it's nowhere near as congested as cities further south. On the city's outskirts you'll find a forest where Moray's own dinosaurs have emerged, and a secluded loch offering lots of bird activity, including rare visitors.

1 ELGIN

🏠 **Moraybank B&B** (page 318)

Some might be surprised by what Elgin has to offer a Slow explorer. Struck through by the A96 and with a range of high street outlets, you'd be forgiven for thinking it's more practical than characterful. However, a little digging reveals a diverse range of restaurants, a museum showcasing Moray's archaeology, art heritage and natural history, and a ruined cathedral destroyed during one of the Wolf of Badenoch's (page 40) temper tantrums.

In the early 1800s, many of the medieval buildings in the centre of Elgin were replaced by large public buildings. Residential streets were built either side of **High Street**, now a pedestrianised thoroughfare with a town square. Part of the city's modern revival involved the demolishing of the original church, the Muckle Kirk. In 1828, a large Greek-style church, **St Giles**, was built in its place and still stands in the town square. There was once a medieval tolbooth in this square too; taxes were collected here and it was also used as a prison before being burnt down by a prisoner in 1701. A replacement was built, but in 1846 a fountain was put on the site instead, which is what you can see today.

A short walk east along High Street from St Giles will bring you to **Elgin Museum** (IV30 1EQ 🖉 01343 543675 ♂ elginmuseum.org.uk ☉ Apr–Oct; see website for times), the oldest independent museum in Scotland. Built in 1842 to house collections belonging to The Elgin and Morayshire Scientific Association, now called the Moray Society, it is managed by volunteers, who also assist the curator with events and exhibitions. The two storeys of displays range in contents from a rare greyware jug and original Pictish stones to a mummified cat. My favourite is the natural history section – a host of British taxidermy specimens have been arranged behind curved glass, replicating a woodland scene. The two Scottish wildcat specimens are particularly exciting.

Fossils have been an important component of the museum since its inception. Many of these are unique to Elgin and the most famous is *Elginia mirabilis* ('the wonder of Elgin'), named by palaeontologist Edwin

---

1 Elgin Museum. **2** Elgin Cathedral. ▶

Newton. *Elginia* was a pareiasaur, a reptile with no modern descendants. Some pareiasaurs weighed up to a metric tonne, but *Elginia* was only the size of a Labrador. Similar to a Triceratops, it had a distinctive frilled skull covered in thick spines that it used for protection. The life-size model on display in the museum was created by Stephen Caine.

Make sure to have a look in the shop before you leave. There are some fantastic publications for sale about Moray history, geology and palaeontology, including a booklet all about the Elgin reptiles.

For a bit of city greenery, backtrack along High Street to take a right down Lossie Wynd. There are several streets called 'wynd' in Scotland and they are typically narrow alleyways off the main road – the most infamous example is 'Butts Wynd' (for obvious reasons) in St Andrews, Fife. At the end of Lossie Wynd, cross the A96 at the pedestrian crossing to reach **Cooper Park**. This is a standard city park with a large duck pond, but it has the added bonus of a path at its northern edge that fringes the endlessly twisting **River Lossie** – this ultimately becomes Lossiemouth Estuary (page 145).

> *"There are several streets called 'wynd' in Scotland and they are typically narrow alleyways off the main road."*

At the southeast corner of Cooper Park is **Elgin Cathedral** (⚲ historicenvironmentscotland; Historic Scotland). Built in the 13th century, it was once described by Alexander Bur, one of Elgin's former bishops (1362–97), as 'the ornament of the realm'. The cathedral was destroyed by the Wolf of Badenoch (page 40) in 1390 and now stands in ruins, but is still a majestic crumbly cluster that reminds me of a small-scale Roman forum. Surrounded by headstones within a gated enclosure stand two towers at one end, a yawning circular aperture at the top of the other, an octagonal chapter house and dozens of narrow stone window arches.

Elgin is said to have more medieval memorials than any other cathedral in Scotland. Particularly notable features dotted among the sections of ruined stone include a Pictish slab showing a rare falconry scene, discovered nearby in 1823, and Scotland's tallest gravestone, measuring over 16ft tall.

Before you return to the city centre, poke your head in the **Biblical Garden** (⊙ May–Sep daily), accessed through a small iron gate on the cathedral's northern side. With vibrant flower beds in summer and

DUKE OF GORDON MONUMENT

Towards the west of Elgin is **Lady Hill**. This natural hillock is named after the Chapel of Our Lady, which was attached to a castle built on this site by King David I in 1130. Partially destroyed during the Wars of Independence, all that remains of Elgin Castle now are scattered sections of stone wall. Still, even from a distance you'll be able to locate Lady Hill because there's a 78ft-high monument on top of it. This is the Duke of Gordon's Monument, erected in 1839 to commemorate George Gordon, 5th Duke of Gordon and first Commander of the Gordon Highlanders Regiment. The statue of the duke was added on top of the pillar in 1855. It's said that on the stroke of midnight he climbs down and drinks from nearby Marywell. Whether that myth tickles your fancy or not, his hill has unrivalled views over Elgin and beyond. The easiest way to reach it on foot is via the stone stairway opposite the Royal Mail depot on the A96 (⏚ feast.placed.woes).

numerous places to perch and watch the birds, it's a peaceful spot tucked away from the city's bustle.

There are some fantastic independent shops in Elgin. From High Street, head south down Commerce Street and you'll reach **Yeadon's of Elgin** (⏚ yeadons.co.uk ⊙ 09.30–16.00 Mon–Sat), a bookseller established in 1887 and twinned with Yeadon's of Banchory (page 269). As with many bookshops in the North East, there are lots of local interest titles. Meeting Commerce Street at a right angle is South Street, and 50yds down here is **Crafted in Moray** (⏚ ⊙ 10.00–15.00 Mon–Sat), with a jolly aquamarine banner. This gift shop sells works from over a hundred Scottish artists and crafters and I've spent ages admiring its crystals, jewellery and fine art prints.

Be mindful of the one-way streets if you're driving through Elgin. It's a lot easier, and more relaxing, to explore on foot. You'll find central parking in the multi-storey car park in South Street, beside TK Maxx. After noon, it's free to park beside the library at the southern end of Cooper Park; this is only a few minutes' walk from town and puts you closer to the cathedral too.

⏚ FOOD & DRINK

Don't miss **Elgin Farmers' Market**, held in the city centre on the third Saturday of each month from 09.00 to 16.00.

The Ditsy Teacup Thunderton Pl, IV30 1BG ✆ 01343 551697 ⏚ theditsyteacup.co.uk ⊙ 09:00–15:00 Mon–Sat. With its crystal chandeliers, Rococo-style mirror and bright décor, The Ditsy Teacup adds a touch of elegance to your day. Choose from petite or veggie breakfasts, smashed avocado, pancakes, paninis, baked potatoes, soup and home bakes (all dishes available until 15.00). The scones – plain, fruit, cheese or a special flavour of the day – are particularly popular, served with your choice of jam made on the premises.

Pancake Place High St, IV30 1BW ✆ 01343 542541 🖰 cafebiba.scot/location/the-pancake-place-elgin. I'm always lured towards a restaurant promising pancakes and this one really delivers. There's a huge range of savoury and sweet options as well as all-day brunch, burgers, baguettes and ice cream. Comfort food at its most indulgent.

Pizzeria Toscana Thunderton Pl, IV30 1BG ✆ 01343 551066 🖰 pizzeria-toscana.yolasite. com 🕐 10.30–14.00 & 17.00–22.00 Mon–Sat, 17.00–22.00 Sun. An authentic Italian tucked on a quiet corner just off High Street, serving perfect-sized portions of pasta, risotto, meat dishes and, of course, plenty of pizzas.

2 QUARRELWOOD

/// imposes.printout.reforming

Four miles west of Elgin, beside the A96, is a fine patch of pine forest. Situated on a hill, Quarrelwood (also called Quarry Wood) has an undulating gradient with steep-sided dells.

"Listen out for woodpeckers and jays but watch your feet as the paths can be rocky and crossed with roots."

Listen out for woodpeckers and jays but watch your feet as the paths can be rocky and crossed with roots. The main trail is a three-mile circular marked with red posts and named the **Elginia Trail** after *Elginia mirabilis* (page 138) was uncovered in the sandstone quarries here. This dog-sized creature's remains are thought to date back 250 million years, long before the appearance of T-Rex. A replica can be seen in Elgin Museum.

As you follow the trail, keep an eye out for a concealed circular clearing. This is the only **henge** to have been discovered in Moray and, unusually for this kind of landmark, it was built on a hill. Originating from the Stone Age, some 2,000 years ago, the henge consists of a circular bank with a ditch running around its circumference. The trail cuts through the middle, banked on both sides by dense bracken. Its size suggests that it held great importance, but its true purpose remains unknown.

To get to Quarrelwood from Elgin, head west on the A96 past Dr Gray's Hospital. After 2¼ miles, turn right at the sign for Spynie Kirk and you'll reach the forest's free car park on the right after half a mile.

3 RSPB LOCH SPYNIE

/// fizzled.advice.excellent ⊘ rspb.org.uk

Halfway between Elgin and Lossiemouth lies Loch Spynie, a secluded nature reserve with a linear trail threading between the reed-lined loch and a narrow slice of mixed woodland. This is a great spot for birdwatching – from the hide tucked into the reeds you can see ducks, swans and maybe even an otter. Surrounded by farmland, the loch attracts good numbers of geese that browse in the fields and swoop over the trees to forage at the water's edge. Tufted ducks, goldeneye and wigeon are all common, with occasional rarities including bearded tits and avocets getting local photographers excited. Bird feeders in the car park attract a variety of tits and finches and the occasional red squirrel. I've taken my best photo of a brambling here – this finch is similar in size to a chaffinch but has darker colouring and only visits the UK during its winter migration. I've also seen fieldfares and redwings in the trees along the reserve access track during this time of year.

"I've also seen fieldfares and redwings in the trees along the reserve access track during this time of year."

To reach Loch Spynie from Elgin, follow Newmill Road north, turn right on to Calcots Road then keep left at the fork, leading uphill to Pitgaveny Road. Follow this country lane for two miles, continuing straight at the crossroads, until you see a gravel farm track on the left with an RSPB sign for the reserve. The car park is half a mile down this track. Watch your speed here, as hasty driving is frowned upon in the neighbouring farms.

LOSSIEMOUTH TO FINDHORN: THE WESTERN MORAY COAST

The following stretch of coastline is superb, encompassing a string of fishing villages where ancient history sits right on the paths, dolphins fling themselves out of the shallows and an outrageous New Year festival takes place on a dark January night. Over a week-long trip you could visit a different beach every day – while they all face the Moray Firth, they each offer their own opportunities for rock pooling, birdwatching or just sun lounging. This section, beginning at Lossiemouth and heading west through Hopeman, Burghead and Findhorn, is walkable from end to end and covers about 16 miles of the 50-mile **Moray Coast Trail** (⊘ morayways.org.uk/routes/the-moray-coast-trail). The route is easy-going, with many stretches of smooth tarmac perfect for cycling.

4 LOSSIEMOUTH

Mounted on a rounded hump on the coast, the village of Lossiemouth, or Lossie as it's also known, lies 5½ miles north of Elgin on the A941. If you hear something thundering overhead here, it's a Typhoon aircraft from **RAF Lossiemouth**, stationed just outside the village. You can get an aerial view of the base from the top of Covesea Lighthouse (page 148).

Although it extends two miles inland, most of Lossiemouth is residential and everything visitors would want to see lies at the water's edge. A good place to start is Pitgaveny Street on the northeast side, where you'll find ample parking opposite a towering stone wall (▥ thundered.teeth.stapled). Some 200yds north along this road you'll reach a skinny **harbour**, now mostly occupied by sail boats.

Modern Lossiemouth is an amalgamation of several old fishing villages: Stotfield, Seatown and Branderburgh. After the original harbour at the mouth of the River Lossie became too dangerous to access, Colonel Brander of Pitgaveny assisted with the construction of a new harbour at Stotfield Point in 1837. It became a successful port, importing salt, barley and coal and exporting herring, whisky and stone among other materials. The buildings overlooking the marina were used for mending nets and storing fishing gear. They became disused after the decline of the fishing industry and are now cafés, shops, flats and the volunteer-run **Lossiemouth Fisheries & Community Museum** (Pitgaveny Quay, IV31 6NT ✆ 01343 813772 ⊘ lossiemuseum.co.uk ⊙ Apr–Oct Mon–Sat). One of the exhibits is a reconstruction of a study belonging to **James Ramsay Macdonald**, who was born in Lossiemouth in 1866 and went on to become Britain's first Labour Prime Minister.

> "Modern Lossiemouth is an amalgamation of several old fishing villages: Stotfield, Seatown and Branderburgh."

Tucked around the southwest corner of the harbour is **The Re:Store Moray** (Queen St, IV31 6NU ✆ 01343 815000 ⬛ ⊙ Mon–Sat), Moray's zero-waste refill shop and an excellent Slow resource for free-range and ethically sourced produce. There's a real sense of community on its

Facebook and Instagram accounts, with stories behind its products and tips for making sustainable lifestyle changes.

Two hundred yards further west down Queen Street, a small green called James Square opens up on the left, bordered by rough stone cottages. In the centre there's a collection of plaques commemorating historical achievements of residents. One of these is for **Meg Farquhar**, who became an assistant to the resident professional at Moray Golf Club in 1929 – making her the first woman in Britain to become a professional golfer.

Backtrack to the harbour and return south down Pitgaveny Street to **East Beach**, accessed via a footbridge crossing the estuary of the River Lossie. During summer, most of my visits to Lossie are spent at this estuary, along with many other wildlife photographers. Stand at any spot next to this 1½-mile narrow water channel from March to late

LOSSIE OSPREYS

Lossiemouth Estuary is a must for birdwatchers, accessed by following Church Street (a side-road off the A941 at the southern end of the village) east to the caravan park. As well as sightings throughout the year of wigeon, teal, grey heron and redshank, every spring there's also a flurry of human activity here when ospreys return to Britain after overwintering in Africa.

Ospreys are the only bird of prey to feed exclusively on fish. As a result of hunting and egg collecting in the 19th century, their numbers were slashed and the last breeding bird recorded in Scotland was in 1916. Almost 40 years later, a pair was observed at Loch Garten (page 48), and a combination of natural recolonisation and diligent protection from egg thieves has resulted in their comeback. The current estimate stands at 250 to 300 breeding pairs in Scotland.

I got to know Elgin-based photographer Liam McBride (📷 @scotland_landscape_ photography) from hours spent waiting for the ospreys to turn up at Lossie Estuary. During a lull in activity, I ask him why this is a good spot for them. 'You've got Findhorn on one side and Spey Bay on the other,' he tells me. 'They have two of the best fishing rivers in Scotland for salmon and trout. At Spey Bay you'll see them taking more trout, but at Lossiemouth I'd say it's 90% flatfish.'

Liam is recognised locally for his osprey photos and I soon discovered how much skill is required to capture these formidable birds slamming into the water, talons first, and emerging with huge flatfish. I can see why they're one of Liam's favourite birds. 'It's the co-operation between them,' he says, 'and how resilient they are. It's the thrill of being able to watch them hunt up close – you don't often get to see that elsewhere in the wild.'

August and you might be treated to **ospreys** diving for flat fish just a few feet away from you (page 145).

Sand dunes were artificially created on East Beach in the early 20th century when railway carriages were used to form a protective barrier for the adjacent cottages. This now makes the estuary a sheltered place to walk, as winds blowing in from the sea get caught behind the dunes.

A large evergreen forest stretches southeast from the estuary towards Spey Bay. Similar to Roseisle Forest (page 158), there are many winding trails to follow in here and World War II pillboxes are dotted among the pines. You can access the forest by walking southeast beside the estuary for half a mile, then turning right into the trees.

The Spynie Canal drains into the estuary at its northwest corner, and just west of this is another small green beside Gregory Place. James Ramsay Macdonald was born in one of the houses overlooking this green. The footpath through the grass was once a railway line connecting Lossiemouth to Aberdeen, operational from 1852 to 1966.

Lossie's other beach, **West Beach**, lies in front of the golf course on the opposite side of the harbour (parking ▥ drew.crows.tennis). Walk along the sand here for just over a mile and you'll reach Covesea Lighthouse.

¶¶ FOOD & DRINK

Catch 79 Seafood Bistro Clifton Rd, IV31 6DP ✆ 07495 190464 ◨ ⊙ 17.00–22.00 Thu–Sat, noon–15.00 & 17.00–22.00 Sun. With just a handful of tables in an intimate, wood-panelled setting, this higher-end restaurant specialises in fresh fish and seafood. Its excellent mixed grill changes depending on what's been caught that day.

The Harbour Lights Pitgaveny St, IV31 6TW ✆ 01343 814622 ◈ theharbour-lights.co.uk ⊙ daily. Enjoy all-day breakfasts, snacks, lunches, home bakes and a range of teas, coffees and alcoholic beverages at this upmarket café on the harbour's edge.

The Salt Cellar Clifton Rd, IV31 6DJ ✆ 01343 813027 ◈ 1629lossiemouth.co.uk ⊙ 10.00–20.00 Mon–Sat. Part of two other adjoining restaurants facing Lossiemouth Estuary: Bridge 45 and Guidi's. An exposed brick arched ceiling and warm lighting give The Salt Cellar an underground feel reflective of its name, with brightly coloured fresco-style wall paintings livening up the space. Serves a diverse range of pasta, risotto, burgers, steaks and fish dishes.

Windswept Brewery Coulardbank Ind Estate, IV31 6NG ✆ 01343 814310 ◈ windsweptbrewing.com ⊙ bar Tue–Sat; shop Mon–Sat. Founded by two former RAF

1 Hopeman East Beach. **2** Lossiemouth. **3** Duffus Castle. **4** Covesea Lighthouse. ▶

pilots, this brewery has a shop selling beers and merchandise and a Tap Room Bar serving cask, keg and bottled beers and a variety of other alcoholic and soft drinks. An hour-long brewery tour and tasting is also available from Thursday to Saturday.

5 COVESEA LIGHTHOUSE

🏠 **Covesea Lighthouse Keeper Cottages** (page 318)
Covesea IV31 6SP 🕿 01343 810664 ⌖ covesealighthouse.co.uk ⏱ Apr–Oct 10:00 & 11:00 Sat; booking essential, entry by donation

Just over two miles from the centre of Lossie, easily walkable along West Beach, is bright white Covesea Lighthouse. Volunteer Rhona Graham took me on a tour, leading the way up 144 steps and two ladders. There have been weddings held here and on one occasion Rhona had to avert her eyes when a group of men in kilts were climbing the ladder in front of her!

Once we clambered through a miniature door to the balcony, all I could see was ocean. 'It's great taking teenagers up here,' Rhona told me. 'They think it's boring and then they get to the top and go "wow!" It really is a spectacular view – I looked north over the Moray Firth and walked around to scan south across open countryside and RAF Lossiemouth.

Covesea Lighthouse's story began with Saint Gerardine, a 'Celtic hermit' who lived in a nearby cave and walked up and down the headland with a lantern to prevent ships from colliding with the rocks. However, multiple ferocious storms resulting in disaster in the 19th century made it clear a lighthouse was needed instead. It was designed and built in 1846 by Alan Stevenson, a member of the 'Lighthouse Stevensons' family who built most of Scotland's lighthouses over a period of 150 years. 'This is where my interest in the story really comes in,' Rhona said. 'His nephew was Robert Louis Stevenson. Sometimes when you're on the beach hearing the waves, you think maybe that's what inspired him to write some of his stories.'

Sadly, Covesea Lighthouse is no longer operational. After 166 years of service, it was decommissioned by the Northern Lighthouse Board in 2012 and replaced by a yellow buoy with a radar signal. The lighthouse and adjoining land were purchased by the local community and now the site is preserved as a learning facility, welcoming school groups, cadets and any other curious visitors. For a heightened experience, you can hire one of the keeper cottages as a holiday rental (see website).

SCULPTOR'S CAVE

Only accessible at low tide, this cave by Covesea is at best difficult to reach and at worst dangerous. It's this remoteness that makes it an appropriate place for the ancient rituals that supposedly occurred here. Many mysterious items have been found inside the cave, such as pottery, Bronze Age arm rings and a large quantity of human remains including children's skulls. Some party.

There's also evidence of Pictish presence here – salmon, crescent, triple oval and mirror case symbols can all be seen on the walls. In such a precarious position between land and sea, Sculptor's Cave is said to represent a gateway between the upper world and underworld.

One archaeologist involved in excavating the site was Sylvia Benton. Born in India and educated in England, she visited Moray often and carried out the first formal excavation of Sculptor's Cave from 1928 to 1930. Later in life she was elected an honorary member of the Elgin Society, now the Moray Society, and also acted as honorary curator of Elgin Museum (page 138). In 1979, at the age of 92,

she returned to Sculptor's Cave during a new excavation by Ian and Alexandra Shepherd. Undeterred by the perilous descent down a 90ft cliff, Sylvia carried out her research then apparently scurried back up again quicker than they could reel in the safety rope. Success ran in the family – her sister, Mary Benton, was Ladies' Champion of the Moray Golf Club on six occasions from 1906 to 1919.

This is a fascinating spot, but I think it's a case of an intriguing piece of history and not somewhere I recommend actually visiting. The cave sits on the Moray Coast Trail, roughly a mile east of Clashach Cove (page 151). A footpath heads down the cliff beside a white coastguard lookout (◼◼◼ stewing. inert.money) and provides a distant view of the cave mouth, but some of the drops here are pretty dicey and the cave itself is at the bottom of a sheer cliff. It's possible to reach it by walking far out of the way and doubling back via a lower path, but those attempting this should be mindful of the tide. I'm happy just to know it's down there, and I have fierce respect for Sylvia Benton.

To access Covesea Lighthouse, travel west from Lossie on the B9040 and turn right into Silver Sands Holiday Caravan Park. Make an immediate left down a gravel track leading to the parking area. Here you'll see the **Royal Navy and RAF Heritage Centre** (⊙ Easter–Oct 11.00–16.00 Sat & Sun), displaying the history of nearby RAF Lossiemouth airbase.

6 HOPEMAN & AROUND

🏠 **Mossyards Holiday Cottages** (page 318)

Continuing west on the B9040 from Covesea, you'll arrive in Hopeman. This small village is halved by Harbour Street, which leads to the waterfront. Hopeman didn't originally have a harbour and fishermen had to haul their boats directly on to the beach. When he purchased the village in 1837, Admiral Duff of Drummuir saw its potential as a fishing port and the original harbour was completed in 1840. By 1888, it was extended to include a west pier. As the tides prevented increasingly larger boats from docking, it became more popular with pleasure boats and small fishing vessels.

At the harbour's edge sits **The Harbour with Footprints Gallery** (✎ 07734 315840), a gift shop selling a range of sea-themed items from 91 local crafters and artists. There are also hot drinks and snacks available and an exhibition space upstairs. On one side of Hopeman's harbour is **West Beach** which, similar to the majority of others on this coast, consists of fine, golden sand. When I visited on a blustery day in October, the shallows were being pummelled by a group of fishing gannets. I watched the birds with a sailor who'd lived in Hopeman for 40 years but had never seen gannets dive so close to shore.

"This sea witch is said to sit by rock pools around Findlay's Bay and snatch unsuspecting children."

On the opposite side of the harbour is **East Beach**. Turn right at the sign for East Beach Promenade and follow a narrow single-lane road round to three parking areas. On sunny weekends these can fill up quickly. In front of the first car park is **Findlay's Bay**, named after John Findlay who operated one of three boatyards in Hopeman in the mid 1860s. A nearby plaque warns parents about a local legend called the **Grin Iron Wife**. This sea witch is said to sit by rock pools around Findlay's Bay and snatch unsuspecting children.

Wander a little further east and you'll see a sign for **Braemou Well**. Partially concealed in a skinny walkway between gorse and a stone wall, this is where fisherwomen and their children used to fetch water in creels and carry them back to the village. During the 17th century, people undertook annual pilgrimages to this well from Elgin. The water is said to have healing powers, so visitors offered coins, pebbles or scraps of silk as gifts to the spirit of the well before drinking from it. People even bathed their babies in the well to try and ensure their future health.

Continuing east on the coastal track from Hopeman past Braemou Well, you'll encounter lots of little bays and fascinating rock formations. Some look like stone bubbles while others are cubic like city skylines.

As always on the Moray Coast, keep an eye out for bottlenose dolphins while you walk. Banks of heather and gorse conceal yellowhammers, stonechats and linnets. Gobble a blackberry or two in autumn – the ones growing here are the sweetest I've ever tasted.

As the winding sand path presses against the golf course, it climbs to a great vantage point for sunrises and sunsets. Then it dips down again into **Clashach Cove**, sometimes referred to as Cove Bay. This sheltered spot is far enough away from Hopeman's East Beach to be nicely secluded and has two caves to explore. You can walk all the way through one of them at low tide, but the other is submerged in darkness. Step inside and you'll feel a noticeable drop in temperature. I've read too many vampire stories not to experience a little shiver standing here, picturing red eyes in the gloom.

"Gobble a blackberry or two in autumn – the ones growing here are the sweetest I've ever tasted."

Just beyond Clashach Cove is **Clashach Quarry**, where fossilised reptile footprints are often uncovered. Sandstone from this quarry was used as part of the extension to Edinburgh's National Museum of Scotland and also in the 9/11 memorial in New York.

If you enjoy exploring ruins, **Duffus Castle** (⬦ visit-a-place/places/duffus-castle; free entry) is a prime example just outside Hopeman. Head east on the B9040 and in less than a mile turn right on to the B9012. Follow this for two miles until you reach a sign for the castle, which you'll soon spot propped up on a hill. The fields surrounding Duffus Castle attract plenty of wildlife, and by walking around the ruin you can scan the reeds for birds and butterflies too.

The castle was originally built from earth and timber in the 12th century by Freskin, a Flemish man sent north by King David I in 1130 as a royal representative. Around 1270, Lord of Inverugie, Sir Reginald Cheyne the Elder, took ownership. It's likely that this was when stone was added. Over time, the north wall of the tower sunk down the hill, succumbing to the fragility of such old earthworks. Visitors can now explore the scant remains of cellars, latrines and the drawing room.

¶ FOOD & DRINK

Hopeman Sands Café Harbour St, IV30 5SJ ✆ 01343 831466 ⏱ Tue–Sun. This dinky café serves delicious breakfasts, sandwiches, scones and cakes – there's always a treat on offer for good pups as well.

Kula Duffus Castle car park, IV30 5RH ⊙ 10.00–16.00 Thu–Sun. This peppermint green coffee hut serves hot and soft drinks, ice cream, cakes and other snacks. It's a great advocate for local produce and sells coffee from Speyside Coffee, close to Spey Bay (page 170), baked goods from Bijou in Elgin, and Stew 'n' Drew's.

Stew 'n' Drew's Harbour St, IV30 5SJ ✆ 01343 830339 ◈ stewndrews.co.uk. If you fancy ice cream, this is the place to get it. Choose from 24 different flavours, all made a few yards away at Stew 'n' Drew HQ using local milk. Imaginative flavours in the past have included whisky and wasabi, but tamer choices such as bubblegum and sticky toffee are also available.

W Reid Butchers Harbour St, IV30 5SJ ✆ 01343 830300 ⊙ Mon–Sat. This award-winning butchers is part of the Scottish Craft Butchers partnership and offers lots of high-quality local produce. As well as meats, you can also get homemade pies and pastries, locally sourced vegetables, baked goods and sauces here.

7 BURGHEAD

I could write a whole chapter on Burghead alone. This quiet coastal village juts into the Moray Firth on a promontory two miles west of Hopeman. With rocky shores, sandy beaches and almost 360° ocean views, it's an unrivalled spot for watching seabirds, seals and dolphins (page 155).

A good place to start your explorations is the white coastguard lookout at the tip of the peninsula, which contains a **Museum and Visitor Centre** (✆ 01343 835518 ◈ burghead.com/visitor-centre ⊙ Apr–Sep noon–16.00 daily). Perched high on the headland, this pocket-sized museum provides snippets of history as far back as AD400. Ascend a spiral staircase next to the entrance for expansive views over the Moray Firth. So good are your chances of spotting marine wildlife here that Burghead is part of wildlife charity Whale and Dolphin Conservation's (WDC) Shorewatch Programme (◈ uk.whales.org). Volunteers scan the horizon for ten-minute periods at designated Shorewatch sites throughout Scotland and record any whales or dolphins they see.

With its easy access to shore, good defences and sheltered harbour, Burghead was frequently fought over and Vikings raided it in the 8th and 9th centuries. Though they mostly settled in the Northern and Western isles, it's thought they may have been responsible for Burghead's name – *burg* is a Norse word meaning 'a fortified place'.

1 The Burning of the Clavie, Burghead. 2 Burghead sea wall. 3 Burghead harbour.
4 Burghead is one of the best places in the North East to see bottlenose dolphins. ▶

THE BURNING OF THE CLAVIE

Although the Picts have faded over time, ancient traditions endure in Burghead. Fire symbolised the sun and was often included in purification rituals. Only a handful of fire festivals still take place in Scotland, but Burghead's version continued even when the calendar changed.

The Burning of the Clavie attracts thousands of visitors each year and is held on 11 January to commemorate Auld New Year, the start of the year according to the old Julian calendar. The Clavie is a tar-filled barrel that the Clavie King (a prestigious title assigned to long-standing Burghead residents and often passed down through generations) sets alight and carries around the village, finishing on Doorie Hill. After placing it on a chimney-like structure, charred black over the centuries, more fuel is thrown on to keep it alight. Once the fire eventually diminishes, many folk scramble to claim a piece of the still smouldering Clavie for good luck.

Covid-19 saw the festival cancelled in 2021 for the first time since World War II, but it was back with its usual outrageousness the following year. Hordes of us huddled at the foot of Doorie Hill as buckets of tar were flung into the air, igniting balloons of flame and screams from the crowd. Health and safety protocol goes flying but it's enormous fun and has to be seen to be believed.

Beside the visitor centre is Britain's largest **Pictish Iron Age fort**. The site is so ancient that Roman maps dated AD86 show a settlement there, although all that remains of it now are steep grassy hills. Thirty stones, each with the same Pictish **bull carving**, with its tail swishing and head held low as if to charge, were found in Burghead during the 19th century, though now only six of the stones remain. Like all Pictish animal symbols, its outline is stencil-like with deep, looping lines. A bull carving hasn't been discovered at any other Pictish fort, and you can see one of the six surviving stones in Elgin Museum (page 138).

Most of the old fort was demolished to build the new village and harbour in the early 19th century. Business boomed and steamers passed through from Inverness, Leith in Edinburgh and even London. It's said the herring attracted as many as a thousand fishing boats to the Moray Firth in 1920, but there's only a handful docked in Burghead's harbour today. Visit on Boxing Day and you might see people among the seals and gulls – every year brave individuals jump in for charity.

Looking east from the visitor centre, you'll spot a charred chimney on nearby **Doorie Hill**. This is where the last witch was burned in Moray in the 17th century and is now the finishing point of Burghead's infamous

Burning of the Clavie festival (see opposite). Another point of intrigue can be found off Church Street, behind Doorie Hill. Turn left on to King Street and follow a narrow alley – behind a locked gate (during summer a key is available at the visitor centre) is a mysterious **well**. Some say it was a shrine to Celtic gods, while others believe early Christian baptisms took place there or even ritual executions.

The village's northern side is what Burghead residents, or 'Brochers', call the **Backshore**: a stretch of boulders and puddles attracting wading birds and welly-clad rock poolers alike. Beside it is a two mile-long coastal footpath connecting Burghead to Hopeman. Oystercatchers and curlews are frequently seen here, but rarities such as purple sandpipers also show up. The side of the path furthest from the shore is dominated by dense thickets of gorse, which buzz with yellowhammers, stonechats and linnets in spring and summer.

Burghead's **harbour** can be found at its southwest corner. Scattered with lobster pots, crab claws and fish nets, it's a bubble of activity. Grey seals and a variety of seabirds are drawn in to feed on stray fish and shelter from stormy weather behind the sea wall. Long-tailed ducks can

FINS IN THE FIRTH

Burghead is one of the best places in the North East to see bottlenose dolphins. Whale- and dolphin-watching guide Steve Truluck has been observing marine wildlife in the Moray Firth since 2014. When dolphins appear, he can sometimes be spotted running along Burghead Backshore with his camera and his springer spaniel Riley in tow.

'Bottlenose dolphins are seen throughout the year,' Steve says. 'It's the sightings of humpback whales and orcas from Burghead Visitor Centre that really get the pulse racing. On one occasion, a humpback whale breached over 60 times in a row. Another time there were two humpbacks in the area for almost a week, delighting locals and visitors who'd travelled from all over to get a glimpse.'

Despite also being called killer whales, orcas are actually the largest member of the dolphin family. They show up on the Moray Coast a couple of times a year, usually between April and June. 'I saw my first orcas from Burghead,' Steve tells me. 'That's a moment that will stay with me forever.'

Steve is a co-author of the *Scottish Killer Whale Photo Identification Catalogue*. This collaborative citizen science project identifies individual orcas using images of their dorsal fins, saddle patches and eye patches. The photo ID data collected improves the monitoring of Scottish orcas in future years. You can see Steve's wildlife photography and follow his updates from all over the Scottish coast on 🆕 Steve Truluck At Sea.

Around Burghead

✻ OS Explorer 423; start: Salmon Green car park, Station Rd (▥ handbags.directly.koala); 3½ miles; ♥ NJ1108968895; mostly easy.

- -

This route follows part of the Moray Coast Trail but also takes in the harbour, visitor centre and Pictish fort. One of Burghead's many qualities is its diverse landscape – sandy beach, pine forest, rocky shore, hedgerow and craggy cliff habitats can all be seen on this circular.

1 From the Salmon Green, put the sea on your right and walk along the tarmac path beside the stone wall. When the road bends left up Clavie Court and a gap in the wall appears on the right, walk through here and follow the path to the beach, descending a concrete ramp on to the sand.

2 When you reach the first World War II pillbox on the left, walk up the dune trail beside it, entering Roseisle Forest. At the bottom of the other side of the dune, turn left and follow an indented path to the main track. Turn right on to this, then in 90yds branch left and take another narrow path that appears just before the main path bends away to the right.

3 You'll soon arrive at the old railway line, its tracks just visible above ground. Through a gap in the fence, turn left and walk along the tracks to a crossroads. Turn right up a short flight of steps and continue straight over a sandy bank with tree roots.

4 After a quarter of a mile, carry on straight across a five-pronged crossroads. The heather is fantastic here in late summer.

5 Once the path opens out, another steep sandy bank appears ahead. Before you reach it, branch left towards the road. When the path forks, bear right uphill.

6 Emerge from the forest at the end of the village, beside the Burghead welcome sign. Turn left on to a narrower trail on a high ridge over St Aethans Road. In a matter of steps you'll be parallel to the turning for the B9040 to Hopeman, which heads uphill from St Aethans Road. Descend a slope to the road, cross over and walk up the B9040. In 300yds you'll pass Burghead Cemetery on the left.

7 After another 250yds, turn left on to Fraser Road, which lies between a row of houses and an open field. Shortly after the road bends left, take a footpath on the right towards the sea. In 50yds this splits in two – turn right and follow a gentle descent through an avenue of gorse bushes that attracts yellowhammers all year round.

8 At the bottom, turn sharply left to join the tarmac path of The Moray Coast Trail. You're now on Burghead Backshore – a superb stretch for wading birds at low tide (page 155). Stay on this path all the way along Burghead's northern flank, sticking close to the water when the gorse makes way for an open green beside Forteath Street.

9 When you arrive at a minimum height barrier there are two options. The first is to continue straight to a circular parking area at the end, then turn left up a narrow footpath winding around the headland to Burghead Visitor Centre. There's a steep drop to one side here so I wouldn't recommend this in strong winds. The alternative is to turn left before the height barrier on to Bath Street and walk up a steep hill. Just up here on the left is the blackened Clavie chimney on Doorie Hill (page 154). At the end of Bath Street, turn right and approach the visitor centre.

10 Whichever route you choose, once you're outside the visitor centre walk south away from it, following the edge of the headland until the harbour appears below. Descend some steep stone steps then turn right down a concrete ramp and another flight of steps. When you reach the harbour, turn left on to Granary Street. Two hundred yards further on, cross over Church Street and you'll see the start point up ahead.

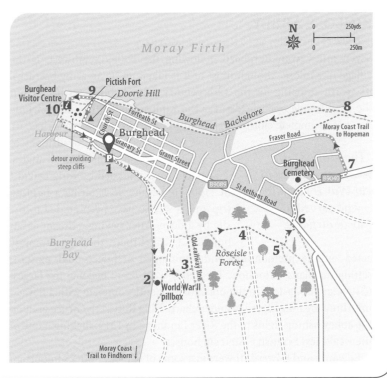

be seen very closely in winter, and there was a flurry of excitement in spring 2021 when a rare Slavonian grebe showed up.

Southeast of the harbour is the **Salmon Green**, where fisherfolk used to lay out salmon nets for mending. At low tide you can access a sweeping **beach** here via a slipway. It has the softest sand I've ever buried my toes in and runs for six miles to Findhorn (see opposite). Be mindful of the tide as it fluctuates widely – on some days the water retreats almost past the harbour entrance but on others it covers the entire beach and the bottom of the slipway.

Half-buried along the beach is a row of anti-tank concrete blocks and pillboxes from World War II. Beyond these is **Roseisle Forest**, planted to avoid a repeat of the late 17th-century disaster in Culbin (page 167). There's a vast network of trails ideal for walking, cycling or wildlife watching – look out for red squirrels and roe deer. Deep in the forest, you'll be walking across sand even when the beach is well out of sight.

8 KINLOSS ABBEY

IV36 3UW 🖉 kinlossabbey.org ☺ always open; free entry

Seven miles from Burghead, following the B9089 southwest, is the village of Kinloss. Though most of it is taken up by an army barracks, it's worth stopping for the 12th-century ruined abbey, set back from the road beside open fields near the Kinloss Burn. The ruins include two near-complete cloister walls and some impressive stone arches. It's possible to walk among the headstones of the cemetery to see the ruin from all angles.

"The grounds are now a resting place for World War II casualties who served at local airfields."

The abbey was founded by King David I in 1150. He became lost during a hunting trip and is said to have been guided to the site by a dove. After having a dream about building a chapel there, the king promptly acted on the premonition and summoned architects and masons, setting his plans in motion. The abbey went on to become the largest Cistercian monastery in the north of Scotland, complete with a library, mill, brewing house, garden and orchard. King Robert the Bruce granted the abbey fishing rights to the River Findhorn in 1312, making it one of the wealthiest Scottish Cistercian houses.

Edward I and Edward III were just some of Kinloss Abbey's important guests. Mary Queen of Scots also stayed here in 1562, even though she was a Catholic and the abbey had already shifted to Protestantism. The grounds are now a resting place for World War II casualties who served at local airfields.

Some of the stones from the abbey ruins were passed on to Oliver Cromwell in 1650 to build Inverness Citadel. Sources differ on whether the stones were bought or stolen, although seeing as Cromwell was involved my inkling would be the latter. I asked Kinloss Abbey Trustee Kirsteen Mitcalfe for her verdict. She told me, 'We think that at the time of the Reformation, the abbey lands were sold to Edward Bruce, 1st Lord Kinloss, who sold them on to Brodie of Lethen. He then sold some of the stones to Cromwell to build the citadel. Of course, it would have been quite easy, once the main part of the abbey was demolished, for dressed stones to be pillaged and I'm sure that many local farmers have part of the historic buildings on their premises. So both versions are probably correct!'

Other pieces of the abbey were used to build a row of cottages on the road to Findhorn. These cottages became a bakery and then a pub in the 1950s, which is the Abbey Inn today.

9 FINDHORN

The village of Findhorn is easy to locate on a map of the Moray Coast as it sits beside an obvious swollen bowl of water on the far west side. This is the River Findhorn right before it spills into the sea, and it's a fine place to watch wildlife. Depending on the tide, it might be dotted with seals or covered in foraging waders. The mouth of the bay is where you'll find the village's restaurants, so you can tuck into an ice cream or a full Scottish breakfast while overlooking the yachts.

Walk around the hook-shaped headland to access a longer beach on the other side, which stretches six miles to Burghead. Here the terrain is layered with both sand and shingle. There are usually lots of rockpooling and shell-foraging opportunities at low tide and the multi-coloured beach huts are particularly photogenic. I had a sunset swim here once and watched sandwich terns diving just a few feet away. If the air is still, you can often hear the haunting sound of seals wailing from their haul-out site further along the beach.

You can watch the Moray Firth's marine wildlife from the water by joining a boat trip with **North 58 Sea Adventures** ($\mathcal{O}$ 01309 690099 $\mathcal{O}$ north58.co.uk $\odot$ Mar–Nov daily; Dec–Feb custom trips only),

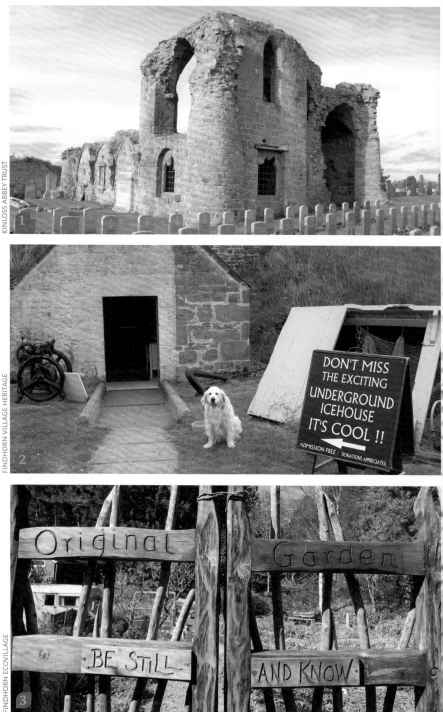

DON'T MISS
THE EXCITING
UNDERGROUND
ICEHOUSE
IT'S COOL !!
ADMISSION FREE : DONATIONS APPRECIATED

Original

Garden

BE STILL

AND KNOW

departing from Findhorn or Lossiemouth. Choose from a two-hour wildlife trip, a four-hour cruise with a stop-off for dinner halfway through, or a custom charter tour if you want a really personalised experience. You can also cross the bay to **Culbin Forest** (page 167) on one of North 58's regular water taxis.

Towards the northern end of Findhorn is the **Heritage Centre & Icehouse** (North Shore, IV36 3YQ ⌂ findhorn-heritage.co.uk ⊙ Jun–Aug 14.00–17.00 daily; May & Sep 14.00–17:00 Sat & Sun; entry by donation). The icehouse was built over 150 years ago to store salmon before it was shipped to London, and the arched chambers are now used to display artefacts from Findhorn's fishing history. You can learn about life in a bothy, Atlantic salmon and how boats were built here. In the Heritage Centre is a Bronze Age burial urn found nearby, natural history exhibits about local marine wildlife, and a range of photographs showing Findhorn past and present.

> "The arched chambers are now used to display artefacts from Findhorn's fishing history."

Just south of Findhorn on the B9011 lies the **Findhorn Foundation** (The Park, IV36 3TZ ⌂ findhorn.org). In 1962, co-founders Eileen Caddy, Peter Caddy and Dorothy Maclean arrived at a caravan park here and grew vegetables, herbs and flowers in the sandy, barren soil. Word spread of their new garden and before long others joined them, keen to follow a similar lifestyle in harmony with nature.

Over time a forward-thinking spiritual community, or Ecovillage, was formed. The Findhorn Foundation was recognised as a non-governmental organisation (NGO) by the UN in 1997 – now it's a place for learning, spiritual inspiration and pioneering sustainability in daily life. The Foundation hosts talks, events and workshops and there are learning materials on its website and social media. **Moray Art Centre** (⌂ morayartcentre.org) is based here and hosts exhibitions and a range of daytime and evening art classes.

Everyone is welcome to stroll through The Foundation during the day – there's a café (page 163), and footpaths leading to the beach and Roseisle Forest. To learn more, you can arrange a tour (suggested donation £10 per person) through the website, or buy a guidebook in

◀ **1** Kinloss Abbey. **2** Heritage Centre & Icehouse. **3** Findhorn Ecovillage.

the **Phoenix Shop** by the entrance to the site, which sells gifts and a range of food and drink.

Findhorn Bay Nature Reserve

/// observers.folks.protect ⌀ fblnr.org

On a crisp December morning, the babble of thousands of greylag and pink-footed geese drifted across Findhorn Bay. I arrived before sunrise but the sky to the east was already glowing. Slinging my camera across my back, I squelched towards the geese, only just able to make out their skinny necks as they stood tightly packed on a sandbar. The tide was coming in so none of us had long.

I set up my tripod and watched a small gaggle take to the air. The birds formed a loose skein that blew across the sky like a stray ribbon. A little while later another group took off, then another. Over the next two hours the crowd on the sandbar diminished, until the bay eventually fell silent.

From October onwards, I often hear geese honking in the dark as they fly unseen overhead. We have them all year round in the UK, but in winter vast numbers arrive from the Arctic during their winter migration. Along the Moray Coast they roost on estuaries and bays such as Findhorn, then move inland at sunrise to browse in nearby stubble fields.

"Over the next two hours the crowd on the sandbar diminished, until the bay eventually fell silent."

Findhorn Bay was designated as a nature reserve in 1998 and can be accessed on the left side of the B9011 as you approach Findhorn. As well as geese, it also provides sustenance and shelter for ospreys in summer, whooper swans in winter and an assortment of other birds throughout the year. There are a few parking spots listed on the website, but for an overview of the whole bay and easy access to Findhorn itself, I'd suggest the car park opposite the entrance to the Findhorn Foundation, which you'll pass on your way in and out of the village.

¶¶ FOOD & DRINK

The Bakehouse Café IV36 3YG ✆ 01309 691826 ⌀ bakehousecafe.co.uk. Originally a sit-in café that transitioned into a market during the pandemic. Offers locally sourced and organic food prepared from scratch each day including hot take-away food. Every Friday and

Saturday is Pizza Night – call ahead to book and either sit in or pick up and take-away. Vegan and gluten-free alternatives are also available.

The Captain's Table Findhorn Boat Yard, IV36 3YE ✆ 01309 690663 ♂ captainstable. uk ☺ 08.00–22.00 daily. The best place to eat in Findhorn. Dog-friendly and heaving on sunny weekends (for good reason), this pub serves full Scottish and vegetarian breakfasts, plus burgers, soups, sandwiches and bar meals by day and a range of cocktails and local ales by night.

Phoenix Café The Park, IV36 3TZ ✆ 01309 690110 ♂ phoenixshop.co.uk/cafe. Located within Findhorn Ecovillage. With both indoor seating and a garden terrace, it serves a range of light lunches, cakes and drinks, many of which are vegetarian. Nearby is the Phoenix Shop, specialising in local, organic and Fairtrade products.

FORRES TO MORAY'S WEST BOUNDARY

Forres is the most westerly major settlement on the Moray Coast, sitting four miles inland, close to the River Findhorn. Culbin Forest and Brodie Castle, an intriguing National Trust property, are also nearby. Two miles further on from Brodie is Moray's western boundary.

10 FORRES

⚐ **The Loft Glamping & Camping** (page 318)

Forres is mentioned in Shakespeare's *Macbeth* as the setting for both King Duncan's Castle and the nearby heath where Macbeth encounters the three witches. In contrast, the town is now famous for its vibrant flowers: a fine showcase can be admired on the green beside Victoria Road, where sculptures of a beaver, peacock and butterfly are filled with multi-coloured petals in summer. Maintained by volunteers, these displays and others around Forres have won the town numerous accolades, including several prestigious **Britain in Bloom** awards. If you visit in early spring before the flower animals are in bloom, you'll still see a splash of colour from mats of mauve and white crocuses beside the road.

One of Moray's larger towns, Forres has smart stone-block buildings lining High Street (the B9011). This widens in the centre beside a fine stone tolbooth with a central clock tower and an intricately spired Market Cross, both dating from the mid 19th century. Several nearby churches provide a touch of elegance – St John's Episcopal Church in particular, overlooking the flower animals on Victoria Road, has a large portico with curved arches and a petaled stained-glass window.

If you're approaching from Findhorn, you'll arrive at the northeast end of town. At the mini roundabout where the B9011 meets the A96 from Elgin, look for a huge stone slab encased in protective glass on a hill up ahead to the right. This is **Sueno's Stone**, considered by Historic Scotland to be 'the tallest and most complex piece of early medieval sculpture in Scotland'. Originating from the late 9th century, the stone depicts a complex Pictish battle with cavalry and foot soldiers. At 21ft, it's the largest stone of its kind in Britain. Like some other Pictish slabs, there are symbols on one side and a holy cross decorated with interlace on the other. Although little is known of the stone's context, one theory is that it marks the 9th-century victory of the Scots over the Picts. You can get a closer look at the stone by continuing straight over the mini roundabout on to Victoria Road and taking the first turning on the right down Findhorn Road. This has space to park and an information board.

"Women suspected of witchcraft were rolled down nearby Cluny Hill in barrels with spikes driven through them."

Less than 200yds further southwest down Victoria Road is the police station. In front, filling a gap in the shin-high wall, is a small boulder and plaque. This unassuming memorial is the **Witches Stone**, marking a grisly time in history. During the 16th and 17th centuries when witch mania was rife in Scotland, women suspected of witchcraft were rolled down nearby Cluny Hill in barrels with spikes driven through them. When the barrels came to rest, they were burned. The stone here marks the place where one of these condemned women met her end.

About the same distance again down Victoria Road, **Grant Park** opens up on the left. Every July, the Forres Highland Games are held here. Unique to this particular Games is the **Message Bike Race**, enabling spectators to compete in a sprint along the field riding a traditional message bike.

On the opposite side of Grant Park you can access a hilly patch of mixed woodland with criss-crossing trails. A short but steep hike up Cluny Hill will take you to **Nelson's Tower** (⊙ Apr–Sep 14.00–16:00 daily; entry by donation), visible from street-level above the treeline.

1 Culbin Forest. **2** Sueno's Stone, Forres. **3** Brodie Castle. ▶

Built as a memorial to Admiral Lord Nelson in 1806, the octagonal tower contains a sculpted bust of Nelson and donated gifts such as silver cups and bronze medals. Visitors can enjoy a 360° panoramic view from the top, including the section of the Moray Firth that lies beyond Findhorn to the north.

As Victoria Road becomes High Street you'll see the flower animals I keep going on about. More evidence of Forres' flower prowess can be admired in the **Sunken Gardens** – a petite square with beds of blooms and a wishing well in the northwest corner. Uncovered during the construction of the gardens, the well was restored by the Forres Rotary Club. It was in use until c1825, when the town's water supply was introduced.

Three quarters of a mile south of High Street is **Sanquhar Loch**, which is connected to nearby Sanquhar Woodlands via the Burn of Mosset. To get there, follow South Street over a mini roundabout onto Sanquhar Road. After passing a fitness centre on your right, you'll reach a couple of parking bays at the loch's edge in 350yds. Completed in 1900, the water from this loch supplied Benromach Distillery – just north of Forres across the A96 – and was acquired by Moray Council in 1969. It's now popular with ducks and dog walkers and has an easy-access trail leading around its northern edge. Before long, the loch constricts to the winding burn, curving into the woods. A map here shows several walking routes, some with patches of uneven steps. In this mixed forest you might spot roe deer, jays or red squirrels.

FOOD & DRINK

Café 1496 79 High St, IV36 1AE ☏ 01309 358120 ⌂ cafe1496.co.uk ☉ check website. A relaxed pace gives this café a European feel. Even on a weekday lunchtime it's almost full – I managed to nip into a window seat just as another customer was leaving and enjoyed a delicious bagel filled with avocado, halloumi, caramelised red onion and a poached egg. Breakfast is served all day and you can choose between big and wee versions. There's a great range of vegetarian and vegan options and also a 'boozy brunch' served from Friday to Sunday – booking advised.

Mosset Tavern Gordon St, IV36 1DY ☏ 01309 672981 ⌂ mossettavern.co.uk. This former mill has been welcoming customers as a family-friendly pub since 1973. It also welcomes dogs and serves delicious meals and local ales. The car park has been converted to an outdoor seating area overlooking the Burn of Mosset, so you can watch the water while enjoying your drink.

11 CULBIN FOREST

forestryandland.gov.scot/visit/culbin

Combining ponds, sand dunes and a muddy bay as well as swathes of mixed woodland, Culbin Forest is vast and varied. It begins across the bay from Findhorn and stretches over eight miles along the coast. During summer visits, I've spotted dragonflies, speckled wood butterflies and wood ants in the dense ground cover beside the paths. It might be tempting to explore the narrower deer trails off the main tracks, but thick mossy patches can sink several inches down and spiderwebs as large as hammocks are slung between pines. So, for ease of walking and to avoid damaging ground vegetation and those diligent spiders' handiwork, it's best to stick to the waymarked trails.

"Wooden structures etched with poetry are partially concealed among the trees beside a cross-section of paths."

I recommend visiting Culbin more than once to really explore it at depth. Forestry and Land Scotland points visitors to the **Wellhill car park** (*III* crowds.hunk.quits) just north of the village of Kintessack. There are picnic areas and toilets here and it's also where the forest's two waymarked trails begin. However, as the main car park it can get busy, especially at weekends, and there are parking charges. For a quieter walk, I suggest starting from the free **Cloddymoss car park** instead (*III* rope.zoned.something; see directions on page 168).

The paths in Culbin are wide and flat, ideal for bikes and wheelchairs. You can often find a handy free leaflet in wooden boxes beside information boards, or you can use the map on Culbin's website. Each junction on the trail network is numbered and this makes the forest easy to navigate even if you haven't been before.

Not far from Cloddymoss is a particularly poignant feature of interest, marked as **Hidden History** on the map. Wooden structures etched with poetry are partially concealed among the trees beside a cross-section of paths – these evocative passages allude to the 17th-century Culbin **sandstorms**. The severity of these sandstorms increased as village inhabitants destabilised the sand by taking marram grass for thatching. On one occasion in 1694, homes were evacuated when they became completely covered in sand. Rumours spread that the sandstorms came because Alexander Kinnaird, one of the owners of the estate, played cards with the Devil on a Sunday.

Partway round the **Hill 99 Trail**, which runs in a squashed circle for 3½ miles near Wellhill car park, is a **viewpoint tower**. Opened in 2008, this wooden structure allows visitors to climb above the pines and gaze across the Moray Firth. Handy etchings in the barrier point out features of the horizon, including nearby Brodie Castle (see below).

Most of Culbin's northern edge is an RSPB reserve with important saltmarsh and shingle habitats for wading birds. North of the viewpoint tower lies a patch of mudflats called **The Gut**. Wooden poles sticking out of the mud here are from World War II, positioned to prevent enemy gliders from landing.

At the forest's eastern edge is Findhorn Bay, where you're pretty much guaranteed to see both grey and common seals. Depending on the tide, they might be bobbing in the water or hauled out on land. Wherever they are, keep your distance to avoid disturbing them. It's a lengthy walk to the bay even from Wellhill car park, but there is the option of catching a water taxi to that side of Culbin from **Findhorn** (page 159).

"At the forest's eastern edge is Findhorn Bay, where you're pretty much guaranteed to see both grey and common seals."

To get to the Cloddymoss car park from Forres, head southwest on the A96. Just after the bridge crossing the River Findhorn, turn right at the brown-and-white sign for Culbin. Ignore another sign for the forest to the right and instead follow signs for Kintessack and then Cloddymoss. After three miles, you'll arrive at a small gravel car park with an information board. This is where horseriders are advised to start – as well as being quieter, there's space for larger vehicles.

12 BRODIE CASTLE

Brodie, IV36 2TE ℰ 01309 641700 ⊙ varies by season, check website for details; access to castle by guided tour only; National Trust for Scotland

Built in 1567, Brodie Castle has been home to the Brodie clan for over 400 years. Although they'd already been occupying this area for centuries before that – the earliest record of a Brodie laird's death is from 1285. The name comes from 'Brothie' and the Gaelic word *broth* means 'a ditch', so it's believed to be derived from the ditch nearby.

A distinctive peach colour, Brodie Castle looks most impressive in spring when bordered by **daffodils**. This is one of the best places in Scotland to see these yellow trumpets, and they are firmly planted in

AN EXPENSIVE MODIFICATION

As well as 6,400 books, there's a portrait in Brodie Castle's library of a deerhound called Driver. The original painting showed Driver standing over a dead deer. Violet, Ian Brodie's wife, was an animal lover and disliked the painting so much that she cut Driver's head out of the portrait and framed that instead. The painter was Edwin Landseer, whose world-renowned works include *The Monarch of the Glen* and the lion sculptures at the base of Nelson's Column in London. Had Driver's painting not been chopped up, it might have contributed handsomely to the castle's upkeep!

the castle's history. Ian Brodie, the 24th laird, was a globally recognised daffodil breeder in the early 20th century. He selected the pollen and transferred it by hand with a fine brush. Over the years this resulted in thousands of hybrids, but only 185 of them met the laird's standards and were allocated names. Since then, other gardeners have created new daffodil varieties based on Brodie's originals. April is the time to see them at their best here.

In the 1960s, after the cost of maintaining the castle became too much for Ian's son Ninian, the 25th and last laird of Brodie Castle, he approached the National Trust for Scotland. Parts of the castle are now open to the public for guided tours, and the laird's wing is available as holiday accommodation. A particularly spectacular feature on the tour is the dining room's highly decorated **17th-century ceiling**. Each corner represents one of the four elements: mermaids for water, pregnant women for earth, cherubs for air and a phoenix for fire. The most recent extension to the castle came in 1846, enabling visitors to pass through a Victorian fireplace into the library.

In the castle grounds, just beyond the visitor centre, is a tunnel leading to the **Playful Garden**. As well as unicorns (Scotland's national animal), a giant chair and table and flowerbeds, there are interactive elements too. Multi-coloured xylophones and zoetropes designed to look like daffodils are innovative and thoughtful additions, tempting both adults and children to have a play.

Before you leave, look for a signposted footpath opposite the white toilet hut at the far end of the car park. Follow a winding grass trail lined with birches, rowans and blackberry bushes to the **Rodney Stone**, which you'll have passed on the way in. Standing over 6ft high, this is another of the North East's many Pictish symbol stones. It shows Pictish beasties and carvings in Ogham – an ancient Celtic alphabet of lines and dashes that we still don't fully understand.

Located between the entrance and exit routes to Brodie Castle on the A96 is **Brodie Countryfare** (IV36 2TD ✆ 01309 641555 🖰 brodiecountryfare.com ⊙ daily), a pricey but high-quality shop selling original local gifts. What I like about it is the undeniable Scottish feel – as well as the obvious tartan and Highland cows, you can also find more subtly themed items such as children's books about kelpies and candles smelling of heather.

Brodie Countryfare is advertised as a day out but you need less than an hour to have a good look around the food, designer clothes and luxury home departments, or perhaps a little longer if you stop at the restaurant. Many of the items are sourced from Scottish suppliers, such as the Isle of Skye Candle Company and Black Thistle Distilleries.

SPEY BAY & THE EAST COAST TO CULLEN

Time to return to the sea, and the following section of the Moray Coast is dotted with several small villages full of fishing heritage and an abundance of antiques. We begin at the shingle beach of Spey Bay, where the River Spey completes its arduous journey. Portknockie is best-known for its tourist-trapping sea arch, but search beyond this and you'll discover mosaic art and a mysterious well. Close to the Aberdeenshire border, the large village of Cullen offers ample vintage shopping, secluded coast paths and a hearty fish soup that you simply have to try.

13 SPEY BAY

/// fruitcake.twitches.escaping 🖰 scottishwildlifetrust.org.uk/reserve/spey-bay

This coastal reserve at the mouth of the Spey contains Scotland's largest shingle beach. The river's constant movement has created a succession of habitats here including grassland, damp woodland and brackish saltmarsh. It's one of those beaches where the pebbles crackle and shift as you walk over them, contrasting with the fine sandy bays usually encountered on the Moray Coast.

The only fisherfolk here now are eider ducks, ospreys, gannets and dolphins, but this estuary was once one of the most important salmon fishing areas in Scotland. In 1768, the Duke of Gordon established a commercial fishing station and **icehouse** here, at the mouth of the bay. Until 1968, ice was collected and stored inside this triple-vaulted building during winter, designed to keep salmon fresh until it was shipped out.

Since 1997, the fishing station building beside the icehouse has been the **Scottish Dolphin Centre** (IV32 7PJ ✆ 01343 820339 ⌂ dolphincentre. whales.org ⌚ check website for opening hours). Run by Whale and Dolphin Conservation (WDC), it has a gift shop, café and interactive displays about marine wildlife. If you've ever wondered what a whale's eardrum looks like, this is the place to find out.

'The river mouth at Spey Bay attracts some of Scotland's most iconic wildlife,' Centre Manager Alison Rose told me. 'We love chatting to visitors about the latest sightings and helping them with wildlife spotting. I remember a bright sunny day when the dolphins were feeding just off the shingle beach. A lovely family who'd never seen dolphins before were delighted and it was so heartwarming to see their reaction!'

The best vantage point to watch for all this wildlife is on the short hill beside the icehouse. As well as scanning the shore for fins, you can look inside the icehouse on a 45-minute guided tour (book through the Dolphin Centre website).

Though only about eight miles southeast of Lossiemouth as the herring gull flies, humans need to loop back inland to get to Spey Bay – take the A96 east out of Elgin and follow signs for Coastal Trail East just before you reach Fochabers (page 125).

¶¶ FOOD & DRINK

Lower Mill of Tynet Farm AB56 5HJ ⌂ lowermilloftynet.co.uk. Just off the A98, 3½ miles southeast of Spey Bay, is the micro-dairy: a 24/7 walk-in vending machine. As well as buying free-range and organic eggs, fresh vegetables, coffee and other bits and pieces, you can also make your own milkshake here. Buy a reusable 1L glass bottle from the vending machine, take your pick of syrup (flavours include creme egg, Turkish delight and banoffee) and fill it up with milk. It couldn't get much fresher – you can thank the cows in the field opposite.

14 PORTKNOCKIE

⌂ **The Victoria Hotel** (page 318)

About 12 miles northeast on the A98 from Spey Bay, the A942 branches left to the village of Portknockie. With its largely residential high street, most interest for visitors comes from the landscape: a small harbour to the west, a string of coastal paths to the east and stretches of shingle in between. It can be an exposed place to live during fierce winter storms, and for this reason some of the traditional stone and clay houses facing the sea are aligned north to south to protect them from winds blowing in from the cliffs. You can walk down narrow alleyways called 'slappies' between some of these old houses. National Cycle Route 1 follows the old railway line linking Portknockie to Cullen (page 174), one mile further east along the coast.

"Now, only a few boats land their creels here and a children's paddling pool has been built in the outer basin."

Founded as a fishing village by three Cullen fishermen in 1677, Portknockie was home to 800 inhabitants by the 1840s, with around a hundred boats using the harbour. Now, only a few boats land their creels here and a children's paddling pool has been built in the outer basin.

The east side of the harbour is sheltered by a 79ft promontory named **Green Castle**. It's believed to date back to the Iron Age and was still occupied as a Pictish fortification in AD1000 when Vikings turned up in longboats to pillage the Moray Firth. The burnt remains of oak-framed walls found here are similar to those uncovered in Burghead's Pictish fort (page 154).

On Green Castle's east bank is an intriguing permanent art piece, unveiled in 2009. Portknockie-based artist Geoff Roberts designed and created two **herring in mosaic** with the help (and handprints) of local school children. Made using recycled tiles, the mosaics measure some 16ft each and reflect the herring seen on Portknockie's coat of arms.

If you walk down Patrol Road facing the sea, you can peer down over **Three Creeks Shore**. From 1883 to 1905, wooden fishing boats were built and launched here, but now it's a place for wildlife. A combination of headland, rock pool and shingle beach makes Three Creeks ideal for fulmars, kittiwakes, eider ducks and gulls. In Portknockie, gulls are known as 'pules' – a Doric word (page 11). From this vantage point, you might glimpse distant gannets plunging into the sea.

A little further east on Patrol Road, down a narrower lane leading to a grassy footpath, you'll arrive at **Bow Fiddle Rock**, the vast natural

1 Portknockie. **2** The Whale's Mouth sea arch. **3** Bow Fiddle Rock. ▶

stone arch for which the village is best known. It's a tourist magnet but still worth a look. In the shape of its namesake, Bow Fiddle is made of steeply folded beds of quartzite and is usually covered in gulls. It was once a rite of passage for local boys to cross over to the sea arch in springtime and search for gull's eggs. Take care around the steep drops, but a glance at the churning water below reveals more fantastic rock formations, sculpted by waves over millions of years.

Once most people get here, they take their photos then call it a day, but there's another impressive arch half a mile away that even some regular visitors don't know about. Walk past Bow Fiddle on the coast path, round the curve of the cliff – you'll get a good view of its side profile here, which isn't often photographed. The ocean yawns in front and you'll spot Cullen on the right. Continue following the path until you reach a steep staircase descending to the left, signposted Jenny's Well. Down on the beach you'll discover you were just walking right over this second sea arch, called the **Whale's Mouth**. You're far more likely to have this one to yourself, as well as a pebbly beach beside it.

Another trail leads south across this beach. About 200yds down, a little stone crescent has been studded with white pebbles to form the words **'Jenny's Well Portknockie'**. Below them is a spout gushing water into a narrow rivet trickling down to the sea. It's not known exactly who Jenny was, but the consensus seems to be that she lived in one of the nearby caves. The well was associated with May Day celebrations and local people used to leave offerings to Jenny. Besides her name in pebbles, there's no information here at all, leaving her story up to interpretation.

Parking can be tricky in Portknockie, as many of the narrow streets are occupied by residents' cars. There's space at the harbour and at the end of Addison Street by the footpath down to Bow Fiddle Rock, but during summer holidays this can fill up quickly. An alternative is to park at Cullen Beach (▥ convey.showed.brochure) and walk back to Portknockie on the coastal trail.

15 CULLEN & AROUND

⌂ **Stravaig B&B** (page 318)

Cullen is a large village at the eastern edge of Moray, just a mile from Aberdeenshire's boundary and walkable via a coast path from Portknockie. It's hilly, with a steep incline from the beach up to its centre, which is arranged either side of Seafield Street. Most of the buildings are the sort with skinny, rough-cut stones submerged in thick layers of sandy concrete, interrupted by dormer windows. Cullen is perhaps best-known for Cullen skink, a thick, creamy fish soup that's a starter staple in this region. Each year a competition for the best recipe takes place in the village (page 18).

Halfway along a straight section of the A98 is The Square (AB56 4SY). Keen shoppers will want to spend some time around here, where gift shops can be found on all sides. Some of these have a vintage theme, and a visit isn't complete without a browse in the small but packed **Bits 'N' Bobs** collectibles shop (The Square, AB56 4RR 🔳) and the sprawling **Cullen Antiques Centre** (Seafield St, AB56 4SG ⌀ cullenantiquescentre. com), 200yds further down the street. This is the largest antiques centre in the North East, lavishly filling the interior of a church, an adjacent bookshop and a salvage yard out the back. You could spend hours rummaging through this alone.

Once you've had your fill of shopping, stretch your legs on the coastal path. Walking northwest on Seafield Street, you'll pass under an arched bridge framing the beach. Cullen is known for its viaduct bridges, built for the Great North of Scotland Railway line in 1886. At over 80ft high, the viaduct crossing the Deskford Burn is the largest and has eight huge arches. The railway was closed in 1968 and the viaducts are now used by walkers and cyclists as part of the **Moray Coast Trail** (page 22).

While admiring the pale, sandy beach, you might notice a row of distinctive rocks sticking out of the sand. These are known as the **Three Kings**, named after Norse invaders who landed in Cullen in AD961. They were defeated a year later by Indulf, King of Alba, during the nearby Battle of the Bauds.

CHARLIE'S CAVE

Beyond Cullen's Giant Steps (page 177) is Charlie's Cave, although its size makes it more of a crevice than an official cave. Known as the 'Cullen Caveman', Charlie Marioni deserted the French Navy during World War I and built a new home for himself in a small gap in the rocks. He caught fish, made furniture from driftwood and grew vegetables, which he took into town to sell. Charlie became so famous in Cullen that people began making special trips to see him. Increased footfall across land that didn't belong to him angered the landowner, who reported him to the authorities. After 13 years in his rustic home, Charlie was arrested and moved to England, where he died a pauper.

Seafield Street bends right at the harbour to join Port Long Road. Down here you'll see some incredible rock formations arranged in diagonal shapes like modern art installations. Not far past Cullen Sea School is a tiny **pet cemetery**. This began in 1992 when a local doctor asked retired street sweeper Stephen Findlay to bury her spaniel. Mr Findlay later buried his own dog Bruce nearby, and the area soon became a resting place for dozens of Cullen pets. Mr Findlay visited the cemetery daily to weed the grounds and care for the graves. As well as domestic animals, he also buried seals, dolphins and even a shark that washed up on the beach. It's said that a police officer travelled up from Birmingham to ensure her cat was buried in view of the sea. Woeful EU regulations introduced in 2019 stated that Mr Findlay would need to start paying for routine inspections. As he maintained the cemetery as a volunteer he made the difficult decision to close it, finally retiring at the age of 81. Fortunately, this remarkable place can still be appreciated in its current state.

It's possible to continue east past the cemetery and walk the coastal path around the rocky headland of Logie Head to Sunnyside Beach, Findlater Castle (page 189) and further into Aberdeenshire, though be aware that there are several steep inclines across uneven rocks and sudden drops on the side closest to the sea. Once the concrete path ends and the grass trail begins, things can get very muddy – so much so that rocks and

> *"It's said that a police officer travelled up from Birmingham to ensure her cat was buried in view of the sea."*

planks have been placed on the ground for easier access. After looping round a small bay, the path climbs and eventually becomes a flight of wide, flattened boulders down to a small beach on the other side. These are the **Giant Steps**, built single-handedly by Cullen resident Tony Hetherington in 1987. There's a plaque commemorating his incredible achievement at the bottom.

Bin of Cullen

/// moderated.utter.clipped

At 1,050ft, the domed hill called Bin of Cullen isn't particularly high, but for someone like me who doesn't fancy mountains, this three-mile walk

---

◀ **1** Cullen Viaduct. **2** The Moray Coast is a prime location for the northern lights across winter and spring. **3** View from the top of Bin of Cullen.

NORTHERN LIGHTS ON THE MORAY COAST

At 20.45 on 5 March 2022 I was standing in the dark on Burghead Backshore, facing north, when the sky flickered. My jaw dropped in a very clichéd way and I squinted hard. Seconds later a row of silvery feathers appeared, shifting across the horizon as a single ribbon. Not clouds, but the northern lights.

It's often possible to see this otherworldly phenomenon in the North East during winter and spring, but you need to find somewhere away from light pollution. This can be tricky in built up areas, but the Moray Coast provides unobstructed views north across the sea.

Creative outdoor photographer Kim Grant has been capturing the aurora since 2014. 'I was looking for something different to photograph and heard there was a chance of seeing the northern lights one evening,' she tells me. 'I went out to try and see it – little did I know, it turned out to be one of the brightest displays we've ever had in Scotland. There was pink in the sky too, not just the green we all know and love. From there I was hooked!'

Kim watches the aurora all along the coast from Moray into Aberdeenshire, but her favourite spots are Burghead, Hopeman and Cullen. Clear, cloudless skies away from streetlights are crucial, but she also recommends looking for places that incorporate the foreground. 'At low tide, if you walk down the beach, away from the village, Cullen is very special. Here you can often see the lights reflecting on the wet sand, which is great for photos.'

If you're interested in photography, Kim offers online mentoring and runs long weekend workshops on the Moray Coast in spring and autumn. To find out more, visit 🌐 visualisingscotland.co.uk and ▶ Visualising Scotland with Kim Grant.

is ideal for getting the heart pumping and admiring prominent views of the Moray Firth.

From Cullen, follow the A98 out of town and turn right on to the B9018. In 2¼ miles, turn right at a sign for Hill of Maud and continue for another 1¼ miles. You'll see a small space for parking on the right by a forestry track with a gate; make sure you don't block access.

Walk along the main track until you cross a bridge over a bubbling burn. Take a left at the crossroads here – after a short incline through patches of mature Scots pines, turn left again once the track levels off. This rocky path carries on to the top, curling around the summit like a drizzle of sauce. Once you break above the treeline you'll have open country views the rest of the way to the trig point. Looking north from the top you can see a broad section of the Moray Firth, including Spey Bay further west. Cullen and its viaducts are clearly visible in front of you. To return, retrace your steps.

FOOD & DRINK

Coffee at the Kings The Links, AB56 4WB ☎ 07799 821488 ⬛ ☺ 10.30–15.30; check Facebook for specific days. This mobile coffee business is run from a vintage caravan on the beachfront. It serves premium barista coffee, luxury hot chocolate and a range of tray bakes.

Deskford Garden Galleries & Willows Tearoom Cottertown of Ardoch, AB56 5XX ⬧ deskfordgardengalleries.com ☺ check website for opening hours. Indulge in a little 1940s glamour at this vintage tea room 3½ miles south of Cullen. Beside several other cottages filled with antiques, collectibles and artwork, its speciality is home-cooked vegetarian, vegan and gluten-free dishes. Take your pick of soup, sandwiches, Sunday roasts and scones. I ordered a pecan pie hot chocolate, described as a 'hug in a mug'. As well as your standard tea room floral plates, Willows has lace tablecloths, 40s music and even tiny cotton handkerchiefs for napkins.

Lily's Kitchen Café Seafield St, AB56 4SH ☎ 01542 488816 ☺ 09.00–16.00 Fri–Tue. Winner of the Cullen Skink World Championships in 2018 (page 18), this small, family-run café offers fantastic breakfasts, freshly made sandwiches and, of course, delicious Cullen skink.

Rockpool Café The Square, AB56 4RR ☎ 01542 841397 ⬧ rockpool-cullen.co.uk ☺ 10.00–16.00 Tue–Sun. Rockpool has a reputation as *the* place to eat in Cullen. Choose from breakfast baps, pancakes and a full Scottish on the breakfast menu, or hot and cold sandwiches, burgers and seasonal specials on the lunch menu. There's also a vibrant array of iced cakes and bakes. Book ahead.

The Royal Oak Hotel 34 Castle Tce, AB56 4SD ☎ 01542 842762 ⬧ theroyaloakcullen.co.uk. This family-run hotel and restaurant is right next to the viaduct bridge and a few minutes' walk from Cullen beach. The food is delicious and the staff are lovely. The Cullen skink is particularly good too.

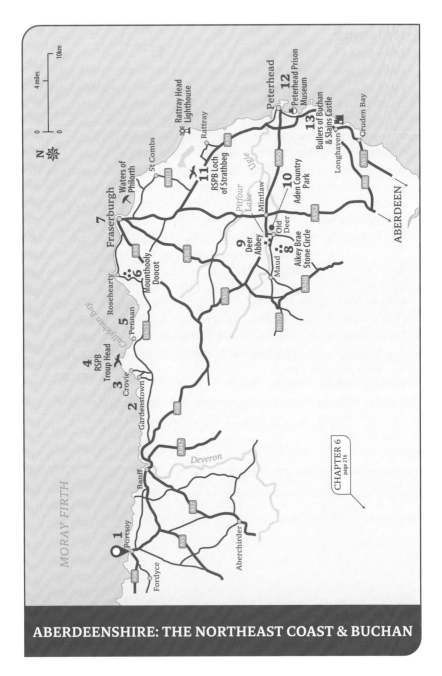

ABERDEENSHIRE: THE NORTHEAST COAST & BUCHAN

MORAY FIRTH

N

0   4 miles
0   10km

1 Portsoy
Fordyce
A98
A97
Aberchirder
A947
Deveron
Banff
A95
2 Gardenstown
3 Crovie
4 RSPB Troup Head
Pennan
5
B9031
Cullykhan Bay
Rosehearty
6 Mounthooly Doocot
7 Fraserburgh
Waters of Philorth
St Combs
B9033
A98
A90
Rattray Head Lighthouse
Rattray
A90
11 RSPB Loch of Strathbeg
Pitfour Lake
Mintlaw
Peterhead
12 Peterhead Prison Museum
13 Bullers of Buchan & Slains Castle
Cruden Bay
Longhaven
A975
A90
A952
10 Aden Country Park
Old Deer
Ugie
A950
A950
9 Deer Abbey
Maud
8 Aikey Brae Stone Circle
B9170
B9148
ABERDEEN

CHAPTER 6
page 216

5
ABERDEENSHIRE: THE NORTHEAST COAST & BUCHAN

This bumpy right angle jutting into the North Sea is the true northeast of Scotland. Extending east along a horizontal shelf to Fraserburgh then curving southeast to Peterhead, it's the same length and half as long again as the Moray Coast. Its varied stretch of coastline offers an alternating mix of buttery beaches, jagged cliffs and grassy headlands buffeted by salt winds. I wouldn't say it's a particularly famous part of Aberdeenshire, but it has some of the finest sandy bays and most impressive coastal birdwatching sites in the book.

Buchan refers to the area on the southeast side, covering a section of coastline but mostly extending inland across an assortment of small villages and settlements surrounded by farmland. Scattered among these you'll find abbey ruins and a stone circle perfectly placed for soaking up spring sunrises.

I think the coast is this chapter's best feature because of its diversity. In some places you can lounge on beaches the colour of Biscoff, gleaming even on an overcast day. In others, you can explore craggy clifftops shaped like giant fingerprints – narrow ridges curved around each other without touching, much to the seabirds' convenience. Shift again and tiny fishing villages appear. Wedged against the cliffs for protection from the elements, they're occasionally so narrow you can only access them on foot.

Outside of the big towns of Fraserburgh and Peterhead, on the northeast and east coasts respectively, this region can be very quiet out of season. You can expect empty harbours and shut-up shops during winter especially, but don't let this put you off. Walking isn't seasonal, and during these lulls in activity you'll often have entire beaches to yourself. Even if amenities are closed, the coast never is.

GETTING AROUND

Shortly after leaving Cullen in Moray, the A98 crosses the Aberdeenshire border and finishes in Fraserburgh, 39 miles east. Many north coast sites listed in this chapter are found on B roads, some with rather thrilling inclines. The main route to the east coast from the south is via the A90, which comes up from Aberdeen and sticks close to the coast past Peterhead and up to Fraserburgh.

BUSES

Stagecoach services from Fraserburgh's bus station on Hanover Street include the 69 to Peterhead via St Combs. Plenty of buses run from Peterhead – the X63 stops at Cruden Bay, providing walkable access to Slains Castle and Bullers of Buchan. Another useful service from Peterhead is the 66, which has a stop next to Aden Country Park and another at Old Deer Parish Church, one mile from Deer Abbey and Aikey Brae Stone Circle. The 35 Aberdeen to Elgin route stops at Portsoy before continuing into Moray.

Cliffside villages such as Gardenstown, Crovie and Pennan are trickier to access by bus (mostly because Crovie and Pennan are too narrow for buses to even get to), but during the week you can take the 272 from Fraserburgh to Cotton Hill Quarry, then the 273 to Gardenstown, and walk from there to Crovie. This is more straightforward on Saturdays as the 273 goes directly to Gardenstown from Fraserburgh.

WALKING & CYCLING

Cyclists and long-distance walkers might consider part of the 53-mile **Formartine & Buchan Way** (aberdeenshire.gov.uk/paths-and-outdoor-access/long-distance-routes/formartine-and-buchan-way). This route follows an old railway line that once stretched from Dyce

---

_i_ TOURIST INFORMATION

The Museum of Scottish Lighthouses Stevenson Rd AB43 9DU 01346 511022
 lighthousemuseum.org.uk
RSPB Loch of Strathbeg Visitor Centre Starnafin, Crimon AB43 8QN 01346 532017
 rspb.org.uk/reserves-and-events/reserves-a-z/loch-of-strathbeg

---

(just north of Aberdeen City) to Fraserburgh, with a side branch to Peterhead. The trail is entirely off-road and suitable for horse riders. It's split into 11 sub-sections, each with its own parking suggestions. National Cycle Route 1 also pops briefly into this chapter area. After passing through Portsoy it bends south, staying inland until Aberdeen.

Coastal paths are excellent here. It's possible to walk from Peterhead to Cruden Bay via a winding trail of 11½ miles, while the clifftop path linking Gardenstown to Crovie is only half a mile and follows flat terrain, making it a decent short route for cyclists too. Portsoy has options for cliff walking in either direction, and I've highlighted one of these in a suggested walk (page 184).

LOGIE HEAD TO TROUP HEAD

Aberdeenshire's north coast is a bumpy barcode of headlands. One of these is Logie Head between Cullen and Portsoy, close to the Moray border. Another is the broad lump of Troup Head. This is one of the region's finest clifftop nature reserves and thrums with the sight, sound and smell of thousands of seabirds. Between the headlands of Logie and Troup is a coast of extreme conditions, where ruined castles dangle off the land and villages are crammed at the feet of cliffs.

1 PORTSOY & AROUND

🏠 **Driftwood Cottage** (page 319)

Five miles east of Cullen, the small coastal town of Portsoy is the first major stop once you cross the border into Aberdeenshire. The A98 cuts straight through the centre and this is where you'll find cafés, a fish and chip shop, bakery and ice cream parlour. Down the side of the Co-op is a little car park beside **Loch Soy**. With benches dotted around, this is a great spot to tuck into an ice cream or a macaroni pie from the bakery, with chatty ducks for company. It only takes a few minutes to walk the loch's 500yd perimeter.

A little further east on the A98 is my favourite street in Portsoy. Church Street has dry-stone cottages with flower boxes on the windowsills, low doorways and matching painted sashes. I grimace at the word 'quaint' but that's what springs to mind here. As you walk north along Church Street, a straight footpath appears on the left, between two high stone walls. This was once the railway route through Portsoy. In

Portsoy with a coastal loop

❄ OS Explorer Map 425; start: Loch Soy car park, ▦ flood.central.crockery; 4¼ miles;
♀ NJ5888865910; easy.

T his easy-going route passes all of Portsoy's mentioned sites of interest and includes a stretch of the coastal path to the east, allowing you to see the town from afar and up close.

1 From Loch Soy car park, cross over the A98 and turn right. Some 75yds along, turn left down Shillinghill, beside the J G Ross bakery. Bend to the right, crossing a stone bridge over the old railway line. At the end of the road, turn left on to Church Street. After 100yds, keep right at the fork.

2 At the end of Church Street is the harbour. Bear right on to Shore Street and follow it for around 300yds.

3 Outside Sutherlands of Portsoy fishmonger's, the road bends right to join Links Road. The large white building on the right, behind a mounted boat named the *Soy Lady*, is The Salmon Bothy (page 186). Continue straight past the museum, following the curve of beach past the caravan park.

4 Cross a little bridge over the Burn of Durn and stick to the beach's edge. Some 180yds later, at the end of the tarmac road, pass through a small car park and join a grass footpath straight ahead. Take the first path branching sharply uphill to the right, marked with a white sign for 'Coastguard Path and East Head'.

5 You'll soon reach a more established grass path at a T-junction – turn left here. There are extensive sea views to your left on this elevated stretch. Bear right at the fork – the left one leads downhill to an isolated cove.

6 After passing through a wooden gate, turn left at the next junction to stay in view of the sea. The path follows the edge of the headland for a while, rising and dipping beside craggy rocks dotted with cormorants.

7 Once you curve round to face east, another white sign for Coastguard Point leads up a trail to the right. At the top is a cordoned square of rope, marking the site of the old coastguard hut. Take the path to the right, back towards Portsoy. This leads loosely parallel to the outward route but slightly further inland. Bin of Cullen (page 177) peeps over the hills.

8 Turn right at the next T-junction and you'll then spot the gate you passed through earlier. Head back through and retrace a brief section of the outward route, passing the turning for the secluded cove again. Instead of returning the way you came, down the trail that's now on your right, continue straight for 300yds.

9 At another T-junction, turn left and carry on uphill. In 300yds, emerge at a gravel vehicle track and turn right on to it.

10 At the end of the vehicle track is the B9139. Before you reach the road itself, turn right down a footpath parallel to the road. Cross over the Burn of Durn.

11 The path meets Aird Street/A98 140yds further on from the burn – turn left and follow it for a quarter of a mile. When you see steps on the right to Portsoy School, just before the road bends left, cross over and follow a cycle bridleway path (National Cycle Route 1) through a gate, bordered on the right by a low stone wall.

12 Turn left to continue following cycle signs past a children's playground and left again past a green-and-white Scout hut. Just beyond this, you'll reach the southern end of Loch Soy. Walk around it to return to the start point.

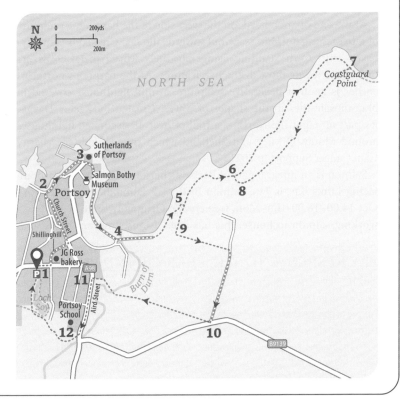

1859, the construction of the railway improved trading links with the rest of the UK and Europe. The trains are gone now, but you can still follow this old line and others throughout the town on foot.

At the end of Church Street is Portsoy's 17th-century **harbour**. It's an oddly complex one, reminding me of the barricades at airports that keep doubling back on themselves. The harbour was extended in 1825 in response to the expanding fleet of herring vessels, but only a couple of boats are moored here now.

As you face the sea, your eye will likely be drawn left to a multistorey listed building with a sign for **Portsoy Marble** (🅕 ☉ check Facebook for up-to-date times), selling crystals, homeware and Peaky Blinders caps (see below). The region is known for its 'marble', although this dark red or green rock is correctly known as serpentine. It has a mottled pattern similar to snakeskin and you can buy smooth pieces of it at the shop, close to where it was once quarried.

At the end of Shorehead, on the west side of the harbour, a sculpture of a **breaching dolphin** leaps out towards the sea. Created by Portsoy-based artist Carn Standing using intricately woven metal cords, it's one of the town's most distinctive features. At the harbour's northeast corner is another decorative sculpture: a mini lighthouse covered in blue mosaic tiles in the shapes of waves. Created by Rachel Davies, it's part of 'Light the North' – a trail of over 45 decorated lighthouses around Moray, Orkney and Shetland which raised funds for charity Clan Cancer Support in 2021.

Salmon is an integral part of Portsoy's heritage. East of the harbour, facing Links Bay, is **The Salmon Bothy** (⌀ salmonbothy.org ☉ Apr–Oct 14.00–16.00 Thu–Mon; free entry). Originally built in 1834 as a working salmon icehouse, this has been a museum, family research

PAY RESPECTS TO THE PEAKY BLINDERS

In 2021, the cast and crew of British gangster drama *Peaky Blinders* arrived in Portsoy to film the final season. Close to the Portsoy Marble shop on the harbourfront you'll see a gathering of flower tributes and slate headstones marking the spot where character Michael Gray was killed. During shooting, two crew members became stranded in blizzard conditions on the A96. Along with almost 30 other stranded drivers, they took refuge for the night in local homes in Huntly (page 249), causing quite flurry of excitement among fans of the show.

base and community venue since 2009. Unlike other, much smaller, icehouses on this coastline, Portsoy's Salmon Bothy is an imposing, domed stone building with cobbled floors. The museum is split across three chambers, dividing artefacts relating to salmon, ships, geology and wildlife. Beneath information boards about Portsoy's fishing history are traditional boat-building tools, nets and model ships. Next door are the old fishermen's sleeping quarters. The bunk beds are still set up inside, but are now covered in gifts, books and other trinkets available to buy.

Fordyce

Three miles southwest of Portsoy is the tiny village of Fordyce. You wouldn't know it was there unless you saw the sign on the A98 towards Cullen, but it's worth an hour's potter. Fordyce's character comes from its tight, single-lane roads curving around old stone cottages. Lots of skilled gardeners live here – a walk through these quiet lanes features flowers of every colour and shape.

"Fordyce's character comes from its tight, single-lane roads curving around old stone cottages."

Just off West Church Street in the centre of Fordyce is a gravel footpath to a small square **Victorian garden**, with benches facing a central island of flowers. This is a tranquil spot to sit and listen to the Burn of Fordyce just beyond. From the garden, you can go for a short stroll beside the water to a tiny woodland, which has an accessible loop that's perfect for children and those with less mobility. To get there, cross a bridge over the burn and walk south beside it. In less than a minute you'll cross another bridge and reach a toilet block. Continue straight and follow signs to a woodland area, now with the burn on your right.

Shortly, the path bends right past a wizened stone wall with two arches, now furry with grass and dandelions poking through the cracks. Just past this is **Fordyce Community Woodland**, the site of a former limestone quarry. It was given to the community in 1999 by the Earl of Seafield to commemorate the 500th anniversary of the village. A flat, stone-lined path takes you on a short loop through the trees, passing a clearing with picnic benches and a wooden platform overlooking the burn. When you're done, return via the outward route.

In the centre of Fordyce, where several narrow streets intersect at a junction some 80yds northeast of the Victorian garden, is **Fordyce**

Castle (⌀ fordycecastle.co.uk). This magnificent pink stone structure has wizard-hat turrets and tiny square windows, contrasting with the more modern houses overshadowed by it. Constructed in 1592 for a wealthy Aberdeen merchant called Thomas Menzies of Kirkhill, the castle and adjoining cottages are now divided between private property and self-catering accommodation.

Left of the castle you'll see the **Old Kirk and Kirkyard**. The most eye-catching part of the church is a tower with an arch cut through the middle. The trees surrounding the kirkyard are home to a large resident rookery, and the birds' throaty caws add a little auditory ambience to the old gravestones.

Findlater Castle & Sunnyside Beach

The best castles are the crumbly ones. Although closer to Cullen than Fordyce, **Findlater Castle** (▥ hoops.hogs.slyly) is in Aberdeenshire so I've listed it here instead. I'd say it's one of the North East's most impressive ruins, and free to visit too. Part of its charm comes from its location – accessing the castle requires a drive through a farm and a walk along a mud track. It appears out of nowhere, precariously balanced on the side of a crag – you'll have the best view of it from the end of this track, where you're far enough back to take in the whole ruin and its ocean backdrop.

The name Findlater may have come from the Gaelic *fionn leitir*, meaning 'white cliff'. There's a grassy trail down to the castle, enabling you to look inside, but due to its ruinous nature and the unkempt access paths, I wouldn't recommend it. Even disregarding the risk to your safety, regular footfall on the ruin causes further damage.

Though it's easy to understand why a castle would have been built on such a tricky promontory, it can't have been easy to achieve. The current ruins date back to the mid-15th century, but by that point the castle had already been strengthened in the 1260s by King Alexander III, in anticipation of an invasion from Norwegian King Haakon IV. This must have helped, as Haakon was defeated during the Battle of Largs in 1263.

At the end of the mud track that ends at the castle viewpoint, a grass trail heads west towards **Sunnyside Beach**. You can also get here along

◄ **1** Findlater Castle. **2** Dolphin sculpture, Portsoy. **3** Old Fordyce Church.
4 Sunnyside Beach.

the coast path from Cullen, but it's a lengthy route over several rocky sections, so starting from Findlater Castle is easier. 'Hidden gem' always triggers an eye roll from me, but that's what Sunnyside is. Follow the grass path for about half a mile as it stretches west then bends downhill. After heavy rain this might be muddy and during summer there may be dense bracken obscuring the path on either side. A bit of sliding and grappling is worth it for the bay at the bottom: wispy fine sand, stirred by the breeze, and wavelets washing over cubic rocks jutting diagonally out to sea. A little further back is a sand bank tall enough to perch on with your feet dangling.

"Wispy fine sand, stirred by the breeze, and wavelets washing over cubic rocks jutting diagonally out to sea."

Long grass flashes in the sun, perhaps with a stonechat or two clinging to the stems. If you're lucky you'll have the place to yourself. Take your pick of rock pooling, paddling or just admiring the views.

Findlater Castle is signposted off the A98, 2¾ miles west of Portsoy. Park beside a farm and go the rest of the way, some 600yds, on foot down the mud track.

If you're wondering what the structure in the field beside the track is, looking like a squat, white sand castle, it's **Findlater Doocot**. *Doocot* is the Scots word for a dovecote, a structure made for housing pigeons and doves. This one dates from the 16th century and is described as a 'beehive' doocot, the oldest kind. There's another, more intricately designed example near Fraserburgh, called Mounthooly Doocot (page 198).

¶¶ FOOD & DRINK

The Old Kirk Bistro Church St, Fordyce AB45 2SL ℰ 01261 843410 ◼ ☻ Mar–Dec noon–16.30 Thu & Sun, noon–21.00 Fri & Sat. Located inside a converted 18th-century church and specialising in seafood. Stylish dishes include langoustine stir fry and hand-dived scallop with cauliflower purée, which taste all the more decadent for being locally sourced and fresh off the boat. B&B accommodation also available.

Portsoy Ice Cream Seafield St, AB45 2QT ℰ portsoyicecream.co.uk ☻ daily; check Facebook for winter hours. The much-deserved winner of several awards in the National Ice Cream Competition, this family-run business has been creating homemade artisan ice creams and sorbets since 2003. As well as multi-coloured ice cream, mini pancakes and bubble waffles for you and Scoop's ice cream for your dog, you can sip an espresso or smoothie in the Coffee Corner and buy other Scottish produce here: fresh fruit and veg, items from the butchers and bakery and gifts such as fudge and whisky.

Symposium Seafield St, AB45 2QT 𝒫 01261 843856 🅵 SYMPOSIUM coffee house (Portsoy) ⊙ 10.00–16.00 daily. Although one of several branches across the North East, Symposium still has an independent feel to it, with tables huddled together and welcoming, chatty staff. Serves pancakes, toasted breakfast bagels, sandwiches and salads, including veggie and vegan options.

2 GARDENSTOWN

🏠 **The Garden Arms Hotel** (page 318)

Gardenstown is stacked against the cliffs, its houses lined along sloping roads that slalom down to the harbour. The best place to park is at the northern end, near Eli's Crafts, Cakes & Coffee (page 192). From here, head southwest on New Ground, walking uphill to join Harbour Road. When the road forks you can either turn right towards the harbour or left up to Main Street. The L-shaped bend signposted 'Braeheid' offers a vantage point over the harbour and Gamrie Bay. The sprawling rock close to the harbour entrance is called **Craigandargity** and was apparently mistaken for a submarine during World War I.

Main Street mostly consists of holiday accommodation and a small convenience store, but at the end is the focal point of Gardenstown's community: **The Garden Arms Hotel** (page 194). Dating from 1743, the building has low, beamed ceilings and uneven floors reminiscent of a fairground fun house, only with peaceful pastels rather than psychedelic hues. Owners Derek and Lorraine Toal take pride in its quirky appearance and have named their two guest bedrooms the Wonky and Squinty Rooms, which share the Crooked Corridor. Guests are invited to join seasoned regulars for events such as the Thursday night quiz, giving this place the welcoming community atmosphere you hope for in a small village pub.

A VISIT FROM BRAM STOKER

With its friendly ambience and cosy décor, guests at The Garden Arms feel more like they're in someone's home than a hotel. I fell asleep to the sounds of creaking floors and murmurs from the bar below during my stay. As if its appearance wasn't alluring enough, Bram Stoker stayed here in July 1896, a year before *Dracula* was published. The author visited Aberdeenshire regularly until his death in 1912. It's said Dracula's Gothic abode was inspired by Slains Castle (page 214), 36 miles southeast, but Stoker also set part of another novel, *The Mystery of the Sea*, in Gardenstown itself.

At Gardenstown's western end is a part of the village called **Seatown**, consisting of a row of houses connected by a very narrow road leading to a turning circle. Barely more than a car's width from the houses' front doors is a sheer drop to the beach below. Prior to the 1940s there wasn't a road here at all, just a narrow walkway. After the last house, the jetty descends to a beach that curves round salmon-pink cliffs. The sand here is darker than at other sites on this coastline, and studded with striated rocks and pebbles.

At the far end of the beach, the ruined **St John's Kirkyard** is visible on the cliff above. Dedicated to St John the Evangelist and founded in AD1004, the church was formerly known as the 'Kirk of Sculls', after three Danish skulls were mounted inside following a nearby battle in the same year. You can get up here via a badly eroded footpath that climbs uphill from the beach, though approaching via the B9031 from Gardenstown is more accessible. From the car park (🄌 tropic. headliner.dodging), follow a gently inclining vehicle track for just over 500yds.

The ruin is worth seeing, but once you get up here your gaze will inevitably drift to the view beyond. From within the churchyard – and slightly past it along a grassy track – you can gaze east over Gamrie Bay. This is an ideal spot for a picnic and dolphin watch.

Standing beside the kirkyard, you'll see a distant row of houses a little further east from Gardenstown. This is Crovie (page 194), and you can walk here from Gardenstown via a half-mile **clifftop path** following a flat gravel track. It starts from the higher part of the village, through a gate at the end of Morven View Road, off Garden Crescent. You can make it into a circular walk by returning on a path at the bottom of the cliff you've just walked over the top of, but this is only possible at low tide so make sure you check tide times before setting off. As well as being accessible at any time of day, the clifftop path provides a much higher vantage point for watching the sea, so I suggest returning the same way you came.

🍴 FOOD & DRINK

Eli's Craft, Cakes & Coffee New Ground, AB45 3YU ✆ 07795 823246 🛐 🕒 Mar–Dec noon–16.00 Thu–Sun. This is a pocket of colour, with almost every inch of space filled with

1 Gardenstown. **2** Crovie. **3** RSPB Troup Head. **4** Gannets at Troup Head. ▶

canvases, ceramics, knitwear, candles and postcards. As well as a tempting cabinet of cakes and bakes, soup, toasties and bagels are also available.

The Garden Arms Hotel Main St, AB45 3YP ℘ 01261 851260 ⊘ thegardenarms.com ⊙ 17.00–22.00 Mon, 17.00–midnight Thu & Fri, noon–late Sat & Sun. During my stay at this wonky hotel (page 318), I tucked into a delicious West African peanut and sweet potato stew – it was refreshing to see creative vegetarian dishes rather than just old faithfuls that happen to not have meat in them. And, with locally sourced eggs and meat, visitors can be assured that food hasn't travelled far here.

3 CROVIE

Only residents and authorised vehicles are allowed to drive into Crovie, pronounced 'Crivvie', and when you arrive you'll see why. It consists solely of a jetty protruding into the bay and a single row of houses squeezed against the base of a cliff. They're arranged with their short, or gable, sides facing the sea, providing the least resistance during strong winds. A narrow concrete path leads to the end of this string of cottages, similar to the one in Gardenstown.

Crovie was established during the 1700s by people who had been cleared out of inland estates to make room for livestock. By the mid 19th century, it had a fleet of nine fishing boats, which increased to 54 by 1890. The majority of catches were herring, whiting and mackerel. As a port too small to accommodate larger vessels, Crovie suffered when steam drifters gained popularity in the 20th century. After World War II there were no boats left in Crovie's fleet and fishermen had to travel to larger harbours such as Fraserburgh.

"Now there are about two dozen inhabited stone cottages, many with terracotta roofs that catch the sun."

In January 1953, a violent storm washed away the footpath to Gardenstown, and several houses in Crovie were badly damaged or destroyed completely. Now there are about two dozen inhabited stone cottages, many with terracotta roofs that catch the sun. Storms still pass through today, and waves smacking the end of the jetty make for some dramatic photo opportunities.

You can access Crovie via a short footpath from Gardenstown (page 191), or by taking the signed left turn off Bracoden Road, about half a mile from Gardenstown. After another half a mile you'll see a sign for **Crovie Car Park & Viewpoint** (⬛ height.saturate.comfort) – from here, you can walk down a steep road that reaches the jetty in 400yds.

4 RSPB TROUP HEAD

/// activates.stressed.storms & rspb.org.uk/reserves-and-events/reserves-a-z/troup-head

The clifftop reserve of Troup Head is the largest mainland gannet colony in Scotland and one of Britain's finest sites for coastal birdwatching. During spring, you'll have skylarks singing behind and seabirds squawking in front. The birds live in segregated neighbourhoods along the cliff: gannets occupy the most space; guillemots and razorbills live on the ground floor; and fulmars have taken over the higher storeys. Birds of every kind swirl in the air, seemingly queuing up to time their landing correctly. Some gannets spend winter here, but in spring thousands of other birds arrive from offshore. By summer, Troup Head turns white with

"Birds of every kind swirl in the air, seemingly queuing up to time their landing correctly."

gannets and you sometimes have to duck as they soar overhead, neon-green-lined feet dangling. At such a high vantage point, you also have a good chance of spotting bottlenose dolphins, porpoises or perhaps a minke whale. Note that you should be extremely careful everywhere at Troup Head, as there are many sheer cliff drops and no fences on the sea-facing side.

You can reach the cliffs via one of two routes. For a more direct path, walk around the donation plinth in the car park to join a farm track heading north, then follow RSPB signs pointing right to another gate. Livestock is kept here so keep dogs on leads. Most of this route is an indented path in the grass.

Alternatively, a longer path winds around the headland between the sea and open fields. This begins through the first gate you see when you enter the car park and follows a flat gravel track, but at the end there's a fairly steep staircase heading up to the gannet lookout point. If you take this coastal route, you'll be able to admire the striated cliffs across Downie Bay. Although the majority of seabirds are found on the cliff jutting further out to sea, small groups of fulmars and guillemots nest here. You can hear them calling several hundred yards away across the bay. At the lookout point on the northeast tip of the cliff, known as the **Hare's Nose**, you can peer down (very carefully, I might add) and see more nesting birds.

Troup Head wasn't always so active. Tim Marshall has been birding around Aberdeen since he moved there in 1982. At that time there was only a handful of gannet nests at Troup Head. 'Getting there wasn't easy,' he told me. 'It was a trek across fields, one of which had quite a large bull in it! There were just four nests in 1988 with a few more birds around. I went back six years later and there were 300 nests.'

Since then, numbers have swelled to thousands of occupied nests. Despite such dramatic rises on this particular cliff, there are still no other breeding sites on Aberdeenshire's coast. I asked Tim why he thinks Troup Head has become such a popular spot for gannets. 'The ledges are fairly deep and there's good feeding in the area. A fresh nesting site between Bass Rock and Noss, Shetland, was very welcome.'

Accessing Troup Head is straightforward if you know how, but first-time visitors might think they're trespassing as the route passes through farms. From Crovie, take a left turn off Bracoden Road when you reach Bracoden School. From here, just keep going and look out for tiny blue RSPB signs pointing you in the right direction.

THE COAST FROM PENNAN TO FRASERBURGH

After Troup Head, the coastline draws back in for a while. Along this dip you'll find several sheltered bays, beaches and fishing villages, concluding with the town of Fraserburgh on a curve of land at the far northeast corner. Until Fraserburgh it's mostly B roads, providing an excuse to travel leisurely through open country. There's a decent handful of castles and other historic monuments to check out here, although some are easily missed – unless you've got yours truly leading the way.

5 PENNAN & AROUND

🏠 **Mill of Nethermill Holidays** (page 319)

All of the houses in Pennan are white and look particularly striking when the sun's beaming off them. The window frames are painted an assortment of turquoise, violet and brown, looking like a row of pale faces with different coloured eyeliner.

Because it consists mainly of houses and holiday lets, this small village four miles east of Gardenstown can be very quiet out of season. In summer, a shack called **Coastal Cuppie** (❚) serves coffee and cake, but for most of the year the culinary theme here is very much picnics. I'd say it's a place to swing into for a short leg stretch before continuing

A FAMOUS PHONE BOX

The most famous part of Pennan is its red phone box, which can be found on the seafront. It's linked to the 1983 film **Local Hero**, starring Burt Lancaster and Peter Riegert. In the film, a Texan oil company intends to build a large oil refinery that will cover an entire fictional Scottish village called Ferness. Riegert plays Mac, who's sent by his boss Felix Happer, played by Lancaster, to negotiate with the village's inhabitants. During his stay in Ferness, Mac takes a liking to coastal life and his loyalty to his company begins to waver.

Pennan provides the backdrop for several of the exterior village scenes in *Local Hero*, although the beach used in the film is actually on Scotland's west coast. A very weathered commemorative plaque can be seen on the wall of the **Pennan Inn**, adjacent to the phone box. Unfortunately the box isn't in the same position as onscreen – tucked in an L-shaped dell in front of a small brown building, it's difficult to get a decent photo of it. A wooden replica of the phone box was built for the film and placed in a more picturesque spot during shooting.

along the coast, with its phone box providing a nugget of movie trivia (see above).

It takes less than ten minutes to stroll from one end of the village to the other. A concrete walkway runs parallel to the road and has a sudden drop down to a pebbly beach on one side. With a row of jagged rocks sandwiched between these pebbles and the water, it's more suited to walks with your shoes on.

Unlike in Crovie, those with smaller vehicles can drive down to the harbour front in Pennan, although there are some tight turns so keep it slow on the descent.

Cullykhan Bay

/// sues.survived.flinches

This secluded bay a mile northwest of Pennan is more a place to potter than a walking location, but it provides dramatic views. From the car park, it's less than five minutes on foot down a shallow-stepped boardwalk to a sandy beach. Only 100yds across, it's hemmed in by cliffs so nicely sheltered. A border of pebbles lines the back and dark rocks dotted with tiny pools bank either side – worth a nosey if you're a keen rock pooler.

Back up the boardwalk, take a path leading right on to a mud track beside a burn running below. As the path climbs up, a wedge of ocean appears through a gap between slanting cliffs before you reach a patch of heather in front of a wooden fence. A vast sea cave pops into view, looking like Tom and Jerry dropped a giant piano into the hill. The partially collapsed cave is called **Hell's Lum** and some say it was once used as a depot for smuggling whisky out and brandy in. In stormy weather, columns of sea spray surge out of the cave, making its name – 'lum' is a Scottish word for chimney – quite apt. Taking care of the sudden drop in front of you, it's possible to walk a little further forward and peer down into impressive ravines below the promontory.

To the right of Hell's Lum, as you look out to sea, is where the late 17th-century coastal battery of **Fort Fiddes** once was. Nothing is visible now and it's just a fenced area of unruly grass ditches, but from this spot you can see Pennan peeking out from behind another headland.

6 MOUNTHOOLY DOOCOT

/// honey.imprints.refutes

This is Aberdeenshire's answer to Rapunzel's tower. The Mounthooly Doocot instantly draws the eye as you approach from the B9031 heading north to the coast, perched high on a grassy outcrop. It was built in mock-Gothic style in around 1800 to house and harvest pigeons, known as doos, for their meat and eggs. The doos kept here would have been semi-domesticated rock doves – ancestors of the modern-day feral pigeons seen in towns and cities. Made of roughly cut beige stones, its four edges are flattened, making it octagonal in shape.

You can see the doocot just fine from the parking bays beside the road (see W3W code above), but for a closer look there's a shallow gravel staircase cut into the hill. Unlike the squat, white doocot near Findlater Castle (page 190), Mounthooly is more decorative: this certainly was a fancy crib for birds. Every face has a circular aperture for them to fly in and out. Arranged around the crenellated top are twelve ball finials representing twelve surrounding estates. Lord Garden of Troup purchased many of these estates from the Crown after they were seized from Lord Pitsligo during the Jacobite Rebellion of 1745. Lord Pitsligo was a Jacobite and acted as General of Horse for the army of Bonnie Prince Charlie.

Mounthooly Doocot looks particularly striking on bright spring and summer days when yellow gorse flowers flare in front of a cloudless

---

1 Pennan. **2** Afternoon tea at Down on the Farm. **3** Mounthooly Doocot. **4** Cullykhan Bay. ▶

REBECCA GIBSON

REBECCA GIBSON

REBECCA GIBSON

REBECCA GIBSON

sky. It's now maintained by Aberdeenshire Council but there's no information on-site, only adding to the intrigue.

Down on the Farm

ᐃ **Down on the Farm** (page 319)

Milestone House, Rosehearty AB43 6JY ✆ 07954 989737 ⊘ downonthefarm.net

A quarter of a mile southwest of Mounthooly Doocot is Stonebriggs Farm. As well as keeping cows, sheep, chickens, dogs, peacocks and ferrets, owners Carole and Matthew Short are keen to promote agritourism and offer tours around their farm, so visitors can meet the animals and even cuddle a lamb or two in summer. Their Dorset Horn sheep give birth twice a year, so there are plenty of opportunities to watch the farm at work. As well as lambing, you can see the sheep being shorn and hop on a trailer and meet the cows. All tours end with tea and cake.

Visitors can also have afternoon tea in a cabin made from an old boat (🕓 10.00–15.00 Mon–Fri), with multi-coloured buoys strung up like bunting. Sunlight streams through a large circular window, and despite gusty winds during my visit I was warm and cosy inside, tucking into Carole's homemade scones.

Upcycling is an integral part of the process for Carole. 'Matthew and I were brought up in frugal households where nothing was wasted,' she told me. 'We were encouraged to make do and mend, so it comes naturally to us to reuse things. It's satisfying seeing something totally transformed into something new.'

If you're looking for a longer dose of farm life, there's a range of glamping accommodation on-site (page 319) such as an off-grid Harvest Hut and two Hideaways, which look like knocked over Pringles tubes. Camping isn't for everyone, so for those who appreciate a roof and a flushing toilet (in this case housed in an old whisky barrel), it's the perfect halfway house.

7 FRASERBURGH

🏠 **Wildflower Eco Lodges** (page 319)

The major fishing port of Fraserburgh is one of the biggest towns in this chapter, providing a string of shops, restaurants and take-aways around High and Cross streets. It's an urban hub, so many of the buildings are modern and lacking in charm, but dotted around there are still old stone cottages studded with sash windows and others made from the uniform granite blocks common in Aberdeen. Similar to Lossiemouth in Moray (page 144) but on a larger scale, much of the inland part of Fraserburgh is residential, and visitors congregate at the waterfront for the town's historic and cultural highlight: **Kinnaird Head Castle Lighthouse & The Museum of Scottish Lighthouses** (Stevenson Rd AB43 9DU ⚓ lighthousemuseum.org.uk). Inside you'll find intricate model ships, displays about the work of the Stevenson family (who constructed the majority of Scotland's lighthouses across nearly two centuries) and artefacts from lighthouses all over the country. The wow factor comes from the collection of lighthouse lenses looking like towering car headlights.

As well as exploring the museum, I recommend joining a guided tour (included in entry price) so you can climb to the top of Kinnaird Head Lighthouse. This striking building is mostly white with sections of mustard yellow. It was once a 16th-century castle constructed by the Frasers of Philorth – this is where the town's name comes from. In 1787 the castle was sold to the Northern Lighthouse Board and converted into their first operational lighthouse. Stop on the way up to look at the keeper's quarters, left exactly as they were when the last keeper vacated in 1991. If you're up for climbing a ladder to the top, you can watch the guide operate machinery that rotates the huge lens above. Back on the

A TALE OF FORBIDDEN LOVE

From Kinnaird Head Lighthouse, a footpath leads around the headland towards Fraserburgh's harbour. Along here you'll see a short square tower with a wooden staircase leading to the first storey and a tiny shoulder-height door on the south side. This is the **Wine Tower** and the exact details of its history are a little foggy. It's believed to have been built by the Fraser family in the 1500s, but ideas for its function range from a harbour building to a private chapel.

What's certain is its tragic love story. According to legend, the laird's daughter fell in love with a piper. Refusing to entertain such a match, the girl's father locked her in the tower's upper chamber and imprisoned the piper in a cave below. He drowned as the tide came in and the girl threw herself out of the window in despair. Until recently, the lighthouse keeper splashed red paint on the rocks below as a tribute to the tale, and you can still see remnants of this on the northern side of the tower. Listen carefully and it's said you might hear music as the piper's ghost searches for his lost sweetheart. Maybe.

ground, calm any wobbly legs by stopping for a coffee in the museum café or browsing a range of lighthouse memorabilia in the gift shop.

Kinnaird Head is also a great spot for dolphin watching all year round: on the grass in front of the lighthouse you have panoramic views of the North Sea. From late spring to early summer you might be jammy enough to see orcas from here as well.

Several car parks in Fraserburgh are pay and display but Castle Street car park, buried down several residential streets, is free and worth hunting for.

From Kinnaird Head, you'll be able to see **Waters of Philorth Beach** stretching in a concave bend to the east of Fraserburgh. It's a nature reserve comprising an estuary of the River Philorth, rolling sand dunes and an assortment of mudflat, reedbed and saltmarsh habitats. A boardwalk climbs a gentle hill before sloping back down to the beach. If the tide's out, the sand spreads far in both directions, its shiny wet surface reflecting the sky. Even at high tide there's plenty of beach to walk on, so no picking your way over slippery boulders required. It's possible to walk all the way into Fraserburgh from here, leaving the sand via the beach car park on South Harbour Road.

Unhelpfully, the turning for the reserve car park (▦ album.dried. bake) isn't registered as a road on Google Maps, but you'll see it on satellite view next to the point where the river crosses the B9033. Beside the road there are narrow brown signs for 'Waters of Philorth' facing both directions, as well as a smaller reserve sign at the turning.

St Combs & Whitelinks Bays

To access the next section of coastline past Fraserburgh, I recommend stopping in the village of St Combs and walking north across two very pretty beaches that face east towards the vast expanse of the North Sea.

Covering a combined distance of 1½ miles, the bays of St Combs and Whitelinks make a shallow backwards 'B' shape, cinched in the middle by a band of cubic blocks and a sprinkling of half-submerged natural stones. Similar to Waters of Philorth, the sand here is fine and golden. Settle against the dunes and you'll be sheltered from the wind on most sides.

---

1 Fraserburgh. **2** The Museum of Scottish Lighthouses at Fraserburgh.
3 Memsie Round Cairn. ▶

MEMSIE ROUND CAIRN

/// ticket.departure.passion

Now for something completely random. If you travel south out of Fraserburgh down the A90 and turn right on to the B9032, a large mound of stones appears on the left as you near the village of Memsie. No it's not fly-tipping from a dodgy builder, but an ancient monument called the Memsie Round Cairn. Sitting in its own field and surrounded by fencing, this sprawling pile of rocks is over 80ft long and nearly 15ft high. Discoveries inside suggest it was used as a medieval burial site. Originally there were two other large cairns here, but they were looted for building materials at the end of the 18th century, so Memsie is now the sole survivor. There's a lay-by beside the cairn where you can pull over and walk up for a closer look.

Depending on the tide, walking across both bays might require wading through an ankle-deep stream running to the sea. Parking isn't widely available, but there's a small area at the end of Gordon Street in St Combs, next to a beige Scottish Water building. From here it's a hop down the steps to the beach.

¶¶ FOOD & DRINK

Peartree Coffee House & Bistro 61 High St, AB43 9ET ✆ 01346 512212 ⬛ ☉ Thu–Sun. Family-run bistro with striking black and lime-green décor, serving fresh seafood sourced daily from local processors or straight from the boat. There's an entire vegetarian & vegan menu with varied options such as sandwiches, burgers and curries, as well as seafood tapas specials every Thursday.

Strichen Lodge Restaurant & Coffee Shop AB43 6TH ✆ 01771 637029 ⬛ Strichen Lodge ☉ 10.00–16.00 daily. Nine miles south of Fraserburgh on the A981, this bright and airy café serves soup, burgers, quiches and other lunchtime dishes, including particularly tasty brie wedges. It sits within Strichen Community Park, which has a little pond ideal for children to see the ducks.

INLAND BUCHAN

While most of this chapter's sites of interest have a coastal theme, there's a cluster of intriguing spots some 14 miles inland, around the parish of Old Deer. This is one of numerous small villages in Buchan, connected to its neighbours by quiet A roads between fields.

As with much of inland Aberdeenshire, the area mostly has flat, rural terrain with plenty of sheep and tractors. Walking and cycling is made easier by the Formartine & Buchan Way (page 182), which has a side branch passing close to a hilltop stone circle and the marvellous, ruined Deer Abbey. Outside of this, travelling on foot usually requires roadside walking, but the popular and varied Aden Country Park offers a mix of paths around a duck pond, courtyard, patches of woodland and a Victorian arboretum.

8 AIKEY BRAE STONE CIRCLE

/// sparkles.deferring.hunk

Every time I hear this stone circle's name, Billy Ray Cyrus pops into my head. Distract yourself from that earworm with a short walk to an ancient monument framed by open fields in the middle of nowhere. This one's particularly special at sunrise; when I first visited, the sky was a blend of tangerine and mustard and the stones cast long shadows across the grass.

Set within a shallow circular dell are three upright standing stones on the northwest side and a single horizontal recumbent with its flankers on the opposite side. Between them lie an assortment of broad, flat stones at knee height. Similar to Aberdeenshire's other recumbent stone circles, Aikey Brae was constructed by farming communities many thousands of years ago and it's believed each stone was strategically placed to match up with the moon's position in midsummer. This is a peaceful spot and clearly a suitable location for ritual and reflection in times gone by. The fact you need to walk a while to reach the circle adds to its appeal.

"This is a peaceful spot and clearly a suitable location for ritual and reflection in times gone by."

From the car park just off the B9029, it's an easy-going stroll up a gently inclining gravel track to the stones. The first stretch of path is buzzing with wildlife – I've had rabbits, yellowhammers, chaffinches, dunnocks and skylarks crossing in front of me and pheasants croaking from somewhere in the gorse.

After less than 300yds, the path splits into a circular, with both forks leading to Aikey Brae. The left track is more direct and passes a pocket of trees to a picnic table at the northern end of the site. When you arrive

at the circle clearing after half a mile, a grassy trail leads to the stones – roots stick up on some of them so watch your step.

9 DEER ABBEY

minds.pavillions.vies 🖉 historicenvironment.scot/visit-a-place/places/deer-abbey
🕓 Apr–Sep 09.30–17.30 daily; Oct–Mar 10.00–16.00 daily; free entry

This beautiful Cistercian abbey ruin stands within a walled field, close to Aikey Brae. The most intact side is at the back – crumbling walls with arched window frames and doorways stand behind a grid of now shin-height partitions that once separated the rooms; a large square lawn in the centre of the ruin was the cloister. In the northwest corner of the field, a miniature portico with four pillars shelters a stone head, an altar slab with a carved cross and other sculpted stones from the abbey.

Deer Abbey was founded in 1219 by Earl of Buchan William Comyn. Home to monks for over 300 years, it fell to ruin after the Protestant Reformation in 1560. Its library is said to have included the **Book of Deer**, a 10th-century Gospel book containing the oldest record of written Scottish Gaelic. Notes within the book say that St Columba and his nephew St Drostan founded a now-lost Pictish monastery in the nearby village of Old Deer around AD580. Allegedly, Drostan cried when his uncle left, and the Gaelic word for tears, *dèara*, inspired the monastery's name.

The lay-by for the abbey is beside the A950. Look for the small sign pointing to an entranceway sheltered by a pillared stone porch.

10 ADEN COUNTRY PARK & AROUND

🏠 **Aden House B&B** (page 319)

Station Rd, Mintlaw AB42 5FQ 🔲 🕓 park & shop year-round, museum summer only

Opened in 1980, this varied 230-acre park sits 14 miles south of Fraserburgh. Similar to Aberdeen's Seaton Park (page 281), Aden has more than you think at first glance. Curled around a wide, white-bricked circular courtyard close to the main car park are slate-roofed buildings with bright red doors. Here you'll find a sweet little gift shop (🔲 thefriendsofaden) selling knitwear, local interest books and postcards.

◀ **1** Aikey Brae Stone Circle. **2** Deer Abbey. **3** Aden Country Park.

What I like about Aden Country Park is its diversity. There are numerous waymarked trails and spots to enjoy a picnic, so you could easily spend a few hours here. Beside the courtyard is a **sensory garden** with narrow brick paths between knee-high hedges, flowerbeds of daffodils and primroses in spring, and benches beneath cosy trellis awnings. Beside the duck pond, a footpath heads northwest through shaded birch forest. As it first bends left you'll see a wooded fence enclosure with a mineral well inside. Beside the overflow car park is the **Fairy Wood**, which needs a sunny day to be appreciated properly as the thick canopy doesn't let much light in.

One mile from the park is **Pitfour Lake** (▦ rooks.gained.diver) – yes, it is a lake, not a loch! Glittering on a sunny day, this is another wild spot worth dropping into for a short walk. You can follow a wide, all-abilities path all the way round. Look for ducks and swans on the water and a range of small birds in the trees.

To get here from Aden, head west on the A950 and take the first right, where the car park appears immediately on the right. Across the road, follow a tiny sign for the lake up an earth track to reach its southeast bank.

SOUTH TO SLAINS CASTLE

🏠 **Cruden Bay B&B** (page 319)

Time to return to Aberdeenshire's impressive coastline. This is the furthest east we will stretch into the North Sea and I find it thrilling that, when facing the water here, the next land visible on the horizon would be Norway. The following section contains Peterhead, the largest fishing port in the UK. The main reason to stop here is the Prison Museum – one of the North East's most unnerving, macabre and fascinating places. Some six miles south, close to the Gothic ruin of Slains Castle, birdwatchers flock to Bullers of Buchan with its puzzle piece cliffs and promise of puffins.

11 RSPB LOCH OF STRATHBEG

Starnafin, Crimon AB43 8QN ⊘ rspb.org.uk/reserves-and-events/
reserves-a-z/loch-of-strathbeg

With its combination of shallow freshwater and surrounding grassland, this windswept reserve's claim to fame is it has the largest dune loch in

Britain. On a map, Loch of Strathbeg is represented by a significant chunk of blue close to the coast, around nine miles southeast of Fraserburgh.

The great thing about this reserve is there's something to see in every season. Over 500 species have been recorded in the range of habitats here, which includes woodland, beach and internationally important wetland. With spring and summer comes the buzzing activity of raising chicks, and migrants such as ospreys arrive. In autumn and winter, up to 20% of the world's population of **pink-footed geese** roost on the wetland, having migrated to Britain from Greenland and Iceland. As well as seasonal spectacles, a variety of ducks and gulls can be seen on the loch all year round. You might also see dusty-coloured horses browsing the fields – these are **Konik ponies** and their grazing provides ideal feeding conditions for wading birds.

Beside the main car park is the visitor centre. Here you can pick up leaflets about other nearby RSPB reserves and borrow a pond-dipping kit to take down to a small platform just along the track. Inside the visitor centre, armchairs have been placed in front of a floor-to-ceiling window on the lower level, revealing dozens of birds flurrying around the feeders. These attract all the usual finches and tits, and a good number of tree sparrows too – similar to the better-known house sparrow, but with a chestnut head instead of grey. The upper level has a stairlift for wheelchair users and looks out over a much larger pond dedicated to birds. Common terns – streamlined seabirds with black caps and scarlet red bills – raise their chicks on the island in this pond in spring and summer.

As with many RSPB reserves, I couldn't decide which hide to visit. In the end I plumped for the **Tower Pool Hide**, a 15-minute walk from the visitor centre. It sits west of the loch and looks out over the Burn of Savoch. To get there from the car park, head back to the road and follow signs for the Wetland Hides. The pool hide is set far back from the water, so I recommend bringing a scope if you have one as it's tricky to watch the birds in any detail through binoculars. You'll see the Dunbar Hide a little closer to the water – a gravel track leads to it from the pool hide.

Rattray Head Lighthouse

Under five miles east of Strathbeg is an isolated lighthouse that requires a drive down a farm track and a walk through the dunes to reach it.

MORWENNA EGAN

LIAM MCBRIDE

VISITSCOTLAND/NORTH EAST 250/DAMIAN SHIELDS

VISITSCOTLAND/NORTH EAST 250/DAMIAN SHIELDS

Rattray Head isn't open to the public, but you can still admire it at fairly close quarters from a secluded sandy beach that's worth a visit in itself.

To get there from Strathbeg, head southwest on Starnafin Road and turn left on to the A90. Take the second turning on the left and follow signs for Rattray. After 1½ miles you'll arrive at **St Mary's Chapel** (▥ goggles.irritable.member) on your right, sitting close to the southern tip of the Strathbeg reserve. There's parking at the end of the road for the lighthouse but, if you value your tyres, I suggest leaving the car beside the chapel instead and walking 1½ miles to the end of the heavily pot-holed track.

"You can still admire it at fairly close quarters from a secluded sandy beach that's worth a visit in itself."

It's worth stopping at the chapel anyway as it's an attractive ruin, now mostly consisting of its two end walls. Believed to be one of the oldest structures still standing in this region of Scotland, the chapel was first referenced by William Comyn, Earl of Buchan, in a note dated 1220. It's said Comyn built it as a private chapel.

If you visit in spring, you'll be rewarded for the extra walk from the chapel with skylarks, yellowhammers and goldfinches. When you reach the lighthouse cottages, the path becomes a narrow grass path. After a few minutes through grassy dunes you'll hit the beach, which has the same gold sand as St Combs Bay (page 202). If the tide is out, the lighthouse will be completely grounded. Similar to Kinnaird Head in Fraserburgh, it's white with a domed cage on top. It was originally built in 1895 and made fully automatic in 1982.

12 PETERHEAD PRISON MUSEUM

South Rd, AB42 2ZX ✐ 01779 581060 ✪ peterheadprisonmuseum.com ☉ daily

The town of Peterhead is the biggest settlement in Aberdeenshire. As you might expect for somewhere so heavily industrial (it's one of Europe's largest fishing ports and also trades in materials such as oil and granite), some parts are nicer to look at than others. However, there's a pretty spot at the southern side called The Lido – this short stretch of beach is sheltered within a rocky border beside the sailboats, making it a safe swimming spot.

◀ **1** Konik ponies at RSPB Loch of Strathbeg. **2** Rattray Head Lighthouse. **3** Slains Castle. **4** Bullers of Buchan.

HOSTAGE ON THE ROOF

The most famous event in Peterhead Prison's history is the riot of 1987. Prison officer Jackie Stuart, who worked there for 25 years, grabbed a blade from an inmate and the block erupted. Windows were smashed, fires were started and officers were pelted with missiles. Jackie was stabbed several times in the struggle but didn't even realise it at the time. After putting him in prisoners' clothes, inmates filled his pockets with lighter fuel and held him captive on the roof for five days. Margaret Thatcher eventually ordered the Special Air Service (SAS) to carry out a rescue. In 2018, Jackie released a book about his ordeal – *Hostage on the Roof* – and he now volunteers at the museum, sharing his incredible story with visitors.

Peterhead's undeniable stand-out attraction is the Prison Museum. It's located inside the real prison building, which was Scotland's only convict prison and considered to be the toughest in the country during its years of operation from 1888 to 2013. In the late 19th century, a granite breakwater was planned at Peterhead to shelter the boats. As an alternative to an expensive labour force, a prison was built and the inmates were used to quarry the granite.

Pick up an audio headset at the gift shop and then you're free to take a self-guided tour through the prison. Learn about the cells, kitchen, laundry room, shower block, exercise yard and other sections from a narrator, interspersed with anecdotes from personnel who used to work there. Less savoury parts of the tour include a cell made up to represent the aftermath of a murder that occurred in the 1970s at the hands of gang leader 'The Red Devil', and foul-smelling wall adornments inspired by the 1980s 'dirty protest' that aren't for the weak-stomached. Some of Scotland's most notorious criminals lived in these exact cells, making the retelling of these events all the more chilling. Walking through a freezing cold cell block while listening to clanging gates and bellowing inmates is enough to set anyone on edge, but it's a totally unique historical experience and ingeniously put together.

"As an alternative to an expensive labour force, a prison was built and the inmates were used to quarry the granite."

After escaping prison, you can warm up in the cosy Refuge Café and enjoy soup, sandwiches and cakes with views across the bay to the breakwater. In here I met Operations Manager Alex Giddes, who was approached in 2014 about the possibility of a museum. 'I invited ex-officers back and consulted them on where the tour should go,' he told me. 'They would say "do you remember when…" and that added to the experience.'

Murder mystery and Halloween events are held at the museum, along with guided night tours in January and February. All events are advertised on Facebook and often sell out within half an hour. Many visitors find the night tours creepier than the Halloween themes. 'They think how they would feel in that situation,' Alex said. 'That seems to be the big impact with the night tours. It's reality, and that's scarier than when you're expecting someone to jump out at you.'

The museum is advertised as a family day out, but considering some of its unsettling content I had my doubts about whether it was suitable for children. However, Alex assured me kids love it. He receives letters after school visits and has been told by some parents that when they ask their children where they want to go for their birthday, they say 'prison'.

It's certainly a unique experience, getting to walk through a real prison and see what it looked, sounded and even smelt like. Alex remembered one visitor from the museum's opening week: 'I try to speak to everyone leaving to get feedback. This one guy stopped and said he'd always wanted to see in it but never wanted to *be* in it. That could be our strapline!'

In the adjoining **lifeboat museum** (included with museum entry fee), the centrepiece is the *Julia Park Barry of Glasgow* – a former RNLI lifeboat active in Peterhead for 30 years in the mid 20th century. After saving almost 500 lives during that time, she has since been restored to pristine condition. As the prison is linked to the seafaring community through the construction of the breakwater, it makes sense to commemorate this and other Peterhead lifeboats here.

The museum is an incredible insight into Peterhead's heritage – I've never been anywhere like it before. A lot of thought and effort has gone in to make this a rare and evocative experience.

13 BULLERS OF BUCHAN & SLAINS CASTLE

/// relate.winds.represent

Some 6½ miles south of Peterhead is a cluster of cliffs arranged in broad, curving dells. At the base of each 'U' shape between the winding ridges are some formidable rock stacks and sea caves, where mottled brown rock is livened by zesty green grass and hardy coastal flora such as campion and scurvy grass. Like Troup Head (page 195) and Fowlsheugh (page 312), Bullers of Buchan is a clifftop reserve home to nesting seabirds during spring and summer.

Great care should be taken on the narrow footpaths, but a stroll here offers opportunities to watch kittiwakes, razorbills, guillemots, shags and occasional rock doves, often staying within their distinct species neighbourhoods. Kittiwakes are particularly abundant – they're the ones that shout their name: 'kitti-wa-AKE!' Puffins show up here from around April each year, and the challenge is finding them hidden in plain sight among everyone else. Look out to sea and you'll see hundreds more birds bobbing on the waves.

From the car park, the path passes between a couple of houses before splitting in two. The left path, heading north, reaches Boddam, a coastal village just south of Peterhead, while the right path leads to **Slains Castle**. If you don't fancy the roughly two-mile walk there along the cliffs, you can drive another mile south on the A975 to the castle car park (**///** skillet.cheeses.went). Slains Castle is half a mile from here, following a flat, gravel vehicle track suitable for cyclists. You'll see the castle from the start, sticking up over the field in front.

This ruin is famous because of **Bram Stoker**. He was entertained near Slains Castle in the 19th century and Count Dracula's castle is said to be inspired by it. Fans of *The Crown* might recognise Slains as one of the filming locations for Castle Mey in season one.

It takes a good twenty minutes to poke your head into all the different fragments of this ruin, but health and safety is non-existent and it's important to be sensible as you explore. The tight spiral staircases have no barriers or banisters and a few platforms have sheer drops into thin air. The main walls are a mixture of crumbly quartz rocks and modern house bricks with lots of archways and turrets. Tufts of sea thrift grow directly out of the rock.

Specifically, this is 'New' Slains Castle and you might also see mentions of an Old Slains Castle, situated a few miles south near Collieston (page 219). This predates New Slains by about 300 years and now consists of a crumbling tower house wall on private land. It was destroyed in 1594 by James VI of England when the castle's owner – Francis Hay, Earl of Erroll – supported the pro-Catholic rebellion of George Gordon, Earl of Huntly. Instead of rebuilding, Hay replaced it with New Slains Castle, which was completed in 1597.

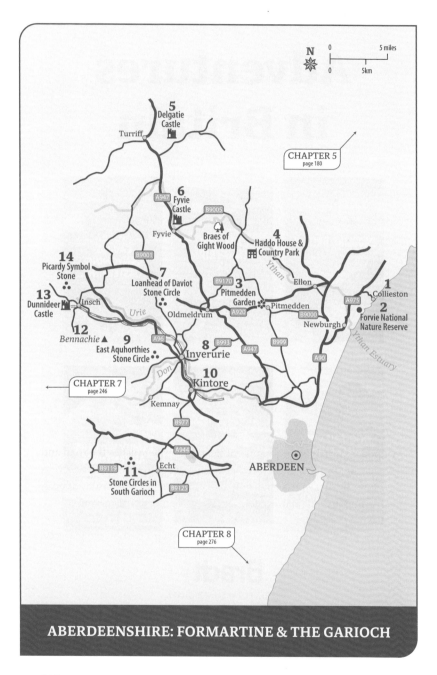

N

0   5 miles

0   5km

5 Delgatie Castle

Turriff

CHAPTER 5
page 180

A947

6 Fyvie Castle

B9005

Fyvie

Braes of Gight Wood

4 Haddo House & Country Park

Ythan

Ellon

14 Picardy Symbol Stone

B9001

7 Loanhead of Daviot Stone Circle

B9170

3 Pitmedden Garden

1 Collieston

A975

13 Dunnideer Castle

Insch

Urie

Oldmeldrum

A920

Pitmedden

B9000

Newburgh

2 Forvie National Nature Reserve

12 Bennachie ▲

9 East Aquhorthies Stone Circle

A96

8

B993

Inverurie

A947

B999

A90

10 Kintore

Don

CHAPTER 7
page 246

Kemnay

B977

A944

11 Stone Circles in South Garioch

B9119

Echt

B9125

ABERDEEN

CHAPTER 8
page 276

ABERDEENSHIRE: FORMARTINE & THE GARIOCH

6
ABERDEENSHIRE: FORMARTINE & THE GARIOCH

This chapter covers the very centre of Aberdeenshire. Formartine is pressed beneath Buchan and the North East coast, holding a slim section of its own coastline just above the Aberdeen city boundary. Pressed against Aberdeen's west edge, the Garioch (pronounced 'Geery') looks like a cartoon paint splash when outlined on a map. A heavily rural landscape, it covers lots of interconnected hamlets, stopping just before Huntly (page 249) to the northwest and just before Banchory (page 269) to the south. Its biggest settlement, Inverurie, is the bullseye.

Both the Garioch and Formartine have lots to offer the curious explorer, with opportunities to hill hike, sip tea overlooking landscaped gardens or rest contemplatively inside a stone circle. In fact, the region is strewn with stone circles and I've included more in this chapter than any other – three of them are only six miles apart. Stone circles around here vary widely in size, complexity and locality: while Sunhoney is sheltered in a pouch of trees on a prominent field, Cullerlie brushes the road and Midmar sits inside a church cemetery. Arguably the most impressive is East Aquhorthies, measuring 64ft across. No matter where they appear, they all add ancient and mysterious history to a countryside walk.

It wouldn't be Aberdeenshire without castles, and I've featured some fine examples here of both ruins and preserved properties. Fyvie Castle has its own tragic ghost, while Delgatie Castle contains one of very few portraits of Mary Queen of Scots in existence. Other historical monuments, such as hilltop forts, Pictish slabs and the dramatic mound of an old motte and bailey site, can all be found nearby.

Over on Formartine's southeast edge is Forvie National Nature Reserve (NNR). Covering 2,000 acres of coastal heathland, the site is best known for its vast shifting sand dunes that have been compared to the Sahara Desert. The adjacent estuary of the River Ythan provides a haul-out site for seals and is an important breeding habitat for a range of seabirds.

GETTING AROUND

Inverurie is the capital of the Garioch and lies beside the A96, 17 miles northwest of Aberdeen. Outside of here, the North East theme of quiet B roads and unnamed single-lane roads continues. This is rural Aberdeenshire, so be prepared to use passing places. The charm of the place is finding a Neolithic monument in a field or a Pictish stone in a lay-by, so keep your eyes peeled for something unexpected while you're cruising behind a tractor.

TRAINS & BUSES

As you'd expect for a rural location, more remote sites in this chapter are tricky to reach on public transport. You can get to Inverurie from Aberdeen via the Stagecoach 37 **bus**. The 49 from Inverurie will take you to the village of Pitmedden, a ¾-mile walk from Pitmedden Garden. Accessing Haddo House Country Park also requires the 49 to Pitmedden, then the 291 to Chapelpark, followed by a 1½-mile walk. Inverurie has plenty to see on foot, and the Stagecoach 37 runs south past Broomend of Crichie Stone Circle and through Kintore, one mile and four miles outside Inverurie respectively.

The Garioch is covered reasonably well by the **Scotrail** Inverness to Aberdeen service, stopping at Insch, Inverurie and Kintore. Insch is a handy stop, as it puts you within walking distance of Dunnideer Castle and Picardy Symbol Stone.

WALKING & CYCLING

Some of the best opportunities for short walks in this area include: the open country hike to Dunnideer Castle; the winding paths in Inverurie's Riverside Park; and the green spaces around Haddo House. If you're looking for walks with waymarkers, Forvie NNR offers a mix through heathland, dune and cliff habitats.

One of the most popular spots for walkers around here is **Bennachie**, a range of hills about 13 miles west of Inverurie. Many aim for the highest point at Oxen Craig (1,732ft), or the Pictish fort on Mither Tap *i* **TOURIST INFORMATION**

Garioch Heritage Centre Loco Works Rd, Inverurie AB51 4FY ☏ 01467 621855
✉ info@gariochheritage.co.uk.
Inverurie Library Market Pl, AB51 3SN ☏ 01467 534784
✉ inverurie.library@aberdeenshire.gov.uk.

(1,699ft), but it's not essential to go puffing up steep inclines. You'll find a range of shorter trails starting from four different car parks, managed by Forestry and Land Scotland. Pop into the visitor centre on the eastern side of Bennachie to stock up on maps and leaflets (page 239).

Roughly a third of the 53-mile **Formartine and Buchan Way** (page 182) crosses this region but doesn't veer close to any sites I've listed. Still, it's a safe, off-road trail from Dyce (outside Aberdeen) to Fraserburgh and worth looking into if you like a long-distance route.

FORMARTINE

Located above Aberdeen City and covering 319 square miles, Formartine is mainly characterised by open farmland, though its small strip of coastline has a fantastic nature reserve dominated by shifting sand dunes. For a bit of interior and landscaped luxury, Forvie Castle, Haddo House and Pitmedden Garden all offer something different.

1 COLLIESTON

The former fishing village of Collieston, at the northern end of Formartine's coastline, occupies a small dell between two headlands. White cottages line just a handful of layered streets, curled around the harbour like raked seats around a theatre. A slipway connects the pavement to a sandy beach about 300ft across, sheltered by a pier curved like a shepherd's crook.

Parking is available at the eastern end of the village, beside **Cransdale Vantage Point** (⊞ bucket.mini.doubt). From here you can look out over the coast and see the dunes and cliffs at nearby Forvie. To the southwest, the sharply angled headland at the back of the closest cliffs is Hackley Head. Beyond this, Aberdeen Harbour and Girdle

Ness Lighthouse are also visible on a clear day, despite being over 20 miles away.

While facing the sea, you'll notice a path passing Collieston's shingle beach on the right, climbing around a grassy hill before threading between cottages and down a stone staircase to the harbour. Here you'll find **Smugglers Cone** (⊘ smugglerscone.com ☉ summer 11.00–16.00 Sat & Sun), an ice-cream parlour and coffee shop. There's also a box containing litter picking equipment; as instructed on the lid, visitors can 'take four for the shore' by borrowing the equipment to pick up four or more pieces of litter from the beach.

2 FORVIE NATIONAL NATURE RESERVE

⊘ nature.scot

Spreading along Collieston's southwest edge, this reserve covers the Ythan Estuary, Forvie Moor and a stretch of sandy beach overlooking the North Sea. It's perhaps best known for its magnificent shifting sand dunes and bird life, including breeding colonies of eider ducks and four species of terns.

There are several places to start exploring the reserve. From Collieston, the first access point is half a mile away at **Forvie Centre** (⊞ likewise. ringside.roving ☉ Apr–Sep, staff dependent), which has educational displays about the site. The main footpath here is the red waymarked **Heath Trail**. This two-mile circular follows a combination of gravel and sand tracks through heather moorland – something you might not expect to see so close to the coast. An all-abilities trail runs for half a mile from the car park to **Sand Loch**, home to swans and ducks. These two trails mostly run at a higher elevation close to the cliffs, so offer more aerial views of the coast.

The heathland is interesting, but if you're hankering for a beach it's best to start at the **Waterside** car park (⊞ truckload.avoiding.froze), just over three miles southwest of Forvie Centre. The 3½-mile blue waymarked **Dune Trail** starting here connects the estuary, a small patch of woodland and the towering sand dunes that Forvie is renowned for, stretching almost as high as buildings in some places. If it's warm enough, whip your shoes and socks off – the sand is cotton-wool soft and

---

1 Collieston Bay. **2** Shifting sand dunes at Forvie NNR. **3** Haddo House & Country Park.
4 Aerial shot of Pitmedden Garden showing the flower designs within each parterre. ▶

deliciously cool on a hot day. Some of the dunes have been blown and moulded into fascinating shapes, with many looking like mini deserts.

Equidistant between the two car parks is **Hackley Bay**, accessible via a half-mile detour south off the furthest reaches of the Heath Trail from Forvie Centre or a similar detour north off the Dune Trail from Waterside. This sheltered beach is a curved sweep of caramel sand cupped by a grassy headland. Because it requires a bit of walking to get there, it's often deserted. A photo of Hackley Bay in bright sunshine could easily be mistaken for a secluded Caribbean cove – it's the sort of beach I can picture a movie heroine galloping along on horseback, hair and impractical dress billowing behind her.

"A photo of Hackley Bay in bright sunshine could easily be mistaken for a secluded Caribbean cove."

From April to August, dogs should be kept on leads around the grassy areas of Forvie to avoid disturbance to ground-nesting birds – eiders, terns and a variety of waders and wildfowl breed here. Dogs can run off-lead on the beach, away from any vulnerable wildlife.

¶¶ FOOD & DRINK

Trellis Coffee Shop Main St, Newburgh AB41 6BL ✆ 01358 789989 ⬀ udnyarmshotel. com/coffee ⊙ 09.30–16.00 Wed–Sun. Situated in a prime location overlooking the Ythan Estuary, this café offers the chance to watch birds and perhaps a seal or two while you sip your latte. The cake cabinet has plenty of freshly made goodies including vegan options. For something larger, pop in for breakfast (09.30–11.30) or choose from soup, toasties and dishes on the lunch specials board.

3 PITMEDDEN GARDEN

AB41 7PD ⊙ late Mar–Jun, Sep & Oct 10.30–16.30 Thu–Mon; Jul & Aug 10.30–16.30 daily; National Trust for Scotland

Nine miles west of Forvie NNR is Pitmedden Garden. This is one of the most distinctive gardens not just in the North East but arguably the whole of Scotland, yet it's vastly overlooked. Thoughtfully designed to replicate its 17th-century origins, Pitmedden is a must for anyone who enjoys immaculate flower beds, shady orchards and little perching lions sculpted from stone. One of the garden's star attributes is the set of large rectangles called **parterres**. Within each parterre are vibrant images created from flowers, including a saltire, thistle and coat-of-arms.

Bordered by box hedges and segmented by turf paths, the parterres are best viewed from above – the guidebook's aerial photos show them well.

Enter Pitmedden through the shop and tearoom and emerge onto the upper terrace. Here you'll see the two newest parterres, planted in 1993 and 1996. Separating these from the four larger parterres of the **Great Garden** below is a wall flanked by a pair of small pavilions. These pavilions are some of the few surviving parts of the original 17th-century garden.

At the end of the last garden, accessible through a gate in the stone wall, is an orchard containing pears, plums and 184 varieties of apple. The orchard provides a handy income source for Pitmedden at its **Apple Sunday** event. Held every September, this market day sells the harvested fruit and is free to attend, with activities provided for children.

Pitmedden Garden was created by Sir Alexander Seton and his wife Dame Margaret Lauder around 1675. The last private owner was Major James Keith, whose father bought Pitmedden from the Seton family in 1893. Major Keith, who was from a farming background, transformed the space into a working kitchen garden. The National Trust for Scotland took ownership of the estate in 1952, a year before Major Keith died. With his approval, the Trust returned the garden to how it would have been during Seton's time.

Pitmedden has since been extended to include the **Museum of Farming Life**, located within old stone buildings and stables beside the herb garden. Inside are traditional farming tools for sowing, harvesting, repairing fences and threshing – a method of separating grain from cut corn. Most of the objects in the museum date from the first half of the 20th century and came from the collections of William Cook, a local farmer.

It takes around an hour to see each part of the garden and have a look at the museum. Starting from the car park, there's also a woodland walk passing through a shady patch of deciduous trees with their roots submerged in wild garlic. The heady scent of this waxy-leaved plant is a sensory staple of early spring.

4 HADDO HOUSE & COUNTRY PARK
🏠 **Goukstone** (page 319) 🏕 **Ythan Valley Campsite** (page 319)
AB41 7EQ ⊙ house: Feb–mid-Dec 11.00–16.00 Fri–Mon (guided tours only); garden & grounds: dawn–dusk daily; National Trust for Scotland

Bucking the trend of turreted and often ruined castles found all over Aberdeenshire, Haddo House is a grand stately home located within an extensive estate, six miles north of Pitmedden. Standing at its northwest side, you can admire the central three-storey block with rows of seven windows, flanked by a pair of two-storey wings. The house was designed in 1732 by William Adam for William Gordon, 2nd Earl of Aberdeen. Matching stone staircases wind up to a balcony on the first floor, which was the original entrance. In 1822, Aberdeen architect Archibald Simpson moved the entrance to the ground floor, where it remains today. Simpson was involved in the design of dozens of other buildings across the North East, including Aberdeen Royal Infirmary and St Giles Parish Church in Elgin (page 138). Many notable visitors have stayed at Haddo House, including Queen Victoria for one night in 1857. The property was opened to the public in 1979 when it was taken over by the National Trust for Scotland.

"Roses and wisteria climb the walls, providing pops of colour against the beige and grey blocks."

A FORGOTTEN CASTLE

Four miles northwest of Haddo House is a simple forest walk with a ruined castle hidden in the middle. **Braes of Gight Wood** (⏵ detained.spurted.until) has a car park beside a forestry gate just off the B9005. From here, head past the gate and follow a wide path downhill. Soon after, it crosses a bridge over a stream – an ideal spot for playing Pooh sticks if you're so inclined. On the other side, a field opens up on the left, banked by trees. You'll then pass through a patch of shady mixed woodland with magnificent beech trees.

About 700yds southwest of the stream, the track leads to the edge of a cow field. You're allowed in, but keep your distance from the cows. In the centre of the field is the fantastic 16th-century ruin of **Gight Castle** (pronounced Gecht), an L-plan tower house draped in ivy. For more than 200 years, the castle belonged to the Gordons of Gight. Its last Gordon resident was Catherine Gordon, who was the mother of poet Lord Byron. She was married to Captain John 'Jack' Byron, who had a taste for gambling. In 1787, Catherine sold the castle to the Earl of Aberdeen to pay off her husband's rising debts. After the Earl's son was killed in a riding accident, the castle was abandoned, left to be claimed by the ivy.

This out-and-back walk to the ruin takes less than an hour. With so many coniferous woodlands in this part of Scotland it's refreshing to see such a fine showcase of deciduous trees for a change.

Within easy reach of the car park and just past the café and shop are the **Formal Gardens**, right in front of the house. Dogs are welcome in here on short leads. Stroll along gravel footpaths and you'll feel like Keira Knightley in one of her period roles. This side of Haddo House has a wide staircase leading to the first floor, aligned symmetrically with a domed fountain in the middle of the lawn. Roses and wisteria climb the walls, providing pops of colour against the beige and grey blocks. When I visited on a muggy day in May there was a sudden downpour, so I ducked under one of the porches and was soon surprised by chattering swallows swooping in and out of their corner crevice nests. Look southeast for views all the way down the Scots Mile, one of the paths through the country park.

To discover the history of Haddo House, join one of the staff for an extensive tour, run several times each day. Intriguing elements include a fireplace in the entrance hall that used to be a bedframe and is in fact older than the rest of the property. Haddo's library is special too. As well as a secret bookcase door, it has one of the biggest chenille rugs in Europe.

My favourite part of the tour was the **Giles Room**, which is covered in 85 small, framed paintings of castles. The artist, James Giles, was a close friend of the 4th Earl, who commissioned him to paint a series of Aberdeenshire castles for a book in the 19th century. The paintings were all done in watercolour and look fantastic displayed together.

"My favourite part of the tour was the Giles Room, which is covered in 85 small, framed paintings of castles."

Art enthusiasts might consider visiting during autumn for the annual **Haddo Arts Festival** (⌗ haddoarts.com), when the historic house hosts a diverse programme of music, poetry, visual art and spoken word events.

5 DELGATIE CASTLE

AB53 5TD 𝒫 01888 563479 𝒶 delgatiecastle.com ☺ early Jan–mid-Dec 10.00–16.00 daily

Set back from a minor road 2½ miles east of Turriff, a small town in the northwest of Formartine, Delgatie Castle has belonged to the Hay family for more than 600 years, although it has been added to over time and at first glance looks far more modern than its 11th-century origins. However, as soon as you start exploring the interior, features such as old stonework and beamed ceilings provide glimpses into its past. When Captain John Hay opened Delgatie to the public, he ran the tours himself. Since his death in 1997, visitors have been guided by information boards in each room, although these were written by Captain Hay so the tour is still effectively led by him.

From the entrance hall, the natural progression through the castle is to branch left past a tiny gift shop to the Yester Room. This has a rustic feel with bare stone walls. A portrait of Captain Hay sits over the fireplace and the heraldic ceiling is split into 128 panels, 48 of which display boldly coloured Hay shields. This room is used for special events, including a monthly afternoon tea.

Almost all of the other rooms in Delgatie Castle branch off a stone turnpike staircase that spirals up and up like Enid Blyton's Faraway Tree. It's decorated with family portraits and travel souvenirs, including a Buddha statue collected by Hay during his travels in India. Many of the rooms have magnificent beamed ceilings with paintings between each panel.

The Ballroom is light and airy thanks to its long bay windows. These were added to reflect the style of Balmoral, a common feature in the 1840s when Albert married Queen Victoria. A long montage hung above the door to the anteroom is believed to portray **Mary Queen of Scots**, who stayed at Delgatie for three days after the Battle of Corrichie in 1562. There are several depictions of her in this artwork, including her wedding to the Dauphin of France and a scene of her on horseback with a falcon flying overhead, reflecting her love of falconry. There's also a head and shoulders portrait of her in the Withdrawing Room. This is believed to be one of only nine known portraits of her in existence. Another notable room in the castle is one completely dedicated to dolls' houses, spanning a century in age all the way to a 1975 Cindy house.

There's a shop and a tea room on-site, serving toasties, baked potatoes and cakes; accommodation is also available (see website).

¶¶ FOOD & DRINK

The Laird's Kitchen Tearoom Delgatie Castle AB53 5TD ⌖ delgatiecastle.com/the-lairds-kitchen ⏱ 10.00–16.00 daily. Although this cosy café with teapot-crammed alcoves and tiny wooden tables is located within Delgatie Castle, visitors can drop in without having to take a castle tour. Serves fresh cakes and scones, hot drinks including vintage afternoon teas, and lunch dishes such as Cullen skink and sandwiches.

6 FYVIE CASTLE

AB53 8JS ⊙ Apr–Dec 10.30–16.30 Thu–Sun; Nov–Dec hours differ; National Trust
for Scotland

Winding gravel paths lead up to the front entrance and gardens of creamy pink Fyvie Castle, 12½ miles south of Delgatie. It's an imposing fortress around 800 years old, surrounded by the River Ythan, stretches of bogland and a small loch. Over the years, it's swelled in size as different owners made their own contributions. According to legend, five different families – Preston, Meldrum, Seton, Gordon and Leith – built each of Fyvie Castle's five towers. This isn't true, although each family's presence is clearly visible in the collection of clan crests on many of the ceilings.

Join a guided tour to explore the castle and you'll see an astonishing number of portraits. These include one of the world's largest collections of works by renowned Scottish artist Sir Henry Raeburn. Fyvie also has one of the finest stone wheel staircases in Scotland. Although tightly coiled like many castle staircases, this one is wide enough for several people to ascend it while standing abreast. It was built in the 1590s by Alexander Seton, Chancellor of Scotland, and the widest of the stone steps measures 10ft. It's said the Gordons once rode their horses up the stairs for a wager, no doubt giving anyone coming down quite the shock.

"Each family's presence is clearly visible in the collection of clan crests on many of the ceilings."

Despite the castle's size and grandeur, many of the rooms feel warm and cosy. Even so, like all good castles, Fyvie has its fair share of ghosts. The most famous is Dame Lilias Drummond, also known as the 'Green Lady'. Lilias was the first wife of Alexander Seton. When she didn't give birth to a son and heir, Alexander kept her captive as 'punishment' and she eventually starved to death. Just a few weeks later, the delightful Alexander married his second wife, Grizel Leslie. On the night of their marriage, the couple heard sighs through the window and in the morning discovered the words 'D Lilies Drummond' etched in the stone on the outside of the windowsill. This is still visible today in the Drummond Room, and it's said that if you catch a random whiff of roses it means the Green Lady isn't far away. If I'd been Lilias, I'd have done far worse to Alexander than a windowsill doodle…

The castle's gardens, sheltered within stone wall partitions, include a Scottish fruit garden and a space dedicated to American trees such as red alder and moose maple, each with a plaque about their properties and uses. This is a particularly good picnic spot, with benches dotted around the clearing and lots of shade from the towering trees.

St Peter's Parish Church

Just over a mile south of Fyvie Castle, at the eastern end of Fyvie village, you'll see a grey stone wall around a churchyard. Built in 1808, St Peter's Parish Church stands on raised land, providing elevated views over a sloping cemetery. The west side of the church looks particularly impressive as the land in front of it drops steeply, requiring a staircase from the roadside to the doors. Its front face is a mirror image, with a pair of double-leafed doors standing side by side, matching pointed arch windows above and two small bells in the bellcote at the top. One of the bells is dated 1809 and the other is inscribed with the words: 'Jan Burgherhuys made me in 1609. Glory be to God alone.'

Some intriguing features are located on the church's back wall, or east gable. Built within the wall itself are four stones far larger than their surrounding granite blocks, loosely arranged in a crucifix shape. The longest was probably the shaft from a Celtic cross, while the other three are Pictish stones. Above the cross is the Rothiebrisbane Stone, carved with a horseshoe symbol over a disc and named after the nearby garden it was moved from. Left of the cross shaft is the Baldyquash Stone, bearing symbols including the Pictish beastie, mirror and crescent. On the right is the incomplete Kirkyard Stone, showing a double disc with an eagle.

Above the stones is the **Tiffany Window**, depicting Archangel St Michael. It was built by American artist Louis Comfort Tiffany, who was best known for his stained-glass work. St Michael stands in armour, wings spread behind him, and is holding a sword in one hand and a banner bearing what looks like the St George's flag in the other. This might seem strange in a Scottish church, but during the Middle Ages St Michael was regarded as the patron of knights. Therefore, the flag most likely represents the Crusaders' banner, which has the same red cross on a white field as the English flag.

1 Delgatie Castle. **2** Fyvie Castle. **3** Loanhead of Daviot Stone Circle. ▶

The Tiffany Window commemorates Lieutenant Percy Forbes-Leith of Fyvie Castle, who died of typhoid fever in 1900 while serving in the British Army during the Boer War. The window was given to the church by American friends of Percy's father, Alexander Forbes-Leith. Because the secret method of producing Tiffany glass was lost after the death of the last family member, the window is now considered priceless.

If you'd like to see the interior of the church, you could either attend a Sunday service or contact the minister (🅕 Friends of Fyvie Church).

7 LOANHEAD OF DAVIOT STONE CIRCLE

Gordon District Daviot Campsite 🔲 birthdays.card.pastels

Travelling south towards Inverurie, you'll reach another of Aberdeenshire's stone circles. I visited this one just as the sun was setting and the rough surfaces of the stones were glistening in yellow light.

Measuring 67ft in diameter, Loanhead of Daviot is a Neolithic structure (4,300–2,000BC) consisting of eight solitary standing stones marking the perimeter and a huge horizontal recumbent lying between two flankers. Unusually, it also contains a striking doughnut shape in the centre made up of dozens of smaller rocks, their edges blended together by moss. In the centre of the doughnut is a bare patch of ground, perhaps marking a place to stand during ancient rituals of the past. Who knows exactly what happened here, but the site was certainly held in high regard by those before us.

Beside the stone circle are the remnants of an ancient cemetery, visible as two stone crescents only around a foot thick. Excavated in the 1930s, it's believed the cemetery was probably used c1500BC. The cremated remains of around 30 people have been unearthed here, including a man clutching a stone pendant.

Loanhead of Daviot is located 6½ miles outside Inverurie. Just north of the small settlement of Daviot, before the national speed limit signs, you'll see a tiny sign for the stone circle on the right.

THE GARIOCH

The Garioch is one of Aberdeenshire's smallest administrative areas and sits right in the centre of the region, sharing a border with the west side of Aberdeen City. Characterised by agricultural land, it consists of the large, central town of Inverurie and a string of satellite villages and roadside hamlets. With a high concentration of Pictish stones and sacred sites, including a crumbling hillfort and a 10ft-tall Greek goddess, there's more here than just ploughed fields and hedgerows.

8 INVERURIE & AROUND

🏠 **Banks of Ury** (page 319)

Inverurie, the Garioch capital, is corralled on two sides by the rivers Don and Urie (or Ury), which converge just south of the town. It's a large settlement yet has pockets of history, nature and heritage all within walking distance of its wide high street. Many of the buildings along here have two halves: modern shopfronts below and handsome granite faces above. You could fill a couple of days exploring Inverurie's heritage centre, riverside park and range of stand-alone historic sites before venturing further afield.

The focus of the town centre is at the northern end of High Street. Three main roads merge at a roundabout beside the war memorial – kept in a little gated green with trees and lined flower beds – and **Inverurie Town Hall**. This Baroque-styled building dominates the eye as you approach it from the south. Built in 1862 from grey granite, it has a symmetrical frontage with tall bay windows and a white clocktower.

The B9001 runs through the centre of Inverurie and it's here that you'll find most food and accommodation options. It's only around half a mile from one end of the High Street to the other, making the town easily walkable.

North of the Town Hall, on the site of the old railway works, is **Garioch Heritage Centre** (Loco Works Rd, AB51 4FY ✆ 01467 621855 ⬧ gariochheritage.co.uk ⊙ check website for details; free entry). This is the place to go for a proper introduction to the region's history. Its striking frontage has beige blocks with powder blue double doors. Downstairs is a gift shop, an exhibition space for temporary shows and a café serving sandwiches, scones and hot drinks. The upstairs gallery is an airy space

"Many of the buildings along here have two halves: modern shopfronts below and handsome granite faces above."

filled with Garioch Heritage Society's collections of tools, photos, maps, sound recordings and information boards. Exhibits are organised into groups, including farming, medicine, children and military life. Many of the items are recognisable, if a little different to modern equivalents,

BRANDSBUTT STONE

/// remarried.costumed.admit

Just over a mile from Inverurie Town Hall is a piece of ancient history as unexpected as the stone circle in the middle of Aviemore (page 32). The Brandsbutt Stone is a Pictish symbol slab, but instead of sitting in open countryside like many others, it's within a small green beside Gordon Terrace in the northwest end of town. Pull into the lay-by beside the green and you should be able to spot it under a couple of trees. A winding serpent symbol is clearly visible on its cracked surface, as well as the hatched lines of the mysterious Ogham alphabet running up its left side. Above the serpent is a crescent overlapped with a V-shaped rod.

The stone was apparently once part of a Bronze Age circle of standing stones that was sadly destroyed some time before 1866. The stones were broken and built into field walls, but fragments of the Brandsbutt Stone have since been put back together and it stands complete again today.

but some were completely alien to me. On the table of mystery items I had to consult the answer sheet to identify a bizarre wooden object with mean-looking pincers. It turned out to be not a torture device but a glove stretcher. I enjoyed the cabinet about curling, which has been played in the Garioch for generations; during winters in the 20th century, tennis courts in Inverurie were flooded to create an icy surface for play.

Having all this history located within the old locomotive works makes the experience even more authentic. The works were closed in 1969, and 48 years later the centre opened in the renovated Carriage and Waggon Workshop. To keep the old railway industry alive, elements such as the 20-ton crane once used to manoeuvre machinery are still present inside.

On the other side of the railway tracks from the heritage centre, and reachable on a footpath leading off Oldmeldrum Road, is **Ury Riverside Park**. I was once greeted here by half a dozen skylarks doing their trademark routine – hovering in the air with shard wings fluttering while they sang a constant burble that lessened the drone of traffic.

The park lies on part of a floodplain and has both rustling, hip-high grass and short tussocks barely above ground. There are patches of woodland and wildflower meadow too, and the river hairpins back and forth along the eastern edge. Walkers and cyclists can explore the park using a network of tarmac and gravel paths – keep to these paths from April to August to avoid disturbing ground-nesting birds and insects. A mix of native trees such as rowan, hazel and birch have been planted to encourage a greater range of wildlife to thrive here.

An intriguing historical site three quarters of a mile south of the town centre is **Inverurie Cemetery**. Its most obvious feature is a huge grass mound standing over 50ft high, looking like a cat under a duvet. Behind this mound is a slightly smaller one, and together they're known as the **Bass of Inverurie**.

In the 12th century, a motte and bailey castle was built on top of these mounds – the motte on the larger one and the bailey on 'Little Bass'. The mounds themselves were natural but their banks were steepened and a ditch was dug around the perimeter to prevent attackers. Now both mounds are bare, but you can still stand on top of the larger one by ascending a steep staircase cut into the grass bank. From up here you have elevated views across the River Urie to the north and over the cyclically-arranged headstones to the south.

"Its most obvious feature is a huge grass mound standing over 50ft high, looking like a cat under a duvet."

Back at the base of the steps, walk all the way around the Bass and on the other side you'll see a glass cabinet tucked between the two mounds. Encased inside are four granite **Pictish stones**. A horse is carved on the far right stone, but it's now faded and difficult to make out. The deeply carved double disc in the stone beside it is much easier to see. The stones were built into the walls of a medieval church that once stood in the cemetery but was demolished. Luckily the stones were recovered and placed here.

Situated on the B993 just north of where the River Urie joins the River Don, the Bass is best accessed by walking south down the B9001 and bearing left at the traffic lights. Continue straight for a quarter of a mile and once you pass under the railway bridge you'll see the cemetery on the left.

Heading south from the town centre, across the River Don, will take you to Port Elphinstone, a small suburb of Inverurie. About 150yds down Mill Road, looking a little out of place within view of a petrol garage and busy roundabout, is **Broomend of Crichie Stone Circle**. It's set within a clearly defined circular henge but contains only three stones, so I guess it's more of a stone triangle. One of them is carved with Pictish symbols, dated AD600, and was moved here in the 19th century after its original site, some 50yds away, was quarried for railway ballast.

In one way it's better that Broomend of Crichie is in situ where it can be admired by passers-by instead of being locked away in a museum cabinet. However, in this case, exposure to the elements in an open field has taken its toll. The carvings are now very worn, but a close look reveals the faint outlines of a crescent and the same V-rod symbol as in the Brandsbutt Stone (page 232), with a Pictish beastie lying horizontally across the top.

Three miles northwest of Inverurie is a hexagonal tower made from large black and rusty red stone blocks. About halfway up is a series of crests around its circumference and below them is the date of the Battle of Harlaw, 24 July 1411. The **Harlaw Monument** (📍 pinging.nibbled. sweeper) was designed by Aberdeen architect William Kelly and erected in 1914. A metal plaque set into a stone plinth beside the parking lay-by tells the story of a bloody clash between Highlanders and Lowlanders. It took place on nearby heathland and both sides claimed victory. Provost Robert Davidson, commemorated in an inscription around the top of the monument, led townspeople from Aberdeenshire but succumbed to the conflict. To get here, follow the B9001 north out of town and follow signs to the monument. As you turn a bend, it appears at the roadside, jutting 40ft into the sky.

🍴 FOOD & DRINK

The Drouthy Laird Blackhall Rd, AB51 3QT 🖋 01467 670790 🖎 thedrouthylaird.co.uk ⏲ Wed–Sun. Family-run pub and restaurant serving wholesome British dishes such as steak and Guinness pie and fresh Atlantic haddock. Breakfast also served on weekends (10.00–noon Sat & Sun), and there's a Sunday carvery (noon–20.00). There's an emphasis on live, local music, including a weekend DJ and live band events. Afternoon tea available if pre-booked online.

Spice of Life Market PI, AB51 3XN 🖋 01467 621144 🖎 spiceoflifeinverurieonline.com ⏲ noon–14.00 & 17.00–22.00 Wed–Mon. Highly regarded Indian restaurant with vibrant décor and food, beautifully presented with sauce added in swirls and patterns around the plate. Dishes include classic favourites, a range of breads and combo platters.

Via Roma Market PI, AB51 3PY 🖋 01467 621378 🖎 romarestaurant.co.uk ⏲ 17.00–22.00 Sun–Fri, noon–15.00 & 17.00–22.00 Sat. I highly recommend this cosy little place, which serves authentic Italian cuisine and has romantically low lighting. You can order take-away from Via Roma Express next door.

◀ **1** Bennachie. **2** Inverurie War Memorial. **3** East Aquhorthies Stone Circle. **4** Kintore in the snow, from Tuach Hill.

9 EAST AQUHORTHIES STONE CIRCLE

/// growl.quieter.rust

Easily accessible and wonderfully complete, East Aquhorthies is one of the North East's best-preserved examples of a recumbent stone circle. Measuring 64ft in diameter, it dates from the Bronze Age and consists of nine solitary standing stones, a broad recumbent and two upright flankers. A low, moss-fuzzed stone wall surrounds the circle, thought to have been added perhaps as recently as the 19th century.

"The stone closest to the triplet of shallow steps leading into the circle is red beneath its lichen crust."

Each stone is a different shape – some finish with tapered points while others are broad and blunt. Each is deeply encrusted with blooms of white, yellow and mint green lichens. The stone closest to the triplet of shallow steps leading into the circle is red beneath its lichen crust – it has a marbled, crackle quartz appearance with criss-crossed red veins. Others have etched lines across their flat faces. The recumbent is made of red granite, most likely quarried from nearby Bennachie (page 239). Its two standing flankers are grey granite. In front of the recumbent are two smaller blocks that make the inner side of the horizontal slab look like an altar space, perhaps giving an indication of its historic uses.

The stone circle was once called Easter Aquhorthies, and despite Historic Scotland now referring to it as East Aquhorthies you might still see references to the older name. The word itself derives from Gaelic, but it's unclear whether it means 'Field of Prayer' or 'Field of the Pillar Stone'. These sites must have held great importance to prehistoric communities, judging by how much time and effort was required to manoeuvre stones weighing several tons into specific positions.

East Aquhorthies is located in open farmland three miles west of Inverurie, signposted off the A96 roundabout as just 'Aquhorthies Stone Circle'. From the car park, it's a quarter of a mile to the stones up a gentle incline. Rather than heading straight back after having a look, it's worth extending your walk into a circular that loops through woodland. To begin, walk west along a mud track on the circle's southern edge. When the path passes under some trees, turn left just before a bench and follow a narrower trail south into a patch of Sitka spruce forest, descending gently.

After about 200yds, turn right on to a more established track. The trail bends to the right soon after and you'll be walking between a line of beech trees on the left and the edge of the Sitka woodland on the right. As you reach the corner of the field, cut through the trees and continue straight up to the fence line, where you'll emerge at an established path. Turn right to rejoin the start of your outward route.

10 KINTORE

The small town of Kintore lies four miles south of Inverurie. Its name comes from the Gaelic *Ceann-an-torr*: *ceann* meaning 'head' or 'end' and *torr* meaning 'hill'. This probably refers to Tuach Hill, a green space accessed by footpaths at the southern side of town, surrounded by the Tuach Burn.

A largely residential area, the main reason to stop in Kintore is to see the splendid granite **Town House** on The Square. Since being completed in 1747, the building has served as a court room, jail, post office, police station and school, but now it's used as commercial offices. Twin staircases curl up to a front door on the first floor, leading into the council chamber. A clock juts upwards in the centre and you can see the coat of arms of the Earl of Kintore's family – the Keiths – at the point where the two staircases meet. A short, triangular stone stands several feet in front

"Kintore was given a Royal Charter in the 10th century, making it one of Scotland's earliest Royal Burghs."

of the staircases and has the same crest and 'Kintore 2000' printed on it, marking the Millennium. Also in this square is a mottled pink-and-black marble fountain, banked at the bottom by a ring of stacked pebbles.

Kintore was given a Royal Charter in the 10th century, making it one of Scotland's earliest Royal Burghs. For a small town, its range of archaeological discoveries is vast and has included Neolithic pottery, a Roman camp and prehistoric roundhouses. One ancient artefact that visitors can see here today is a Pictish stone inside the courtyard of **Kintore Parish Church**, across the road from the Town House. Above the roadside gates is an angular white arch serving as the town's war memorial, with the names of those lost printed on either side. Like many buildings in the region, the church is made of large granite blocks and has pyramid-shaped pinnacles on each corner. Above the double-leafed door on the west gable is a narrow bellcote. Each of the pointed arch windows has a white lace design across the front. Built in 1819, the church was designed by Archibald Simpson, who was also involved with renovations at Haddo House (page 223) and many other buildings throughout the North East.

The Pictish stone is tucked down on the right side of the church gates, close to the perimeter wall. It has a crescent and Pictish beastie on its front face and a salmon and cauldron on its back face. All the symbols are faded and tricky to make out, but the diagrams on the plaque help to pick out the main lines.

11 STONE CIRCLES IN SOUTH GARIOCH

Some of Aberdeenshire's many stone circles are tucked away on private land, but there are three easily accessible examples towards the southern border of the Garioch, eight miles south of Kintore. They all date to the Bronze Age, making them around 4,000 years old.

Stone circles were often placed prominently on the brows of hills, in clear view of the sun and moon, so they could be used to chart the seasons like prehistoric calendars. **Midmar Stone Circle** is unusual, as instead of being perched prominently on a hill it's located within Midmar Parish Churchyard (▥ whiplash.given.corded). The circle has five solitary stones and a horizontal recumbent with a flanker stone on each side. These flankers are particularly intriguing as they bend inwards, a bit like

"The monoliths stand in a jumbled order like a family photo, and it's suspected that at least one has been moved."

fangs. It's a peculiar juxtaposition to see an ancient monument – looking a little vampiric I might add – beside a Christian place of worship. Built in 1787 to replace another church some distance away, Midmar Kirk is made from old stone blocks and has been given dabs of colour with periwinkle blue doors and window frames. It's not known exactly what the motive was for choosing a location practically on top of the stone circle, although perhaps it was an attempt to quash old pagan beliefs.

Stone circles of this type are usually arranged in size order, with the smallest stones furthest from the recumbent. This isn't the case at Midmar though, where the monoliths stand in a jumbled order like a family photo, and it's suspected that at least one has been moved. To get here, take the turning to Midmar Church on the B9119; there's a little parking area under the trees, past a stone wall.

Just over a mile southeast along the B9119 from Midmar is **Sunhoney Stone Circle** (▥ songbirds.leans.pigtails). This one's in a far more conventional spot, located in the crosshairs between four square fields. Sunhoney has nine solitary stones and a wide but short recumbent with its two flankers. The ground inside the circle is completely grown over with grass, making it look unkempt in the best way. As it's surrounded on all sides by farmland, it's refreshing that this site has been largely left alone, sheltered within a ring of trees. Aside from the whisper of the road, the only sounds are hidden great tits overhead.

Sunhoney is a trickier stone circle to find but only takes ten minutes to access on foot. From Midmar, turn left on to the B9119 and after a mile you'll see a tiny sign for Sunhoney Farm on the left. While it's possible to drive up the track here and park at the end, space is limited and it's important not to obstruct any farm traffic. Instead, head to an established car park down the track

"Aside from the whisper of the road, the only sounds are hidden great tits overhead."

opposite the farm turning. Return to the road on foot and cross over, following the farm track past some cottages until you reach a sign for Sunhoney pointing through a gate. The stones appear about 200yds further up.

On the border of the Garioch, five miles east of Sunhoney, is **Cullerlie Stone Circle** (▥ moderated.selling.contact). This also sits beside a farm and is one of those surprise features you wouldn't think to find at the roadside. The main circle is made up of eight boulders but unusually it also has eight smaller circles within it, made from a mixture of rocks and pebbles. Excavated in 1934, the eight cairns are thought to have been used as cremated burial sites. The circle is signposted off the B9125, just south of the hamlet of Garlogie.

12 BENNACHIE

Forestry & Land Scotland ⌖ forestryandland.gov.scot/visit/bennachie-visitor-centre

Bennachie is the collective name of a group of large hills some 13 miles west of Inverurie. At 1,732ft, **Oxen Craig** is the highest point, but many visitors also make a beeline for the Pictish fort on **Mither Tap** (1,699ft), a more distinctive, knobbly summit. You can reach this via four different car parks surrounding the hill, but first time visitors are best off starting at **Bennachie Visitor Centre** (▥ headrest.croutons.animals

⊘ bennachievisitorcentre.org.uk ☉ Apr–Oct 10.00–16.30 daily). This is situated on the east side of the hill range and has toilets, a gift shop, education resources and trail leaflets.

The Centre is thoughtfully catered to children with interactive screens, games, books, a forest kitchen and nature table. Here you can also learn how people have lived and worked on Bennachie for thousands of years. This is evident not just from the Pictish fort but also the remains of stone walls built by 19th-century settlers, visible on the 2½-mile Colony Trail. From the visitor centre, you'll be on the shortest route to Mither Tap via the 3¾-mile Timeline Trail, although the reduced distance is counteracted by a steeper climb.

Many people come to Bennachie for a hike, but there are several shorter waymarked trails around the visitor centre where you can enjoy the sight of those hulking hills without the slog. One of these is the all-access **Discovery Trail**, looping behind the visitor centre through mixed woodland for half a mile. Dotted throughout this short circular are posts with engraved wildlife for children to take rubbings from – collect paper and crayons from the visitor centre before you set off. This trail reminds me of Abernethy (page 48), with tall pines obscured at the roots by thick clumps of heather. In spring I see willow warblers, chiffchaffs, treecreepers and woodpeckers here.

Each of the other three car parks has its own version of the Mither Tap walk. To the northwest is **Back o'Bennachie** (⧈ dressy.sheepish.putter), which takes in Oxen Craig on the way. At **Rowantree** (⧈ degrading. prancing.clustered), three miles north of the visitor centre, it's a more gradual journey along the Maiden Causeway – a popular starting point for families. **Donview** (⧈ division.steadier.flinches), five miles southwest of the centre, has another, less known, summit on the way to Mither Tap called Millstone Hill. This stands at 1,341ft, so only take on this route if you're ready for a big day out. Back o'Bennachie has pay and display parking but Rowantree and Donview are free.

Although none of the individual summits at Bennachie are tall enough to be Munros (elevations of 3,000ft or more), the mountaineering risks of hazardous terrain and unpredictable conditions still apply. Wear appropriate clothes and footwear, and be aware of potentially dangerous weather.

---

1 Dunnideer Castle. **2** The Picardy Symbol Stone. **3** The Maiden Stone. ▶

Maiden Stone

III supported.hinted.deeply ☺ covered during winter

About two miles north of Bennachie Visitor Centre is another fine example of a Pictish symbol slab called the Maiden Stone. Standing just over 10ft tall, this impressive structure is made of red granite and dates to the 8th century. It's an example of a Class II Pictish stone, meaning it features both Pictish and Christian symbols. On one side is a Celtic cross and on the other is a range of symbols including a Pictish beastie, mirror, double-sided comb and a centaur-like figure.

There's a triangular notch missing from one side of the column, alluding to an **eerie legend**. The story goes that a maiden placed a bet with a stranger, saying she could bake a bannock – a type of flatbread – before he could build a road to the summit of Bennachie by sunset. Unfortunately for the maiden this stranger was the Devil, so he won the bet and came back for his prize. The maiden attempted to escape but the Devil turned her to stone. It's said the stone's notch is the place where he seized her.

There's another intriguing stone sculpture 100yds from the Maiden Stone. Head west along the road verge and look through the trees on your right before you reach a driveway. She's standing within the grounds of a private house so stay on the road, but you should be able to spot a stone woman between the trees. This is the **Statue of Persephone** and there are a few parallels with the Maiden Stone. The Greek goddess Persephone was also known as a maiden, and in this depiction she's holding a mirror similar to the one in the Pictish carving. She was completed in 1961 by sculptor Sean Crampton using over eight tons of millstone grit.

"Unfortunately for the maiden this stranger was the Devil, so he won the bet and came back for his prize."

Lots of Crampton's work was influenced by religious and spiritual themes. The statue is wonderfully curvy and has the same blank stone eyes as other sculptures of Greek deities. She's wearing a silky dress lying in coiled folds across her body. The fact she's concealed in trees makes her even more enchanting.

There's a row of parking bays with interpretation boards beside the Maiden Stone. Visitors should be aware that the stone is enclosed in a protective box during winter so can't be seen at all. There's a QR code at the site so you can access an online 3D model of the stone at any time, but this isn't the same as seeing the real thing.

13 DUNNIDEER CASTLE

🏠 **Edgehill B&B** (page 319)

⏹ closet.meal.initiates

The ruined castle of Dunnideer stands on top of the Hill of Dunnideer, just under two miles from the small village of Insch, on the western edge of the Garioch. Visible for miles around, its largest remaining wall looks like a 30ft-tall slice of toast with a hole in the middle.

Evidence of a settlement dating back to the Iron Age has been found here, but it's the ruined castle, one of the oldest tower houses in Scotland, that's the most visible. Sources differ on its exact origin, ranging from Pictish nobleman Gregory the Great in AD890 to David, Earl of Huntingdon and Garioch in AD1178. However, the first official written evidence of a castle on this site puts it in the mid-13th century.

"The ground is also studded with rabbit holes, so watch your feet to avoid any comedy trips."

Circling the wall fragments are the remains of defence lines from an earlier hillfort, although these are mainly stony banks and difficult to make out. The innermost line includes a vitrified stone wall – vitrified stone has a glassy appearance caused by exposure to intense heat. This happened as a result of the timber framework within the wall being burned.

From the roadside, the castle appears deceptively close, but the grassy access track from the car park (on the bend of Western Road) is steep. Luckily there's plenty of countryside to admire if you need to catch your breath. The ground is also studded with rabbit holes, so watch your feet to avoid any comedy trips.

Once you arrive at the top, other fragments of the ruin appear. Several pieces of crumbling wall are just tall enough to use as a windbreak on gustier days. From up here you'll have panoramic views over patches of woodland, farmland and clusters of houses. Dunnideer Castle is a scheduled Historic Scotland Monument and protected by law, so please don't stand on any of the walls. Note that fires and camping are also prohibited. Take care coming down – as the grass is cropped almost smooth by those bob-tailed scamps, it doesn't have much grip.

¶¶ FOOD & DRINK

Butterfly Effect Commerce St, Insch AB52 6JB ✐ 01464 829276 ￭ butterflyeffectinsch
☉ 10.00–16.00 Tue–Sat. This tiny café is subtly placed in the otherwise nondescript village
of Insch, but provides a one-stop-shop for stocking up on sustainable supplies and cosying
up for a hot drink and snack. Combining a café and refillery, there's a variety of options on
the breakfast and lunch menus including pancakes with your choice of sauce and toppings,
such as bubble gum, Biscoff and unicorn glitter, and some wild tea flavours. Keep an eye on
its Facebook page for events such as cupcake decorating.

14 PICARDY SYMBOL STONE

/// enough.televise.opponent

Just over 6ft tall, the Picardy Stone stands within a square metal fence
close to the edge of a farmed field – you can get a closer look at it by
hopping over a stile. On the side of the stone facing the field, Pictish
symbol carvings are clearly visible: a double disc, a coiled serpent, a
round mirror with a thick handle and several Z-rods. The Z-rod shows
up on a few Pictish stones – it has tiny curls twisting away from both
of its horizontal lines and a teardrop-shaped spear head at one end. It's
often seen overlapping a double disc or serpent – in fact the majority
of double discs have Z-rods accompanying them and the serpent is
the only animal symbol associated with rods. As the rod looks like a
broken spear, it could either represent death or a ruthless warrior who
was a breaker of their enemies' spears. Although the meaning of these
beautifully intricate symbols remains largely a mystery, it's believed they
could represent particular people linked to the stone and what their
tribal status might have been.

The Picardy Stone stands on the remains of a small burial cairn dating
back to around AD600. Very few Pictish symbol stones mark burial
places, making this one particularly special. It's also still in its original
position, unlike stones such as the one at Broomend of Crichie (page
233) that has been relocated. As time passes, some of these ancient
carvings are becoming more and more difficult to see, but the Picardy
Stone is a pristine example and it's hard to believe it was carved some
1,400 years ago.

You can find the stone three miles from Dunnideer, by passing
through Insch and following Largie Road north.

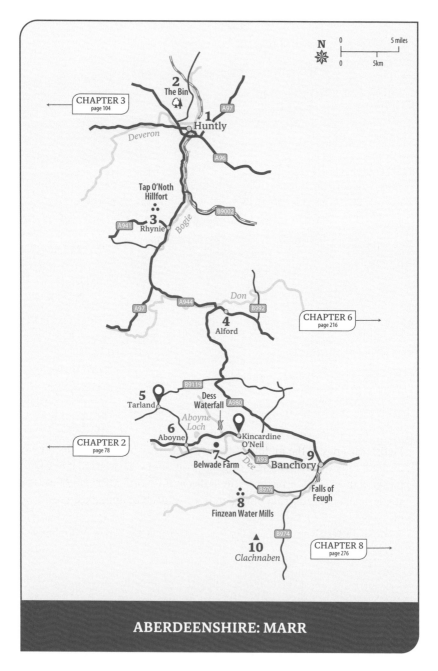

N

0   5 miles

0   5km

2
The Bin

CHAPTER 3
page 104

A97

1
Huntly

Deveron

A96

Tap O'Noth
Hillfort

B9002

Bogie

A941

3
Rhynie

Don

A944

B992

A97

CHAPTER 6
page 216

4
Alford

B9119

5
Tarland

Dess
Waterfall

A980

Aboyne
Loch

6
Aboyne

Kincardine
O'Neil

CHAPTER 2
page 78

7
Belwade Farm

Dee

A93

9
Banchory

Falls of
Feugh

B976

8
Finzean Water Mills

10
Clachnaben

B974

CHAPTER 8
page 276

ABERDEENSHIRE: MARR

7
ABERDEENSHIRE: MARR

After rushing down from the mountains, the rivers Dee and Don run parallel across Marr on their way east to Aberdeen and the coast. Like neighbouring Formartine and the Garioch, much of Marr is farmland – though it might not seem the most intriguing of landscapes at first, on closer inspection you'll find it rich in ancient and often isolated landmarks, making it particularly satisfying from a Slow point of view.

Marr encompasses a vast chunk of western Aberdeenshire, including all of Royal Deeside and as far as Ben Macdui in the Cairngorms. Because the national park is covered in its own chapters, for the purposes of this chapter I've focused on everything up to the park boundary. The main settlements are Huntly in the north, Alford in the centre, and Aboyne and Banchory at the southern end.

In my experience, this is not a part of Aberdeenshire where visitors accumulate – they're typically drawn either side, to Braemar and Aberdeen. With a bit of digging and exploring on foot, you'll be rewarded with unexpected surprises here: waterfalls submerged in woodlands; Pictish carvings in the middle of fields (where they belong, I say); and disused water mills still in their original positions by the weirs that once powered them. One of my favourite walks in the North East is in Marr, at Clachnaben; the surrounding glen is a vast daub of unmarked green on the map, within squinting distance of the Cairngorms. In fact, when it comes to relatively short walks with photo-worthy views, Marr has plenty to offer.

GETTING AROUND

Because of this area's rural nature, it can take some time getting between the groups of sites I've clustered together. Huntly sits on the A96, the main route to Aberdeen from Moray, but apart from that Marr

***i* TOURIST INFORMATION**

Banchory Library Bridge St, AB31 5SU ✆ 01330 700441
✉ banchory.library@aberdeenshire.gov.uk.

is characterised by smaller A and B roads, many of which are single lane. However, these are well-kept, quiet and bordered by countryside scenery, making driving enjoyable.

TRAINS & BUSES

I said driving was enjoyable in Marr. Public transport? Not so much. Getting from Alford to Aboyne for example – a distance of 15 miles – means a four-hour bus trip to Aberdeen (26 miles east) then back out to Aboyne. Accessing Banchory and Tarland from Alford requires the same Aberdeen detour. The only **train station** is in Huntly, but it sits between Keith and Inverurie so bypasses the rest of this chapter area. Don't let this dampen your enthusiasm though. I've deliberated chosen locations that offer multiple walking routes and things to see, so once you've based yourself at a particular town or village you can spend a while there.

The Stagecoach 201 **bus** is handy for linking some of the sites I've featured. This travels from Aberdeen to Braemar with stops in Banchory, Tarland, Kincardine O'Neil (the start point for the Dess Waterfall walk I've featured) and Aboyne. The 10B stops in The Square at Huntly on its way between Inverness and Aberdeen.

WALKING & CYCLING

For those interested in long-distance routes, the 13-mile Banchory to Aboyne leg of the 41-mile **Deeside Way** crosses through the southern end of Marr. This is the longest section of the trail, with several hilly sections, but its paths are also suitable for bicycles. There are great options for short **walks** too, and I've described a number within this chapter including at The Bin, Tap O'Noth, the village of Tarland and, my personal favourite, the peaceful, forested glen of Clachnaben.

Exploring on foot and by bike in this region usually involves an open country vista, but the scenery isn't all farmland. Many circular routes also take in multi-layered woodland, butterfly-rich meadows and more intriguing topographical features such as waterfalls. **Cycling** isn't always care-free when paths are veined by tree roots or in open patches that succumb to boggy mud, but the Deeside Way and other more established trails follow wheel-friendly terrain.

HUNTLY & AROUND

Eleven miles southeast of Keith (page 120) on the A96, Huntly sits at the confluence of the rivers Deveron and Bogie, with evidence of settlements dating back to the Neolithic period. Perhaps best known for its ruined castle – easily the highlight of a visit here – Huntly is also the birthplace of Scottish author and poet **George MacDonald** (1824–1905). MacDonald was a pioneer in the genre of fantasy literature and a mentor to Lewis Carroll. Surrounding Huntly, you'll find a hillfort, forest walks and a fine showcase of Pictish stones.

1 HUNTLY

Located at the edge of the **Malt Whisky Trail** (page 19), Huntly is well-placed for exploring both the southern half of Moray and northwest Aberdeenshire. Its central square is surrounded by old stone buildings, including the post office and library. Without the parked cars, this square would look like an old-fashioned postcard. It has two small pavement islands, one with a memorial statue of Charles Gordon Lennox, 5th Duke of Richmond, and the other with a memorial fountain commemorating James Robertson, a bank agent in the 19th century. The fountain was gifted to the town by his widow in 1882; it's a striking square-shaped monument made from polished granite, with thick grey pillars at each corner and arched beams slanting upwards to meet at the top. Biblical quotes related to water are etched in gold on three sides.

Beside the post office is **Orb's Bookshop** (The Square, AB54 8BR ✆ 01466 793765 ◉ orbsbookshop.co.uk ◷ 10.00–16.00 Mon–Sat), which has a special emphasis on North East Scotland titles, both new and secondhand. When founders Annie and

"Without the parked cars, this square would look like an old-fashioned postcard."

John Lamb retired and could no longer keep the shop running, their friends from local writer's group Huntly Writers stepped in. Since then, the bookshop has been run entirely by volunteers, with profits going towards maintaining the shop and community projects.

If you turn left out of Orb's Bookshop and left again down narrow Duke Street, you'll reach **Ethical Gift Shop & Refillery** (Duke St, AB54 8DL ✆ 01466 799059 ⌂ ethicalgiftshop.uk ☉ Mon–Sat). Here you can purchase a huge variety of sustainable toiletries, stationery, clothes and even bamboo socks, as well as over 300 refillable products from dried fruit and spices to shampoo and deodorant (bring your own containers). Owners Ellie and Martyn Turner began the business in 2007 when they noticed a lack of Fairtrade items in their local area. 'We stock unique artisan products from around the world that have been made with the planet in mind,' Ellie told me. 'We also stock the work of more than 80 local artists and crafters who produce eco-friendly, recycled and sustainable items – there are no harsh chemicals or wasteful industrial plants involved.' It's a shop full of treasures and one of my favourite places in Huntly.

Half a mile north of the town centre is a playing field with a row of parking bays, convenient for a walk beside the River Deveron. This is also the best place to access the ruins of **Huntly Castle** (Castle Ave, AB54 4SH ⌂ historicenvironment.scot/visit-a-place/places/huntly-castle ☉ Apr–Sep 09.30–17.30 daily; Oct–Mar 10.00–16.00 Sat–Wed), visible through the trees. You can explore the castle on your own or join a volunteer for a guided tour, starting from the ticket kiosk.

The first thing I noticed about the castle was the jumbled arrangement of black, smoky grey and chestnut stones in its walls. Surrounding the ruin are steep grass mounds, built artificially in the 1630s for mounting cannons. There were originally six levels to Huntly Castle, although various

"Many of the doorways and windows were made from soft sandstone, which is why so many of them are now crumbling."

sections are now missing with only clues remaining in its foundations. Embedded in the ground are more stones spiralling around a well. Many of the doorways and windows were made from soft sandstone, which is why so many of them are now crumbling.

Three different castles, home to six earls of Huntly and possibly three marquises, have stood on this site: a motte in 1188, a tower house in 1400 and the current castle since 1445. The most dramatic changes came from the 6th Earl; inspired by the châteaux of France, he redesigned the

◀ **1** View towards Tap o'Noth Hillfort, Rhynie. **2** Huntly Castle.

building in the French image to celebrate his new title of 1st Marquis of Huntly in 1599.

Along the wall of one of the corridors are scratchings of medieval graffiti. While some are scribbled letters, others are intricate designs of boats and men dressed for battle. At the end of this walkway is the dungeon pit, where two mannequins slouch at the bottom looking very sorry for themselves. The only living occupants in Huntly Castle now are bats, complementing the ruined aesthetic nicely.

¶¶ FOOD & DRINK

Café India Gordon St, AB54 8ES ✆ 01466 792667 ⌂ cafeindiahuntly.co.uk. With a long interior that creates a spacious feel, this restaurant offers wonderfully light and flavourful Indian dishes and friendly service. I indulged my sweet tooth with a Kashmiri dish made with banana and lychees.

The Merry Kettle Tea Shoppe Duke St, AB54 8DL ✆ 01466 792108 ⨍ ⊙ Mon–Sat. A couple of doors down from the Ethical Gift Shop, this is one of those cute vintage establishments with waxy tablecloths, pastel bunting, a sign for the powder room and a tinkling bell as you walk in. Offers a selection of cakes, soups, jacket potatoes, sandwiches and burgers.

2 THE BIN

/// refills.warmers.continued ⌂ forestryandland.gov.scot/visit/the-bin

For those scrunching up their nose at the title, 'bin' is a variation of the Scots word for 'hill'. This forest, 2½ miles outside Huntly, gets its name from the 1,023ft-high hill at the northwest corner of the site, which is also called The Bin.

It's the diversity of trees that makes this place special. While padding these footpaths I spotted beech, Scots pine, Sitka spruce and silver birch, each with a combination of silky saplings and wizened grannies. Among these are boulders as large as tables and also some of the country's oldest firs, originating from the 1840s.

Several trails start from the large car park (note that overnight parking is not allowed here). If it's just rained it can be boggy in places, but the paths are even and wide enough for horses. You can hike up the yellow-waymarked **Gallon of Water Trail** – a four-mile circular through the forest to a viewpoint at The Bin. Standing on a platform of rock, undulating with puddle-filled wells and spongy tussocks, you can admire a lumpy landscape of pine woodland and scraps of farmland topped with turbines. The gallon of water reference comes from a pool near the viewpoint that's thought to have healing powers, but you have to work hard to earn that magic because I couldn't find it.

This trail is described as strenuous but I wouldn't say so; aside from the occasional steeper rocky section, the route generally follows forestry vehicle roads, wide gravel tracks and winding footpaths at gentle inclines.

On the eastern side of the forest, shorter plods can be enjoyed on the blue-coded **Queen Tree Trail** and red-coded **Ferny Knowe Trail**, which run in two overlapping loops. Stone walls camouflaged in moss trace the direction of the trails, sinking out of sight beneath carpets of orange beech leaves.

Walking the Queen Tree Trail involves following the first half of the Ferny Knowe Trail. After stepping off of this shorter loop and continuing east on Queen Tree, you'll soon see a thick grey slab of a bench on the right. Beyond this is **White Wood**. Described as a living monument to peace, the wood was developed by artist Caroline Wendling and the community of Huntly as a place to reflect. It combines oaks from Germany, stones from France and soil from Scotland, and all of the native trees, wildflowers and shrubs here have an element of white to represent peace. Currently it's an open clearing of oak saplings surrounded by high grass, but in centuries to come the wood will be thriving and dense. Follow the indented line in the grass over planks and tussocks to a 5ft-long boulder in the centre of the clearing: 'White Wood' has been etched in capital letters on its broad flat face.

Further along the Queen Tree Trail is a half-mile path leading to the B9022 just north of Huntly, or you can bear left up a brief steep section to carry on through the forest on the blue trail. At various points you can peek out over open fields, where you might spot roe deer browsing. On the Ferny Knowe Trail is a lookout point with a picnic bench and views towards Huntly over open farmland.

The Bin is signposted as 'The Bin Forest Walks' just off the A96, 2½ miles northwest of Huntly.

3 RHYNIE & AROUND

⚑ **Tap o'Noth Forest Garden Farm** (page 320)

Rhynie is a small village nine miles south of Huntly, intercepted by both the A941 and A97 with the Water of Bogie running down its eastern side. The clear highlight is its collection of finely preserved Pictish stones, located next to **Rhynie Churchyard** (commented.abundance. bronzed) at the southern end of the village. Three Pictish carvings are displayed within a wooden shelter in a car park at the end of Manse Road, which reaches a dead end at the churchyard. Several symbols will be familiar from other carved stones in the area, including mirrors, combs and double discs. The Pictish beastie can be seen on the smallest one, made from pink granite, but the largest stone shows a different mythical animal with a longer neck and two flipper-like appendages.

One of the most famous Pictish stones discovered here is called the Rhynie Man and shows a figure with a goblin face and pointed beard, carrying an axe. This sadly now stands in the reception of an Aberdeen council building of all places. Luckily, another of Rhynie's Pictish discoveries, the **Craw Stane**, is still in situ. It's not in the shelter with the others but on the crest of a hill less than 500yds south.

To see it, turn away from the three stones and continue down the track to the churchyard. It's worth a brief nosey in here for the row of 18th-century gravestones leant against the back wall. Although their inscriptions are mostly illegible, some have carved skull and crossbone symbols, which supposedly reminded the living of their mortality and that, regardless of status or wealth, everyone's fate is the same. Reminders of death strike me as a trifle unnecessary on gravestones, but the carvings are beautiful and almost cartoon-like with their bubbly outlines. I was particularly taken by this engraving on one of the newer gravestones:

Take me to the mountains
For that's where I belong
Just birds and trees
And wind and leaves
And silence as my song.

To carry on to the Craw Stane, take a narrow footpath pressed against the north side of the churchyard's stone wall, leading to open fields. You'll see the stone sticking up on the hill, looking like another gravestone. For a closer look, continue up the path until you reach the A97. After passing through the wide metal gate beside the road there's another immediately to your left. Head through here, shutting it behind you, and walk uphill to the stone.

The Craw Stane is made from grey granite and believed to date from the 7th century. On its front face are the faint outlines of a Pictish beastie and a salmon carving. Over its shoulder is the heathery mound of **Tap**

o'Noth Hillfort. It might look intimidating from here but it takes less than an hour to ascend at an ambling pace. At the top you'll be rewarded by expansive views in multiple directions and an ancient Pictish fort to boot.

The walk up to Tap o'Noth begins at a small car park (⚏ workshop. agreed.dugouts) 1½ miles northwest of Rhynie on the single-lane A941. It's a three mile out-and-back route with a fairly constant but moderate incline.

From the car park, follow a hillfort sign through a gate and along a narrow path between two fields. This leads through another gate to a straight grass section branching left. In summer, this stretch is lit up by rosebay willowherb, a tall colonising plant with brilliant pink clumps of flowers shaped like candles. This species is capable of growing on burnt ground, which inspired one of its other names: fireweed. During late summer, you'll also find clumps of wild raspberries here. I don't condone hoarding whole baskets of berries as wildlife needs them more than we do, but pluck a couple to nibble as you walk because wild raspberries are so much softer and sweeter than the ones you pay for in supermarkets.

"The stonework here has been burnt, initially believed to be the result of an enemy siege."

When you reach the next gate, the trail continues right towards the hillfort, becoming rockier and skirting around the summit with views of rolling waves of pines to the left. At the top is a slightly indented rectangular platform containing the remains of the fort, bordered by a circular bank of rocks almost 10ft high in places. The time and muscle required to haul these up here is remarkable, and it's a testament to the fort's strategic position and prominence that the inhabitants went to such an effort. The stonework here has been burnt, initially believed to be the result of an enemy siege. However, the exact and thorough nature of the burning has led experts to think the walls were burnt on purpose to fuse the rocks together and strengthen the walls against attack. This process is called vitrification, and can also be seen at Dunnideer Castle (page 243).

Lying 1,847ft above sea level, Tap o'Noth is Scotland's second highest hillfort after Griam Beg in Sutherland, and also one of its largest. The site's exact age is unclear, but Iron Age objects uncovered during excavations have placed it within the range of 1000BC and AD1000.

Walk along the trodden grass path through the middle of the fort to a stone plinth, visible from the car park. This was erected in 2020 to mark a century of Girlguiding. By walking around the top you can have a look-see in every direction; the view changes from stacks of pines to sand-coloured fields interrupted by wind turbines and dry-stone walls. The Cairngorms National Park boundary lies just nine miles to the southwest, with significant summits including Lochnagar and Mount Keen, within the Glen Tanar NNR (page 90), visible from here.

CENTRAL MARR

The main village in this section is Alford, 18 miles south of Huntly. A key part of its identity stems from Aberdeen Angus cattle, and you can see lots of this farming heritage first-hand at its superb heritage centre. Fourteen miles southwest, near the Cairngorms National Park boundary, a variety of open country and woodland around the village of Tarland provides excellent walking opportunities.

4 ALFORD

Just south of the River Don and 13 miles southeast of Rhynie, Alford is a large village looking like a bunch of grapes on a map, with clusters of cul-de-sacs surrounding the central stalk of the A944. It's said to be where **Aberdeen Angus** beef originated from, and a life-size bronze statue inspired by a real bull called Jeremy Eric can be seen at the east end of the village on Aberdeen Road (🗺 growth.

"This museum keeps on going round corners and down corridors like an optical illusion."

pollution.earmarked). Sculpted by David Annand, the monument was unveiled in 2001 by the then Prince of Wales and the Queen Mother.

There's a number of independent businesses on Main Street/A944, such as the fabulous vintage shop **Evelyntreasurefinder2** (✆ 07880 790027 ◷ 10.00–16.00 Tue & Thu–Sat, noon–16.00 Sun) that sells clothes, jewellery, accessories and art. Alford's highlight lies just off this main thoroughfare: **Alford Heritage Museum** (Mart Rd ✆ 01975 562906 ⌂ alfordheritagemuseum.com ◷ Apr–Oct noon–16.00 Thu–Sun). Though it doesn't look big from the outside, this museum keeps on going round corners and down corridors like an optical illusion. Each room is dedicated to an aspect of North East heritage and culture, with specific emphasis on Alford and Donside, the area of Aberdeenshire surrounding the River Don. There are displays on farming, photography, poetry, tailoring, laundry and a room packed with old tinned foods that have familiar names but very different packaging.

The museum is housed within the old market building, where Aberdeen Angus cattle and other livestock were displayed and sold from 1905 until business ceased in 1986. Local landowners and enthusiasts rescued the building from being sold off, and the museum opened to the public in 1991, now preserving much of Alford's history. Visitors can walk through the original auction sale ring with its banked stairs encircling the pen and weighing scales still mounted on the wall.

Elsewhere in the museum is a 1930s schoolroom containing rows of wooden desks and leather satchels hung on the walls. The three-legged stool belonged to the dominie (headmaster) and has one worn leg as a result of its owner rocking back and forth. It's said if the rocking grew faster he was in a temper, serving as a warning to the children that a blackboard eraser might come flying. In the farm kitchen, there are traditional sewing machines, a tea set with crocheted cakes on china plates, and a humongous old pram that no doubt provided an effective bicep workout for the owner.

One of my favourite exhibits is a model railway that almost fills one room. The background images were taken by members of the Donside Camera Club, which gathers here weekly. The model has all the scrumptious detail you'd expect, including milk pails, golfers mid-swing and herds of tiny red deer.

"It's said if the rocking grew faster he was in a temper, serving as a warning to the children."

As well as 20th-century farming industry, Alford also has visible links to far older communities. Not far outside the village is a megalithic monument in its rightful place in the middle of nowhere (indulge me – it's been all of 18 pages since the last stone circle). There's no designated car park or signs for **Old Keig Stone Circle**, but if you park in a lay-by (🔳 regulator.penned.capillary) five miles north of Alford on an unnamed road, you'll be 300yds away. To reach the stones, walk down a grass path directly opposite the lay-by, following a line of beech trees between two fields.

It's more of a stone line than stone circle, with five standing boulders in a jagged row. The star is the recumbent; at 53 tonnes, it's the largest in

Aberdeenshire. Longer than a car and almost as tall, it was supposedly transported to this site from the Don Valley, six miles away, taking the Neolithic people who constructed the circle unimaginable effort to manoeuvre into position. To emphasise their age, all of the stones are coated in splotches of grey, black, white and tennis-ball-yellow lichen.

5 TARLAND & AROUND

🏠 **The Commercial Hotel** (page 320)

With a centre of stone-wall houses and narrow streets, the village of Tarland sits two miles from the Cairngorms National Park boundary. The Square, on the corner of Aberdeen Road, is where you'll find parking, a convenience store and Tarland Tearooms (page 262).

Before your mind wanders to tea and cake, there are two historical landmarks worth visiting on the way in to Tarland if you're approaching from the northeast via the B9119. The first is **Corse Castle** (▥ bonfires. claims.node), a 16th-century ruin half-hidden in the trees down a side road just beyond the Corse Burn. You can park in a lay-by 100yds away and walk to a gap in the fence on the left, which leads up to the ruin.

With its walls at right angles to each other and a mixture of irregularly sized and placed window frames, Corse Castle reminds me of a clump of Tetris pieces. Walk beneath the doorway to see the interior, where a menagerie of ivy, nettles and bracken grows out of the cracks. The entire spiral staircase has gone, leaving a clear view up the remaining column.

The castle belonged to the Forbes family for generations, its current form built in 1581 by William Forbes. Above the doorway is an inscription with that year, his initials and the initials of his wife, Elizabeth Strachan. William was the 4th Lord of Corse. His great-grandfather Patrick, the 1st Lord, was armour-bearer to King James III. It was to Patrick that the Barony of O'Neil and Corse was initially granted. After lots of sons named after fathers – an imaginative bunch to be sure – Corse Castle was abandoned in the 19th century, when a more contemporary mansion house was constructed elsewhere.

About 3½ miles further southwest on the B9119 is the second intriguing spot before you reach Tarland: **Culsh Earth House**. Parking isn't straightforward here as the earth house is right on the roadside, and

---

1 Tomnaverie Stone Circle. **2** The auction ring at Alford Heritage Museum. **3** St Mathuloch's Church, Tarland. **4** Corse Castle. **5** Culsh Earth House. ▶

Tomnaverie Stone Circle & Drummy Wood

✿ OS Explorer map OL59; start: The Square, Tarland AB34 4TX; ♥ NJ4812404387; 3 miles; easy.

This three-mile circular links a stone circle (surprise surprise) and Drummy Wood, which contains mountain-bike paths known as Tarland Trails. Horizontal recumbent stones are usually positioned deliberately, and in Tomnaverie's case it seems to have been laid so that Lochnagar – the broad mountain 20 miles southwest – is framed within it. At the notice board in The Square you can pick up a leaflet called 'Walks Around Tarland' that covers the range of trails on offer here (page 262), including this circular. However, I think its estimate of an hour is a big fib, fellow amblers, as I took almost two.

1 From The Square, walk south out of the village, following Bridge Street across Tarland Burn until a footpath signposted with a black waymarker branches off to the left.

2 Follow this path through several gates and across the B9094 – it continues on the other side and follows the road east for some 200yds. After crossing a stile, the path veers right away from the road to climb a short grassy hill crossed by a farm track. At the top you'll reach Tomnaverie Stone Circle. Like others in Aberdeenshire, it's perched prominently with open views in every direction. Unlike others, it has far more stones making up the outer ring and a sprinkling of additional stones within. This is because the site has gone through two phases. Originally it consisted of a central cremation pyre with a ring of kerb stones surrounding it, used as far back as 2500BC. During excavations in the 1990s, a collection of burnt soil, bone and charcoal was unearthed in the middle. The circle of standing stones, in line with what can be seen at other similar sites, came in the second phase, placed around the smaller stones. It's believed that cremation burials took place here until the 17th century.

3 The footpath continues on the other side of the stone circle. About 100yds further on, in a fenced enclosure on the right, is a Royal Observer Corps nuclear bunker used in the Cold War, visible as two stone blocks with vents. Once through the next pedestrian gate, bear left across a rough open patch to another pedestrian gate. Follow a narrow grass path downhill, over a

the brown sign for it points down a private driveway. Your best bet is to park in a lay-by next to this driveway (▥ sleepers.waxer.scribble).

Walk down a short slope from the lay-by and you'll see the entrance to the earth house behind a small grass bank. Despite being called earth houses, these underground chambers weren't lived in but used as cellars

stile built into a stone wall and around a stand of birch trees. Hop over another stile and turn right on to a vehicle track.

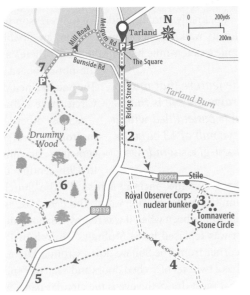

4 Follow this track for 300yds until it bends right. Bear left here to pass through another pedestrian gate and follow the edge of the next couple of fields beside a dry-stone wall.

5 When you reach the B9119, cross over and follow the next black waymarker post into Drummy Wood. This is mostly coniferous with the occasional birch bucking the trend. The path bends right before emerging at a vehicle track. Turn left on to this, then right on to a narrower footpath that appears after 100yds, just as the wide track bends in the other direction. Bear left again at the next clearing, passing between broom bushes.

6 Follow the next two waymarkers by continuing straight, ignoring two other paths branching left. In less than 400yds, the path bends left, close to the edge of the forest. Tarland appears on the right, and after 560yds you'll arrive at a parking area for Drummy Wood.

7 From here, take the single-lane road heading northeast away from the forest and, at the end, turn right on to Burnside Road. After 100yds, take the first left on to Mill Road, following it round to the right for 250yds before turning right again on to Melgum Road. In another 200yds you'll be back in The Square.

as long ago as the Iron Age. There aren't many of them left in Scotland that can be safely accessed, so switch your phone torch on and make full use of the opportunity to skulk around inside. You'll have to bend double to enter the crawlspace and follow a stone-lined corridor with a gravel floor around the corner to a dead end several feet further along.

So far there isn't any evidence to show exactly what was stored in earth houses, but the cool temperature suggests things like grain. Being so big, it's likely they were shared by a few farming families.

So, finally into Tarland. The main reason to visit this small village is for its walking trails, ranging from an all-abilities route of less than a mile to a ten-mile hike into the hills. There's a stash of trail maps beside the notice board on the eastern corner of The Square, including for Tomnaverie Stone Circle (page 260).

"The feature that most draws the eye is the circular panel filled with a honeycomb of 13 circular stained-glass windows."

Across Aberdeen Road, camouflaged in front of the stone wall surrounding a cemetery and ruined church, is a memorial to 19th-century fiddle player Peter Milne, known as the '**Tarland Minstrel**'. The church is **St Mathuloch's**, now limited to its exterior walls. The date 1762 is inscribed, although this may have been when it was renovated, not built. It fell into disrepair after it was replaced by **St Moluag's Church** in 1870 – located around the corner from The Square down Cromar Drive. This impressive building has a twin set of arched doors and a narrow spire on one side. The feature that most draws the eye is the circular panel filled with a honeycomb of 13 circular stained-glass windows of various sizes. Behind St Moluag's is **Muirton Wood**, a patch of mixed forest most easily accessed by a footpath opposite School Road, the street next to Cromar Drive.

FOOD & DRINK

Tarland Tearooms The Square, AB34 4TX ✆ 01339 880132 ⓕ. Winners of 'Best Tearoom' in the 2022 Aberdeen Business Awards, this spacious café provides the perfect boost after a long walk. I tucked into a huge omelette and crisps, or you can choose soup, bagels, paninis or a hefty slab of cake.

SOUTHERN MARR

At the bottom half of Marr you'll enter Royal Deeside – an area beside the River Dee from Braemar to Aberdeen. The following section covers 14 miles, from Aboyne in the west to Banchory in the east. Sites of interest here include a wonderful horse charity, a waterfall hidden in the forest, historic water mills beside the road and one of my favourite half-day hill walks.

6 ABOYNE

🏠 **The Boat Inn** (page 320)

Sandwiched between the River Dee to the south and a bunch of small hills to the north, Aboyne lies six miles southeast of Tarland and is one of this chapter's larger villages. A small green stretches across its central belt, near a free car park and a knot of streets lined with independent cafés and shops. The Tarland Burn cuts through to the east, drifting beneath Ballater Road before joining the Dee just outside the village.

Similar to Tarland, most of Aboyne's appeal comes from its assortment of waymarked walking trails. These range from an all-abilities 1¾-mile loop of mature oak woodland to a 6¾-mile out-and-back ascent to Mortlich Hillfort. Several of the routes follow the Deeside Way, which slices the village horizontally en route between Aberdeen and Ballater. Aboyne is home to the oldest golf club in Royal Deeside and is only four miles from Glen Tanar (page 90) and eight miles from Muir of Dinnet NNR (page 91), making it a handy base for exploring the eastern Cairngorms National Park.

My favourite spot here is **Aboyne Loch** at the northern end of the village. As the A93 bends left, just before a petrol station, there's a pedestrian path branching left under a stone bridge half-hidden in the trees. This is part of the **Old Deeside Railway Line** – follow this between the road and the golf course for half a mile to reach the loch. It's an ideal path for hot days, sheltered on both sides by silver birches, sycamores and Scots pines.

When you spot the loch, climb over a stile and follow a path to the water's edge. The loch is a wobbly C shape with a clump of trees in the centre, screening a caravan park behind. The occasional swan threads its way through mats of lily pads dotting its surface. In summer, the fringe of rosebay willowherb surrounding the loch is a magnet for bees, butterflies and dragonflies. If you stay close to the loch, another path branches back to Aboyne through the middle of the golf course. However, if like me you don't fancy 20 minutes of involuntary ducking each time a ball is struck, you might prefer to return via the more relaxing wooded path.

¶¶ FOOD & DRINK

At the Sign of the Black Faced Sheep Ballater Rd, AB34 5HN 𝒫 01339 887311 ⊘ blackfacedsheep.co.uk ⊙ Thu–Tue. Coupled with a gift shop and laid out on two banister-lined wood-floored levels, this coffee shop has just a few tables and serves breakfast, bagels, bruschetta, soup, teas and coffees, and very generous slabs of cake.

Deeside ReFill North Side Station Sq, AB34 5HX ✆ 07989 965551 ⬛ Deeside Re-fill ⊙ Tue–Sat. An ideal place for those self-catering to stock up on zero-waste pulses, spices, seeds, nuts and dried fruits, as well as household cleaning products, toiletries and more. These are all refillable using your own containers, or you can buy a glass bottle to use again.

7 BELWADE FARM

AB34 5BJ ✆ 01339 885398 ⬦ worldhorsewelfare.org/visit-us/belwade-farm ⬛ World Horse Welfare Belwade Farm ⊙ 11.00–16.00 Wed–Sun; dogs on leads allowed

Three miles east of Aboyne is this fantastic visitor attraction that's essentially Battersea Dogs & Cats Home but for horses. Of the four rescue and rehoming centres run by international charity World Horse Welfare, Belwade Farm is the only one in Scotland. Within its 170 grazing acres, there can be up to 65 horses here at any one time. Some arrive malnourished and mistreated, while others have been well-loved but left as a legacy gift in wills.

Visitors can wander freely around the site. There are a few waymarked trails stretching into surrounding woodland, but you don't have to walk far to meet some of the horses – I made a fuss of three Shetland ponies right next to the visitor centre. Beside a miniature stone circle opposite the car park, the Unicorn Trail heads through a tiny wood dotted with fairy houses and painted horseshoes that my six-year-old self would have loved. Who am I kidding, I loved it now.

As well as all the outdoor paddock space, Belwade has a large indoor school so the horses can be exercised in any weather. Visitors can watch through a gallery window inside the bistro café, or sit outside on the decking and take in the Deeside Valley views. Although the barn has restricted access, it's possible to see inside by joining a guided tour with a member of staff. These are available on selected dates and are bookable through the website.

I was taken on a tour of the site by Lisa Gardiner, who worked as the Centre Promotions Officer for eight years until the end of 2022. She initially became involved with the charity over two decades ago when she worked on the farm. 'We're definitely an outdoorsy visitor attraction,' she said. 'You have to be willing to put your boots on! We've

1 Aboyne. 2 Belwade Farm. 3 Dess Waterfall. ▶

Dess Waterfall

❄ OS Explorer map OL54 or OL59; start: Kincardine O'Neil village hall car park ▥ anchovies. remotest.misty; ♥ NO5903999674; 4 miles; easy.

The village of Kincardine O'Neil lies close to the River Dee and is about equidistant between Aboyne and Banchory. It's the oldest village in Royal Deeside and easily the prettiest, with a high street of large stone cottages and a 14th-century ruined church at its eastern end. This walk follows the Deeside Way as it passes through the village. It's a straightforward route out and back to Dess Waterfall, which is buried within nearby Dess Wood. A range of local walk leaflets can be found in the red telephone box outside The Old Smiddy on North Deeside Road.

1 From the village hall, turn left on to North Deeside Road (A93) and after 100yds take the next right on to Pitmurchie Road, passing Christ Church on the corner. This church catches the eye with pops of army green on its gate, entrance porch and other detailing. You'll pass a set of houses and emerge beside open fields.

2 Follow the fork for the Deeside Way footpath on the left. This passes between a row of gardens and an open field. While walking down here in August, all I could hear were yellowhammers, lawnmowers and the sound of broom pods popping in the sun.

3 After about half a mile, at the next fork, bear left to stay on the Deeside Way. This continues through farmland, crossing a minor country road after 200yds and threading down an avenue bordered by thistles and raspberry bushes. Trees and bracken soon take over, sheltering the path as it enters Dess Wood. Keep on the same Deeside Way path through the forest for three quarters of a mile.

4 After descending a gentle slope, a wooden bridge over Dess Burn appears on the left. The Deeside Way continues across here, but stay on this side of the burn and carry on straight. The path becomes more uneven and planks have been laid for when it's muddy. The burn chats away as you twist through the pines.

got lots of wildlife here too and many people come for the walking trails to see what they can spot.' In 2021, World Horse Welfare requested that each of their four sites undertake wildlife surveys to find out what wild animals and plants can be found on their farms (page 268). Turns out, there are absolutely loads.

Horses are cared for at Belwade until they can be rehomed, sometimes as a ridden or driven horse or perhaps as an invaluable companion. Depending on the case, a horse can stay at Belwade for up to two years,

5 After 200yds, a fence appears in front of a steep drop over the burn and Dess Waterfall emerges around the corner. Two water channels course down the rock into a shallow pool. The path is set quite far back from the falls so you'd need a zoom lens to get a close photo. There is a path down to the water's edge but it takes a bit of scrambling and because the ground is so sandy it's a little dodgy to descend. It depends how willing you are to slide down on your bum and risk being giggled at by other walkers (one of many reasons I advocate early morning walks). Once you've had your fill of the falls, continue straight, veering almost directly over the water.

6 In another 200yds, take the first path right, which bends back on itself and leads uphill through a clearing to a patch of Sitka spruce. Carry on for 600yds, ignoring any lesser side paths coming in on the left.

7 When the more established path of the Deeside Way appears perpendicular to your track, turn left to join it. This puts you back on the trail that you followed on the outward journey. Retrace your steps from here back to Kincardine O'Neil.

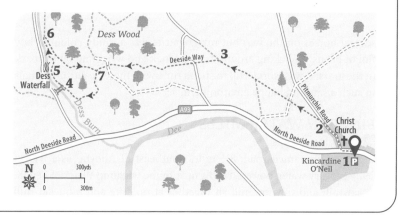

making goodbyes difficult for staff who have worked with them for so long. 'There are maybe only about two staff members that haven't rehomed from us,' Lisa laughed. 'You get a special bond with them. Ultimately the job is to make these horses' lives better and give them that one-to-one attention. It's a happy and sad day when they go to a new home.'

After enjoying a filled roll in the café, I strolled down the track leading to the Tarland Burn, running along the farm's southern edge. I met

BELWADE BIOBLITZ

After enrolling the help of local wildlife expert Harry Scott, Belwade Farm staff undertook a year-long 'BioBlitz' to locate, identify and record every form of life that was seen or heard within the farm boundary in 2022. I chatted with Harry in the bistro, after he'd investigated a mystery moth that had landed outside. He explained that his initial goal of recording 500 species across the year was surpassed by June. At the end of 2022, well over 700 species were identified, including 29 different mammals, 7 different ladybirds and an impressive 287 different moths. 'Everything's here,' Harry said, 'it's just a matter of looking for it. The paddocks are a monoculture but it's a haven for wildlife in the farm's boundary fringes.'

I asked World Horse Welfare's Senior Media Officer Su Delve how the BioBlitz will affect future visitors to Belwade. 'We're committed to managing our farms in the best way for the horses but also in the most environmentally sensitive way,' she said. 'Harry and the Belwade BioBlitz team are helping to inform the charity's wider environmental development, and there are plans for a wildlife interpretive board to be installed at Belwade later in 2023. This will allow visitors to find out more about the wildlife they might encounter while exploring the paths around the farm.'

several horses on the way but my favourite was a sandy-coloured boy full of beans, frolicking around the paddock and wriggling on his back in the grass. It was wonderful to spend time with these beautiful animals in such a safe and happy environment.

8 FINZEAN WATER MILLS

/// custodial.became.letter

Beside an unnamed road, 8½ miles southeast of Aboyne, is a trio of 19th-century water-powered mills next to the wiggling Water of Feugh. A sawmill and turning mill sit together at one site and a bucket mill is located a little further upriver. It's a similar setup to Scalan Mills & Seminary (page 98), where the original buildings have been left in situ and largely intact, and if you ignore the parked cars you could be fooled into thinking it was the 1800s. The mill buildings are built from wooden planks and have red, triangular corrugated iron roofs. Swallows zoom in and out of the rafters in summer and water courses through the lade beside the water just beyond, but mostly it's quiet and still.

It's said these are Scotland's only surviving woodworking mills of this kind. The listed buildings and adjacent weirs form a large part of the local area's heritage – it's particularly impressive that they've managed to stay together in their original setting and can still perform their original function. Dating back to the 1820s, the sawmill was used to cut timber. Some of this ended up in the floor of the main chamber around the Presiding Officer's Chair in Holyrood, the Scottish Parliament building in Edinburgh.

Built a few years later, the turning mill was originally used to make brush heads and herring barrel bungs, then switched to domestic utensils in later years. Buckets were produced at the third mill, a mile down the road, as late as the 21st century. Finzean's water mills were the subject of several paintings by Scottish artist Joseph Farquharson (1846–1935). His preference for painting moody and sheep-speckled winter landscapes earned him the nickname 'Frozen Mutton Farquharson'.

¶¶ FOOD & DRINK

Finzean Farm Shop Balnaboth Steading, AB31 6PA ⊘ finzean.com/farmshop. This place won me over straight away. Lying just over a mile northeast of the water mills, the converted granite steading isn't huge but has so much packed inside: fresh fruit and vegetables, ice cream, cards, books, sustainable toiletries, meat, dairy and preserves. It also sells a range of pulses, nuts and grains from the Finzean Estate. Everything has its place without feeling cluttered. Beside all this amazing local produce is the café, where breakfast, lunch and cakes are served both inside and outside. Sip a brew and admire the view across the Feugh Valley to the distinctive summit of Clachnaben (page 273).

9 BANCHORY & AROUND

⅄ Feughside Caravan Park (page 320)

Banchory is the last major town before you move across the boundary into Aberdeen City, hanging in a hammock of the River Dee as it flows east. Close to neighbouring villages and with the granite torr-topped hill of Clachnaben nearby, Banchory is a handy base for exploring this part of Aberdeenshire. It's also your best bet for shopping, with a range of gift shops lining High and Dee Streets and one of the two excellent Yeadon's bookshops – its sister branch is in Elgin (page 141).

With the exception of a few supermarket and charity chains, most of Banchory's shops are independent. Even better, there seems to be real camaraderie between these small businesses, and this becomes particularly apparent when the town hosts its annual **Summer Shop Window Competition**. Each participating shop conceals an item in its window that's out of place. Some, like a kettle in a bike shop, are pretty obvious, while others demand a sharper eye, such as a single piece of hidden Lego.

The competition is free to enter and certainly not restricted to kids – pick up an entry form from the library (just off Bridge St), Continental Cream ice parlour (Dee St) or Taylors of Banchory (High St). Your task is to find each random item and write it down next to the corresponding shop's number. All correct entries are put into a prize draw. In a time when the humble high street struggles to compete with internet shopping, this is an ingenious way of encouraging visitors to actually stop and look in shop windows. More towns should follow suit.

By happy accident, I found my favourite part of Banchory while tracking down the library, located within a pedestrianised area called **Scott Skinner Square**. Named after one of the greats of Scottish fiddle music, James Scott Skinner (see below), the square is accessed through an alleyway off High Street or up a short flight of stairs off Bridge Street on the opposite side. It contains a selection of small businesses arranged around a mini amphitheatre of steps, including **Butterfly Effect Banchory** (🅕 ☉ Tue–Sat). All sorts of plastic-free and sustainable goodies are available at this zero-waste shop and refillery, such as Kombucha drinks, organic toiletries and vegan sweets. Note that there's another Butterfly Effect refillery 30 miles north in Insch (page 244).

Cubic stools and benches fill the open space beside the steps in Scott Skinner Square, made from a seemingly random arrangement of

THE STRATHSPEY KING

James Scott Skinner was born in Banchory in 1843. By the time he was eight years old, he was playing the cello at dances across Deeside, along with 'Tarland Minstrel' Peter Milne (page 262). Cello playing wasn't the only string to Skinner's bow though (pun unashamedly intended). He also trained as a dance teacher and was even invited by Queen Victoria to teach the children of Balmoral Estate in 1868. Skinner kept on recording music until 1922, five years before he died. In Skinner Square is a tiny garden containing woven sculptures of a fiddle and treble clef musical note, created by Ayrshire-based willow and steel artist David Powell. One of Skinner's most famous pieces, *Bonnie Banchory*, inspired the creation of three abstract columns around the square's curved steps. On the top of each column is a stack of different-sized rods, which represent the sound waves of this song.

wooden and metal slats. A keen eye will notice that engraved on some of these slats are quotes from the Banchory community about their town. Mounted into one of the access ramp walls opposite the library is a drinking fountain from Banchory Railway Station, recovered and brought here after the line closed in 1966. Perhaps it's the combination of history and art in one tiny space, or just the fact it's a peaceful place to sit away from busier streets, but I warmed to Scott Skinner Square instantly.

"The water surges in two channels around rocky contours before crashing into a slower pool and continuing under the bridges."

If you walk south on Dee Street you'll soon cross the river. Half a mile further along is a T-junction, where the left branch passes over the Water of Feugh. Running parallel to the stone road bridge is a newer footbridge where you can peer down at the **Falls of Feugh** below. The water surges in two channels around rocky contours before crashing into a slower pool and continuing under the bridges. In autumn, this is a good spot to look for leaping salmon.

If you visit, please don't put padlocks on the wire mesh of the footbridge, as their accumulated weight causes structural damage. There's a polite sign asking couples to refrain from doing this but it's frequently ignored. Cuddle up and take a selfie instead.

Allow me to squeeze just one more stone circle into this book. **Nine Stanes Stone Circle** isn't advertised or obvious, but it's conveniently close to an unnamed road passing through a Sitka spruce plantation 5½ miles south of Banchory. Park in a lay-by (pocketed.cries.faraway) beside the road then walk for 100yds up a forestry track to the circle. There are six standing stones, a chunky recumbent and two wonky flankers, making up the nine stones in its name. There's also a mini cairn of smaller stones within the larger circle, an intriguing feature not seen in other examples.

When I visited, I'd just experienced an assorted delight of road closures, cafés shut when they shouldn't have been and insufferable August heat (I have about the same heat tolerance as a Mars bar). I arrived at Nine Stanes a sweaty, irritable mess and, although sitting in the middle of the circle with grasshoppers boinging around my feet didn't make me any less sweaty, it was a serene way to end the day. Stone circles are good at that. This one was arranged some 4,000 years ago, used as a burial place and to mark the movement of the moon

throughout the year. Its stones now have mossy beards and grassy feet, but after all that time they're still standing.

Sitting alone in the solitude of the forest, I found it easy to imagine that the people who put this structure together were hidden in the trees, waiting for me to leave. There isn't much that's survived so long that we can still see so clearly.

ᵀ FOOD & DRINK

Birdhouse Café High St AB31 5SS ☎ 01330 828456 ⌕ birdhousecafe.co.uk ⊙ Tue–Sun. Sustainably minded with seasonal and plant-based menus and compostable take-away packaging, this dog-friendly coffee shop offers breakfast, grilled sandwiches, burgers, speciality coffee and sourdough bread baked on-site most days.

Continental Cream Dee St AB31 5ST ☎ 01330 825733 ⌕ continentalcream.com
🅵 ⊙ daily; check Facebook for times. On hot summer afternoons there's a queue down the street for this place. It's not just excellent ice cream on offer either – it also sells artisan chocolates and weigh-out confectionary of the big glass jar variety too.

10 CLACHNABEN

🏠 **Glen Dye Cabins & Cottages** (page 320)
Glen Dye free car park ⧇ submerged.reshaping.stuffing

This is one of my favourite walks. At 1,932ft, Clachnaben is one of the region's shorter hills but still rewards those who hike to the craggy granite tor on its summit with biscuit-tin views across Aberdeenshire. The 5½-mile route is out-and-back, but with a mix of open glen, pine woodland and heathery hills, the landscape transforms as you walk so there's plenty to see both ways. I've said before that I'm no mountain goat, but this is a hill not a mountain so I felt up to the challenge.

The path begins with a mixed jumble of pines, spruces, heather and blaeberry bushes standing shoulder to shoulder. At the end of this forest, continue straight at the crossroads. Look right and you'll see your destination, its craggy outcrop sticking up on top of the hill. Walking parallel to and downhill from the summit for a while is a little disheartening, but once you cross a small footbridge, the path bends right and finally turns towards Clachnaben. Beside the path, long grass conceals anonymous twittering. Strips of pine woodland and bracken

◀ **1** Falls of Feugh, Banchory. **2** Clachnaben is one of the region's shorter hills.
3 Finzean Water Mills.

NATURE IN STERLING SILVER

Bright Star Jewellery ⟨⟩ brightstarjewellery.co.uk

Depending on where you are in Aberdeenshire, you could be looking at mountains, trees, rivers, lochs or the ocean. It's this blend of wild places that inspires jewellery designer and maker Catie Gandhi. Based near Banchory, Catie discovered jewellery making ten years ago and found it was the perfect contrast to her job as a doctor. 'If I've had a tough day at work, there's nothing quite like hammering metal for a bit of stress relief! My favourite pieces are the ones I cast from natural objects, because I love preserving a little bit of nature's beauty.'

Catie creates simple, elegant sterling silver jewellery inspired by leaves, ice, petals and more. 'I love to look for textures and patterns in nature,' she says. 'Really slowing down and paying attention to my surroundings is a great way to relax. If you look closely, you'll find lots of textures in nature – veins in leaves, ripples on water, patterns in sand as the tide goes out… All these details give me inspiration for my designs.'

Catie's process can begin with as little as a seed pod: 'An idea usually starts with something I've seen on a walk. I sketch out some ideas, make a test piece, then refine the design before settling on the finished product.'

As well as using recycled silver and melting down scraps for future pieces, Catie also has fully recyclable packaging including ribbons made from wood pulp. You can see her jewellery in Studio 1 in Banchory's Scott Skinner Square (page 270) and she's also involved with markets throughout the year. For details, see her website and social media.

beds cover the landscape's middle section, while hills tinged green and purple stand behind.

Keep right at the next two forks and cross a stream via three more footbridges. After these, it's just the one path to the top. Pass through a gate into **Black Hillocks Forest** – a quiet patch of pine woodland. The path loops around its southwest edge, offering moorland views on the left with the stream in between. The summit shifts again, now appearing on the left like a wily Whac-A-Mole.

Once you break out of Black Hillocks, the path turns to rocky steps, curving around the hill and back towards the summit. I never look back when I'm hill walking so I can get maximum satisfaction when I reach the top, puffing like a bellows. On this occasion, I really felt like I'd achieved something.

To the east was the route I'd just walked, with Black Hillocks Forest now shrunk to model railway size. The knobbly summit to the north is

Bennachie (page 239). What surprised me most was the ribbon of baby blue on the eastern horizon. Despite being 16 miles inland, the sea is visible from here on clear days. The western side of Clachnaben faces the Cairngorms and has a distinct lack of anything other than hills and heather. No doubt you're in wilderness here.

On my way back down, I passed a dad with his young child making their ascent, and the boy gave me a luminous smile and a wave. This was adorable yet a little bruising to my athletic ability when, if positions had been reversed, all I'd have been able to offer was a gasping grimace.

Jokes aside, this is a really enjoyable walk. Apart from the last section up the rocky steps, most of the route is level or gently climbing, and the walk there and back took me just under three hours.

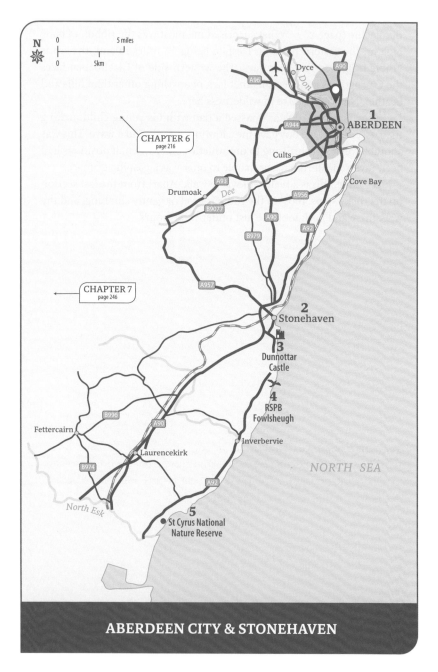

N

0   5 miles

0   5km

Dyce

Don

A90

A96

1
ABERDEEN

A944

CHAPTER 6
page 216

Cults

Cove Bay

A93

Dee

Drumoak

A956

B9077

A90

A92

B979

CHAPTER 7
page 246

A957

2
Stonehaven

3
**Dunnottar
Castle**

4
**RSPB
Fowlsheugh**

B996

A90

Fettercairn

Inverbervie

NORTH SEA

B974

Laurencekirk

A92

North Esk

5
**St Cyrus National
Nature Reserve**

ABERDEEN CITY & STONEHAVEN

8
ABERDEEN CITY & STONEHAVEN

Some disregard Aberdeen as simply 'The Granite City' – an unimaginative and tedious nickname, if you ask me. While I wouldn't consider myself an urban dweller, I developed an immediate fondness for this city. As well as museums and galleries, there's a great deal for outdoor enthusiasts to enjoy here: you can walk through a cactus forest, pass seals hauled out on riverbanks and watch dolphins leaping by the harbour mouth. There's also fantastic culinary diversity, particularly in the centre, with everything from Scottish ice cream to Turkish breakfasts to Argentinian sandwiches.

Aberdeen is an architectural sock drawer. Muscling in among 12th-century churches and the third-oldest university in Scotland are eclectic 21st-century examples of art, sculpture and design. Pioneers in a range of scientific and creative fields are celebrated in a wonderful museum opposite the second-largest granite building in the world and a two-tonne steel leopard. A place of contrasts, for sure.

Aber is a Pictish word for 'river mouth'. This makes Aberdeen an appropriate name for a city that sits beside the mouth of not one but two of the North East's largest rivers. The Don cuts across the northern end, completing its journey at Donmouth Local Nature Reserve, while the Dee flows into the harbour at the southern end.

This sprawling port was once simply the estuary of the Dee, and suffered greatly from weather changes and shifting sandbars. One notable calamity occurred in 1637, when four anchored ships were swept out to sea by a rogue wave along the river. A year later, ships were stranded completely as the harbour mouth became blocked. An impressive feat of engineering saw the Dee diverted, the sandbanks removed and the harbour doubled in size. Aberdeen now has the largest berthage in Scotland – its fishing and offshore oil and gas industries have defined it as a world-class port.

ℹ TOURIST INFORMATION

Aberdeen iCentre Union St AB11 5BP ✆ 01224 269180 ✉ aberdeen@visitscotland.com.

In addition to Aberdeen, this chapter also highlights locations in and around the peaceful coastal town of Stonehaven, 15½ miles south. Here you can witness one of the North East's most dramatic Hogmanay traditions and see the castle on the cover of this book – the rather glorious ruin of Dunnottar.

GETTING AROUND

The main routes into Aberdeen are the A92 from the north and south and the A96 from the northwest. As you'd expect in a big city, traffic can build up and there isn't always a parking space where you want one. One of the most central places to park is the pay and display multistorey in Union Square shopping centre (AB11 5RD), next to the train station. From here, it's less than two miles to the Maritime Museum, Greyhope Bay, David Welch Winter Gardens and other sites of interest. For easy access to Old Aberdeen, you can park for free in Seaton Park.

TRAINS & BUSES

Scotrail services link Aberdeen to Stonehaven, Inverurie, Elgin and Inverness, among others. Apart from a connection to Dyce, for Aberdeen Airport, no trains run within the city itself. Union Square Bus Station is next to the train station. From here you can catch a range of services, such as the Stagecoach 201 to Braemar (via Banchory, Aboyne and Ballater), the 10 to Inverness (via Inverurie, Huntly, Keith, Elgin and Forres) and **Megabus** (⊘ uk.megabus.com) services to a range of destinations across the UK including London, Manchester and Birmingham.

Numerous inner-city services are run by First Bus Aberdeen (⊘ firstbus.co.uk/aberdeen). If you plan on catching a few buses, you might consider getting a **GrassHOPPER Pass** (⊘ grasshopperpass.com), though note that this can only be purchased when boarding a First or Stagecoach service. Pick a day or week ticket and the zone you'd

---

1 Aberdeen cityscape. **2** Seaton Park. **3** Cross the Brig o'Balgownie to reach **4** Donmouth Local Nature Reserve. ▶

MUST SEES

Aberdeen has something for every traveller, whether you're drawn to history, architecture, food and drink, arts or wildlife. These are my top five suggestions for more unique discoveries in and around the city.

1. **Brig o'Balgownie** Once the main route across the River Don, this 14th-century arched bridge is now a peaceful pedestrian crossing; page 285.
2. **City of Aberdeen Distillery** Run by two friends who are passionate about excellent gin, with the chance to design your own; page 296.
3. **Old Aberdeen Bookshop** A tiny place lined with towering shelves and crammed with secondhand titles; page 289.
4. **Provost Skene's House** This remarkable museum celebrates the works of great minds linked to the North East, both past and present; page 295.
5. **Tollohill Wood** A small tangle of trees containing rocky dells stuffed with bracken and even a miniature Neolithic cairn; page 304.

like – these range from Zone A within Aberdeen City to Zone C, which covers travel within Aberdeen and as far out as Fraserburgh, Keith and Braemar.

WALKING & CYCLING

For a less stressful and more immersive visit to Aberdeen, ditching the car and **walking** is the answer. Despite being Scotland's third-largest city, the central hub of Aberdeen is easily walkable. It's only four miles from the most northerly point of interest I've listed in Old Aberdeen to the most southerly in the city centre, with plenty to explore in between.

Seaton Park and Hazlehead Park provide flat paths ideal for exploring by **bike**. National Cycle Route 1 slices down the middle of the city before continuing south to Stonehaven. National Cycle Route 195 runs from Aberdeen's Duthie Park to Ballater, 41 miles west.

1 ABERDEEN

There were originally two settlements in Aberdeen. The city centre, or 'New Aberdeen', is located by the River Dee and is mostly characterised by high street retail, but also conceals many pockets of ancient history.

Further north, the area beside the River Don known as Old Aberdeen offers a far quieter, often cobble-stoned walking experience. The two were combined as the collective City of Aberdeen in 1891, and now this central region has been joined by surrounding residential suburbs and green spaces to form a vast urban catchment covering some 70 square miles. In these outskirts you'll discover wilder spots that the city centre's bustle can't reach.

OLD ABERDEEN

🏠 **Alba Guest House** (page 320)

Old Aberdeen is characterised by chunky stone buildings with low doorways, lining cobbled streets that make cars sound like swarming insects. Most of the sites of historical and architectural interest here lie along a single street that runs parallel to King Street, one of the main routes south into the city centre. Many monks and scholars settled in Old Aberdeen because of St Machar's Cathedral (page 282) and King's College (page 287), established in the 1130s and 1495 respectively.

Seaton Park, the largest green space in Old Aberdeen, sits beside a dangling loop of the River Don. Its name comes from the Gaelic for 'peaceful retreat'. As well as open grass for children and dogs to let off steam on the eastern half, there are splashes of colour from flowerbeds, a high-quality riverside footpath leading to an arched pedestrianised bridge, and several features of historical interest tucked away in the avenues of trees

"Archaeological studies revealed that Tillydrone might have been a defensive site as far back as the second century."

on the western side. One of these is **Tillydrone Motte**, looking like a human-sized anthill. Motte castles were introduced to Scotland in the 1100s, often consisting of wooden structures on top of conical hills. However, archaeological studies revealed that Tillydrone might have been a defensive site as far back as the second century, with perhaps even earlier origins as a prehistoric burial place.

Close to Tillydrone Motte is **Wallace Tower**, also known as Benholm's Lodging. 'Tower' is a little misleading – the building is essentially a tall stone house with a cylindrical turret-like section attached to either side. Originally located in the city centre, it was dismantled brick by brick and reconstructed on the western boundary of Seaton Park in 1964 to make way for a Marks & Spencer store. Standing in an alcove on the

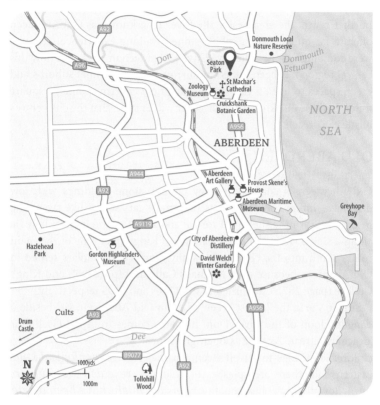

exterior eastern side is a stone carving of what appears at first glance to be the Michelin Man. It's actually Sir Robert Keith of Benholm who constructed the building in the early 1600s, dressed in armour. There's a common belief that any figure in armour is William Wallace, so this is probably where the Wallace Tower name originated, although there's no link to Wallace at all.

Just south of Seaton Park is **St Machar's Cathedral** (⌖ stmachar.com). Its most notable feature is the twin set of towers on its west-facing side, built in the fashion of 14th-century tower houses. There's been a place of worship on this site as far back as AD580, but it first became a cathedral in the mid 1100s. Inside, mounted above the studded Vestry door, is a Pictish cross carving that was uncovered near the park in 1932. This was installed inside the cathedral by the university in 1995 to mark 500 years since the cathedral has been associated with nearby King's College.

Move along the north aisle and you'll see a small square alcove beneath the third stained-glass window. This contains an engraved glass sculpture of the cathedral by local artist Ian Hadden, donated to St Machar's in 2006. Backed by black brick, the silver lines remind me of the etching art kits you can buy, but this exquisitely detailed piece was created freehand.

If you walk south from the cathedral, you'll join **The Chanonry**, the most famous of Old Aberdeen's attractive cobbled streets. Lined by stone walls too high to peer over, it's not really even wide enough for two cars to pass each other. Two hundred yards down, The Chanonry meets St Machar Drive/A978, which is a rude awakening after the peaceful cathedral and paved lane.

Before reaching this though, turn right through a gate to the Cruickshank Building, part of the Department of Plant & Soil Science. This is one of two adjacent University of Aberdeen buildings open to the public, which are well worth visiting for the absorbing insights into natural history that they provide. Follow the path beyond the gate and you'll see a sign with free maps of **Cruickshank Botanic Gardens** (⊘ abdn.ac.uk/about/campus/cruickshank-botanic-garden.php ⊙ Apr–Sep 09.00–19.00 daily; Oct–Mar 09.00–16.30 daily; free entry).

Sometimes botanic gardens can be a little monotonous but this is a particularly diverse one. There are some open lawns and tended flower beds but most of the site is the good kind of unkempt, where you can wind around rockeries, ponds, patio spaces and a large arboretum and Scottish meadow with maze-like paths cut into the grass. It's easy to spend an hour or more here.

"You can wind around rockeries, ponds, patio spaces and a large arboretum and Scottish meadow with maze-like paths."

On the western boundary of the botanic gardens is one of the entrances to the adjoining Zoology Building, home to the excellent **Zoology Museum** (⊘ abdn.ac.uk/museums/exhibitions/zoology-museum-588.php ⊙ 10.00–16.00 Mon–Fri; free entry). The majority of the museum is contained in a single room that's split into lower and upper galleries. On the ground floor, the eye is drawn to the horse, camel, rhino and hippo skeletons in the centre of the room, and the sei whale skeleton suspended from the ceiling. Make sure you peer into the cabinets along the walls too: these are crammed with items, including minuscule amphibian bones, corals

Seaton Park via Donmouth Local Nature Reserve

❋ OS Explorer map 406; start at Seaton Park car park ⅲ baked.strong.beside;
📍 NJ9413709039; 3½ miles; easy.

This diverse circular walk begins at Seaton Park's free car park, accessed via Don Street. It follows the winding River Don to its end point at a sandy beach.

1 Walk west past the children's play area, following the tarmac road. After 200yds, Cathedral Walk opens up on your left. This long avenue has circular flower beds and helter-skelter hedges down the middle.

2 Follow Cathedral Walk until you see St Machar's Cathedral ahead. Here, the path climbs a brief slope to a map of the park and the Granite Garden – a rockery containing boulders from quarries across the North East, including red ones from Peterhead and grey-blue ones from Dyce. Bear right to continue along the path, now running parallel to a stone wall.

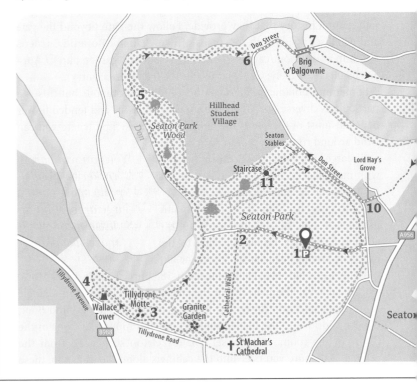

3 After ascending a short hill, you'll spy Tillydrone Motte (page 281) hunched in the trees, looking like a 23ft-high mole hill. About 150yds further down the path, screened by more trees, is Wallace Tower (page 281).

4 Emerge at Tillydrone Avenue and turn right immediately after joining the pavement, following a narrow alleyway then a shallow set of steps to the Don. Turn right to join a tarmac footpath leading back into Seaton Park. When the path splits as the river bends north, bear left and stick to the water's edge for half a mile.

5 Climb some gravel steps heading right, lifting you higher over the river on a sandier path. Birdsong and the heady scent of wild garlic fill the air in early summer and the path is kept cool by a canopy of deciduous trees.

6 Half a mile later, bear left on to Don Street. With their low doorways and sash windows, the cottages here are as different from the city centre apartment blocks as night from day. Past these cottages, cross over Brig o'Balgownie, a single-arched bridge of pinkish blocks softened with age, completed in 1320. Now pedestrianised, it was once the main crossing point over the river until the larger five-arched Bridge of Don was built half a mile downstream in 1830.

7 On the other side of the old bridge, turn immediately right down a flight of stone steps. Now the trills of wrens and blackbirds are joined by less melodic squawking from black-headed gulls. From here it's one mile to the sandy beach at Donmouth Local Nature Reserve. To reach it, continue along the river footpath then carefully cross Ellon Road/A956 and follow Donmouth Road to the end.

8 Once you've had enough time on the beach, retrace your steps down Donmouth Road to Ellon Road. Cross back over and turn left to walk south across the road bridge. Keep an eye on the island to your right for hauled out seals. ▶

Seaton Park via Donmouth Local Nature Reserve (continued)

9 ▶ On the other side, at the wooden sign for Donmouth Local Nature Reserve, follow a trodden grass footpath right, connecting to a tarmac path that bends left around a patch of trees. When it forks, branch right through a gap in a low dry-stone wall.

10 Stay straight across the T-junction of Lord Hay's Grove, then turn right on to Don Street, joining a footpath climbing parallel to the road. After 100yds, cross the road to re-enter Seaton Park via the shaded avenue of Seaton Stables.

11 Head up a short stone staircase on the left, leading to a gate through walled gardens bursting with hydrangeas in summer. Emerge at the far end and bear left gently downhill, back on the tarmac path. Soon you'll see the car park and start point up ahead on the right.

with astonishing detail, and a troupe of fish you wouldn't want to meet down a dark alley.

The upper gallery is an ornithologist's delight, with taxidermy specimens ranging from goldcrests to golden eagles. With the exception of two cassowary and ostrich skeletons, every bird on display can be seen in Britain. For those who didn't grow up watching birds with something close to adoration (as I did), perhaps seeing them all displayed here might provide inspiration to venture into the wild and look for the real thing. I can hope anyway.

Appropriately for a university attraction, there's a real emphasis on education throughout the museum. Beside the entrance to the lower gallery is a **Biodiversity Centre**, containing even more skulls, skins, shells and stones. As long as you're gentle, you're able to touch the specimens in this room. I particularly enjoyed a cabinet in the entrance hall displaying student field notebooks. Presented among branches of foliage and muddy rucksacks was a selection of open journals with notes, sketches and natural materials taped to the pages.

While I love sprawling sites like London's Natural History Museum, Aberdeen's is just the right size for a child's attention span. There's lots to see but it's all compact, making it ideal for a burst of scales, fur and feathers that captivates rather than overwhelms.

When you leave, either return through the botanic gardens or exit via the western entrance on to Tillydrone Avenue. Look left here and you'd be forgiven for thinking you were witnessing an alien invasion.

The gigantic blue-barcoded cube beside Bedford Road isn't a threat to civilisation but in fact the university's main academic library. Opened in 2012, the **Sir Duncan Rice Library** is named after one of the previous university principals. Designed by Danish architects Schmidt Hammer Lassen, the building has eight floors, 760 panels of glass, 22,000 tonnes of concrete and 4,700 lights. Whether you love or hate the design, you can't deny it turns heads.

Return east along St Machar Drive to The Chanonry but turn right and cross over at this point, back on to cobbles on High Street. In the widened area on your left are the remains of the **Market Cross**, erected at the start of the 16th century. The cross stands in front of the **Old Town House**. This smart Georgian building was constructed in 1788 and has nine identical sash windows on its front face, topped in the centre by a clock. Above the doorway is a crest with a Latin inscription meaning 'little things increase through harmony' – a fitting motto for a part of the city that was once an independent burgh (town). Over the years, the Town House has had several different purposes including a police station, when it's said a handcart was kept by the front doors to pick up drunks off the street and take them to the cells to sleep it off.

"Above the doorway is a crest with a Latin inscription meaning 'little things increase through harmony'."

Fifty yards further south on High Street is **Blackwell's University Bookshop** (🖪 BlackwellsAberdeen) on the right. It'll come as no surprise that I had a browse in here – there are lots of local interest titles I hadn't seen elsewhere, and it's also dog friendly.

After another 30yds down High Street, look left to see two pedestrian side streets. The name of the first, Wrights' and Coopers' Place, reflects the once popular trades of woodworking and barrel-making in Old Aberdeen. The single-storey houses of the second lane, Grants' Place, have distinctive overlapping roof tiles with curved edges, known as pantiles.

Continue south on High Street for 300yds until **King's College** appears on the left, providing a wonderfully old-fashioned aesthetic. It was founded in 1495, making the University of Aberdeen as a whole the third-oldest university in Scotland after St Andrews and Glasgow. This is one of the most striking buildings in Old Aberdeen, with an enclosed crown tower, entrance arch dated 1825 and a typical college

quadrangle for lounging between lectures. On the lawn beside the arch is a monument for **William Elphinstone** (1431–1514), who was Bishop of Aberdeen, Lord High Chancellor of Scotland and founder of the university. Sculpted by Henry Wilson in 1926, this elaborate marble-and-bronze sculpture is coffin-shaped and portrays the bishop lying across the top and a series of smaller figures below.

After King's College, High Street becomes College Bounds. Eighty yards south of the Elphinstone monument are two pale columns jutting out of the wall on the right. These are elaborate Turkish-style minaret turrets standing either side of a gateway known as the **Powis Gates**. Finishing with an elaborate flourish, each turret has a gold weathervane topped with a crescent moon. Above the grey archway connecting the turrets is the crest of the Fraser Leslie family, representing Hugh Fraser Leslie of Powis House, who erected the gates in 1834.

Two hundred yards further down, after the street is renamed again to Spital, you'll find **Old Aberdeen Bookshop** (✆ 01224 732184 🖮 oldaberdeenbookshop.co.uk). This tiny secondhand shop has two skinny walkways between towering bookshelves. Its focus is on academic literature, classics, and Scottish and local interest, but you'll find a vast assortment of titles. It's worth noting that the shop is run by one person and may not always follow the opening times advertised on its website.

🍴 FOOD & DRINK

Shelter Coffee High St AB24 3HE 📷 @sheltercafeabdn. Located on the cobbles beside the Old Town House, this small establishment is a popular student spot. There are two outside tables and a mezzanine upper level inside, which was fully occupied when I visited. Take your pick of homemade cakes, breakfasts, soup, sandwiches, paninis and salads – a few have a Turkish theme.

ABERDEEN CITY CENTRE

🏠 **Skene Terrace Apartments** (page 320)

As you'd expect, the centre of Aberdeen is where you'll find high-street shops and most of the restaurants and cafés – each with a mix of mainstream chains and more characterful independents. Many of these line arrow-straight Union Street, a main thoroughfare that transformed

---

◀ **1** The interior of St Machar's Cathedral. **2** Cruickshank Botanic Gardens.
3 The Zoology Museum.

THE WIZARD OF THE NORTH

The **Kirk of St Nicholas** – accessible via a stone archway on Union Street or smaller gate entrances on Back Wynd, Correction Wynd and Schoolhill – is also known as the Mither Kirk, a Doric phrase meaning 'mother church'. It has stood in this central location since the 12th century, surrounded on all sides by gravestones. There are so many belonging to notable people that a map by the Schoolhill entrance shows which is which. The grave I came to find is in the northern half of the churchyard: a relatively fresh-faced slab of pale stone with large black text. It belongs to Scottish magician **John Henry Anderson** (1814–1874), who made significant waves on the 19th-century magic scene and became known as 'the Wizard of the North'.

Born some 30 miles west of Aberdeen, near Kincardine O'Neil, Anderson created a name for himself by performing tricks of illusion in the street and letting word of mouth do his publicity for him. After such humble beginnings, he went on to perform for Queen Victoria and tour the world. One of his best-known feats was the Great Gun Trick, where he seemingly caught a bullet between his teeth.

Among his fans was Harry Houdini, who paid a visit to Anderson's grave in 1909 during one of his own magic shows. However, back then any talent for magic was believed to go hand in hand with devilry, and Anderson wasn't popular with everyone. In his excellent book *The Guide to Mysterious Aberdeen*, Geoff Holder writes that a landlady evicted Anderson once she discovered who he was, saying she could 'smell the brimstone on him'.

the city's geography at the turn of the 19th century. Well-known town surveyor Charles Abercrombie reputedly called the roads leading to Aberdeen's centre 'crooked, narrow, tortuous and hilly' during a council meeting in 1794. Plans for a vast and elevated new road were put forward, and people's houses, medieval streets and even hills in the existing landscape were removed to make way for it. Copious miscalculations and underestimates during the construction of Union Street are considered some of the key factors leading to Aberdeen declaring bankruptcy in 1817.

The centre of Aberdeen has a strange assortment of buildings. Many are made from the grey blocks that inspired the 'Granite City' nickname, but there are also transparent offices with square courtyards reminiscent of London. As an extra architectural contrast, nearby or sometimes directly opposite these modern builds are magnificent old colleges and churches with narrow spires and ornate detailing. Perhaps the most elaborate example is **Marischal College** (Broad Street, AB10

1AB), stretching far along the road with dozens of slit windows and an arched entrance.

The eye is drawn upwards to rows of thin, intricately carved pinnacles lining the roof like a crown. It may come as a surprise to discover that these are also made from granite, despite looking vastly different to the chunky bricks seen elsewhere. The use of granite here is particularly impressive, as its firmness makes it challenging to work with. In front of the college is a statue of Robert the Bruce on horseback, sculpted by Alan Beattie Herriot, and the sort of multi-jet dancing fountain built into the ground that children can't help but run into.

Founded in 1593, Marischal College was combined with King's College (page 287) almost 300 years later to form the University of Aberdeen. Additional construction throughout the 19th and early 20th centuries made Marischal the second-largest granite building in the world – the top spot belongs to Palacio de San Lorenzo de El Escorial near Madrid, if you're wondering.

Since 2009, Marischal has been the headquarters for Aberdeen City Council. It has a combination of architectural features: the older, more modest elements are by Archibald Simpson, made using Rubislaw stone from nearby Rubislaw Quarry on the western side of Aberdeen. Now filled with water and described as the deepest artificial hole in Europe, this quarry is where much of the city's granite was sourced between the mid 18th and late 20th centuries. The newer Gothic-style Kemnay granite of Marischal College is the work of Alexander Marshall Mackenzie. Born in Elgin in 1848, Mackenzie was involved with several significant buildings across the North East including Crathie Kirk, the place of worship for the British Royal Family when they stay at Balmoral.

Aberdeen Art Gallery

Schoolhill, AB10 1FQ ⊘ aberdeencity.gov.uk/AAGM/plan-your-visit/aberdeen-art-gallery
⊙ 10.00–17.00 Mon–Sat; 11.00–16.00 Sun; free entry

Appropriately for a space that exhibits both traditional and contemporary artwork, this gallery (located a quarter of a mile southwest of Marischal College) combines a 19th-century granite frontage with modern twists such as its shard-like glass balcony. The original building was one of Alexander Marshall Mackenzie's creations (see above); following extensive redevelopment, the gallery won the Andrew Doolan Best Building in Scotland Award in 2021. It was commended for conserving the building's heritage while introducing new exhibition spaces and improving its environmental performance. Featuring works spanning some 700 years, the interior showcases Scottish artists including Henry Raeburn and Samuel Peploe, as well as other world-renowned names like Barbara Hepworth and Francis Bacon.

I found the visitor sketchbooks tucked into bench pockets a thoughtful touch, ready in case you feel spontaneously inspired while walking round. If, like me, you're sceptical of canvases painted red and entitled *Oak Tree*, fear not: there's all sorts in this gallery, so something is bound to make you look twice. The diverse representation of genres and styles is summarised perfectly in the **Exploring Art** gallery, which focuses on artistic inspiration. Peer inside a viewfinder on one of the table displays to see a painting of New Aberdeen by Robert Seaton in 1805. Turn the handle and the view stays the same, but the artwork morphs between pop art, Modernism, romanticism, pointillism, Fauvism, Cubism, surrealism and abstract styles. It's an excellent whistle-stop art-history tour and a fun interactive element for younger visitors.

I spent a while admiring the light, circular **Remembrance Hall**. It was visited by more than 15,000 people the day after it was opened by King George V in 1925. Inside is a piece called *Forget Them Not*, created by Fraserburgh-born artist Gordon Burnett as part of the gallery's post-renovation reopening in 2017. Commemorating those lost in conflict, it symbolises the three realms where battles are fought: it's made from granite to reflect land, sculpted in the shape of a Spitfire wing for air, and features a mosaic wave at the bottom for water. Studded across its face are hundreds of enamel forget-me-nots, which are available to purchase in memory of lost loved ones.

Aberdeen Maritime Museum
Shiprow, AB11 5BY ⬙ aberdeencity.gov.uk/AAGM/plan-your-visit/aberdeen-maritime-museum ⊙ 10.00–17.00 Mon–Sat, noon–15.00 Sun; free entry

An integral part of Aberdeen's identity is its maritime heritage, and there's no better place to learn about this than the Maritime Museum. Located close to the quay on the other side of Union Street from the art gallery,

---

1 Marischal College. **2** *Poised* – a two-tonne leopard sculpture created by Andy Scott. **3** Aberdeen Maritime Museum. **4** Provost Skene's House. **5** Girdle Ness Lighthouse at Greyhope Bay. **6** Aberdeen Art Gallery. ▶

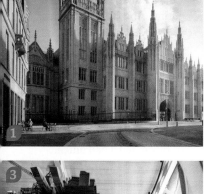

it's housed within three adjacent but very different buildings: Provost Ross's House (1593), which has creaky floorboards and low doorways; the former Trinity Congregational Church (1877); and the glass-fronted Link Building (1997). Exhibits in all three outline Aberdeen's seafaring history, from trading and shipbuilding to the discovery of North Sea oil and gas.

A huge range of memorabilia is on display here, including tiny model ships, silver snuff boxes and even a whale's eardrum from the regrettable whaling era. Hear stories of the seafaring community's often bizarre superstitions – while pigs were considered pretty unlucky, mentions of hares or foxes were believed to doom a ship. Meeting a person with red hair or flat feet on the way to a boat was also considered a bad omen.

The bulk of the museum is arranged on three levels, with a model of the Murchison Oil Platform threading through the middle of them. The model is big enough, but the real thing, situated in the North Sea near Shetland, stretches some 833ft down. Much of the third floor is dedicated to the evolution of Aberdeen Harbour. A port was first established here in 1136 by King David I of Scotland, and through the museum's windows you can look out over today's harbour – a view that's changed dramatically over the centuries.

A display of herring barrel stencils feature specific terms from the Fishery Board's selection standards that were used to describe each barrel's contents. A 'mat-full' was a herring at least 9¼ inches long when cured, with roe clearly visible, while a 'large spent' was an empty fish without roe. Herring inspired many a folk song – the 19th-century tune *Caller Herrin* ('Fresh Herring') was written by Scottish songwriter Carolina Nairne about the laborious and often dangerous work of fishermen and their wives.

POISED

Something you might not expect to find among Aberdeen office blocks is a two-tonne leopard. Opposite Marischal College is Marischal Square, a small outdoor courtyard surrounded by offices and Mackie's 19.2 ice cream parlour (page 300). Look up and you'll see the leopard, peering down from its 50ft-high plinth, with its tail hanging beneath its paws. Unveiled in 2017, *Poised* was created in steel by Scottish sculptor Andy Scott, inspired by the two leopards featured on the City of Aberdeen's coat of arms. Scott's more famous sculpture is the pair of huge steel horse heads beside the M9 in Falkirk, known as *The Kelpies*.

Provost Skene's House

Marischal Sq, Guestrow AB10 1AS ✆ 01224 641086 ⊘ aberdeencity.gov.uk/AAGM/plan-your-visit/provost-skenes-house ⊙ 10.00–17.00 Mon–Sat, 11.00–16.00 Sun; free entry

This creatively presented museum is a celebration of people from, or linked to, Aberdeen and the North East, who have brought pioneering changes to the city and, in many cases, the world. It's particularly remarkable because parts of the house date back to 1545 – one of Aberdeen's few examples of pre-Industrial granite use. More decorative features are made from softer sandstone. The building is named after one of its owners, Sir George Skene, who was Provost of Aberdeen from 1676 to 1685. Destined to be demolished in 1940, it was saved after a public campaign and opened as a museum in 1953.

If you approach from Marischal College, which is directly opposite on Broad Street, you may notice a grimacing face mounted on the corner of the museum. This is a stone imitation of **George Russell**, who owned a bakery in the now non-existent Ragg's Lane in the 19th century. His premises were close to a sewer and eventually shut by the town council. Suspecting that his neighbour had complained about him to the council, Russell sculpted his snarling face and mounted it on the wall of his bakery.

"One moment you're using touchscreens and the next you're gazing at a painted ceiling dated from 1626."

Whenever his neighbour passed by, he would see Russell sneering back at him. I actually think it's cute that he went to so much trouble for a supposed enemy. After Ragg's Lane was demolished in 1959, the Russell Head was moved to the exterior of Provost Skene's House.

This museum is such an interesting mix of old and new. One moment you're using touchscreens and the next you're gazing at a painted ceiling dated from 1626. The building might be centuries old, but I was greeted by the sound of Eurythmics in the Hall of Heroes corridor. Born in Aberdeen, singer-songwriter and political activist Annie Lennox was one of the 'Heroes' selected by public vote, represented by light shows, video clips and auditory displays. At the end of the corridor you can vote for the next set of Heroes.

Each room of the museum is dedicated to a different industry: literature, music, science, medicine, natural history, travel and more. Highlighted people include Leslie Benzies, who produced the *Grand Theft Auto* video games, and Margaret Myles. After losing her son to

EYES TO THE SKIES

One of the celebrated minds in Provost Skene's House (page 295) is scientist and mathematician James Clerk Maxwell, born in Edinburgh. In 1856, aged just 25, he became Professor of Natural Philosophy (Physics) at Aberdeen's Marischal College. Albert Einstein later described Maxwell's work as the 'most profound and the most fruitful that physics has experienced since the time of Newton'.

During his time in Aberdeen, Maxwell studied the motion and composition of Saturn's rings to determine why they didn't drift apart or collide with the planet. This was a subject that had mystified scientists for two centuries, and in 1859 Maxwell won the prestigious Adam's Prize for his essay on the stability of the planet's rings. In the 1980s, over a hundred years after Maxwell died, *Voyager* space probes proved his theory to be correct.

pneumonia in 1924, Myles became a tutor in midwifery and promoted formal midwife training around the world. During a time when many women and babies died in childbirth, Myles's work helped reduce this number.

There's so much for children to do here – they can look through viewfinders showing 19th-century stereoscopic photographs, watch lights zoom around Saturn's rings to demonstrate how they are formed (see above), and put on a puppet show inspired by Catherine Hollingworth, a 20th-century pioneer of children's theatre.

Provost Skene's House showcases a spectrum of talent in such a thoughtful and stylish way. Because the building is so old – the oldest surviving town house in the city in fact – lift access cannot be installed. For those who can't reach the upper levels, an Access Gallery has been set up on the ground floor with information from the rest of the house and a virtual tour. Large text leaflets and audio transcripts are available for those with sight and hearing issues.

City of Aberdeen Distillery

Palmerston Rd, AB11 5RE ☏ 01224 589645 ⊘ cityofaberdeendistillery.co.uk
⊙ noon–17.30 Tue–Sun

Where else in the North East can you sip Scottish gin beneath a railway arch and design your own gin from scratch? Opened in 2019, the City of Aberdeen Distillery was the first in Aberdeen in 80 years.

Owners Alan Milne and Dan Barnett met at the University Wine Society and share passions for drink and craft. 'My uncle made wine when I was a teenager – that's what sparked my interest,' Alan told me. 'Dan's made beer for years. We realised the flavours I was putting in my wines and he was putting into his beers were also being used to make gin, so that's how we made the crossover.'

All the gin here is distilled on-site – the front half of the railway arch has a shop, botanical garden and gin-making bench that visitors sit at for the Gin School Experience. The gin is distilled in a production area at the back, which guests can also see. Dan and Alan use organic alcohol and source local ingredients as much as possible. Aberdeen identity is evident in the beautiful stencil decoration on each bottle, featuring emblems such as the leopards seen on Aberdeen's crest, and knotted rope, anchors and compasses to represent the city's seafaring heritage. The seal has been designed with an oval notch at the top so when broken, the label on the neck becomes a tiny train ticket – a nod to its unique location in the railway arch.

"The front half of the railway arch has a shop, botanical garden and gin-making bench."

As I sipped a delicious gin made using Scottish bramble and warming spices (black pepper, cubeb berries and cassia), Dan showed me a scrapbook of photos taken as they designed the space from scratch. 'When you've got an empty arch, any idea can be entertained,' he said. 'We introduced wood elements and shades of green to get a nature-meets-industrial look. The floor's uneven so we got all the table legs custom-welded to make it level.'

My eye was drawn to a table displaying a pick and mix of over 100 berries, nuts, fruits, fresh citrus and spices that Gin School guests can choose from to flavour their gins. 'I'm proud of our Botanical Garden,' Alan said. 'Hopefully if you can name it, we've got it here.'

The distillery offers three experiences. The 45-minute Discovery Tour outlines Aberdeen's distilling history, finishing with a tasting from the range of gins on offer that day. The 90-minute Gin Tasting Masterclass encourages visitors to hone their smell and taste. In the three-hour Gin School Experience, you can distil your own gin from scratch using botanicals you've chosen, then bottle it, name it and take it home.

Greyhope Bay

Two miles east of Aberdeen's train station, just past the harbour entrance, is a grassy promontory jutting into the North Sea. On a map

I think it looks like an earless pig's head, with Greyhope Bay forming the curved dell above its upturned snout. Despite its small size, this headland has a sandy beach, two lighthouses, a disused artillery battery and an excellent café.

You can access the beach by cutting through a gate on Greyhope Road to a narrow footpath at the water's edge. A range of seabirds gather in the shallows by the rocks here and it's a great spot to look for dolphins too. There's a nondescript white lighthouse at the end of the South Breakwater, but tucked further around the headland is **Girdle Ness Lighthouse**, peeping over the hill. One of many Robert Stevenson-designed structures, it has similar white and yellow colouring to Fraserburgh's Kinnaird Head Lighthouse (page 201), but isn't open to the public. Protruding between Greyhope Bay to the north and Nigg Bay to the south, Girdle Ness was requested when only two out of 45 crew members on board the *Oscar* whaling ship survived a shipwreck close to shore in 1813.

"I think it looks like an earless pig's head, with Greyhope Bay forming the curved dell above its upturned snout."

Once you're done at the beach, make sure to visit Liberty Kitchen at **Greyhope Bay Centre** (page 300) up on the promontory – the first and currently only café in Aberdeen that functions off-grid with hybrid energy and circular rainwater treatment technology. It also has views to the north and east through floor-length windows, making it the perfect spot for cosy, indoor wildlife watching. I tucked into a Biscoff rocky road as a pod of dolphins came surging through the bay.

The café is located within the defensive structure of **Torry Battery**, which has overlooked the harbour since 1860. After defending the city during both World Wars, it was decommissioned in 1956 and is now a scheduled monument. The battery was once armed with guns capable of attacking ships more than ten miles out to sea, but now the only danger here is eating too much cake.

David Welch Winter Gardens

Polmuir Rd, AB11 7TH ⌖ aberdeencity.gov.uk/services/leisure-culture-and-parks/parks-and-gardens/duthie-park ⊙ Mar–Oct 10.30–17.00 daily; Nov–Feb 10.30–16.00 daily; free entry

Forget Kew Gardens. On Aberdeen's southern side you can wander through one of Europe's largest indoor gardens for free, exploring a warren of greenhouses containing tropical flowers, roses, ferns and a fierce squadron of carnivorous plants.

David Welch Winter Gardens lie within **Duthie Park**, which is cupped by the River Dee as it curves north towards Aberdeen Harbour. The park was officially opened by Queen Victoria's daughter Princess Beatrice in 1883, with the gardens added later. I spent an unholy amount of time in the Arid House, where there is every sort of cactus and succulent you can think of – with more than 750 species, it's one of the largest such collections in the UK.

Varying in shape from globes to furry javelins to Mickey Mouse faces, cacti have got to be some of nature's most exquisite creations, not to mention master survivalists. Their spines and fine hairs create a humid micro-habitat around each plant and protect them from herbivores, while their waxy skin acts as a waterproof layer. Most cacti and succulents photosynthesise using a process called crassulacean acid metabolism. To reduce water loss, they absorb CO_2 at night when temperatures are lower, and store it as acid until they can photosynthesise the next day.

Seeing such an impressive display of cacti here makes you realise how big they can grow if given the chance. Walk along the winding footpaths and you'll see some no bigger than a finger and others towering some 15ft tall. If I haven't sold this place enough already, there's even a pond containing teeny tiny terrapins sunning themselves under heat lamps.

The Winter Gardens are about a mile from the city centre. The most picturesque walking route here follows the River Dee on North Esplanade West and Riverside Drive before turning right on to Polmuir Road.

¶¶ FOOD & DRINK

Books & Beans Belmont St, AB10 1JH ℘ 01224 646438 ⊘ booksandbeans.co.uk. Fuel up with Fair Trade coffee, breakfasts, toasties, burgers, omelettes or pancakes before heading to the first floor to browse 10,000 secondhand books.

Cup Tea Salon Little Belmont St, AB10 1JG ℘ 01224 637730 ⊘ cupteasalon.com. *Alice in Wonderland*-themed interior and outside seating in a peaceful pedestrianised side street in view of St Nicholas Kirk. Lunch options include soup and sandwiches but there's also afternoon tea and a wide range of brunch and vegan choices available until 16.00.

Latinway Belmont St, AB10 1JE ℘ 01224 611707 ⊘ latinway.co.uk ⊙ noon–19.00 Mon–Thu; noon–20.00 Fri & Sat. Fabulous authentic Latin American food, to take-away or eat in. Perch at mini-bar tables to feast on tacos, quesadillas and more as Latin music plays.

Liberty Kitchen at Greyhope Bay Greyhope Rd, AB11 8QX ⏁ greyhopebay.com ⏰ 10.00–16.00 Wed–Sun. A cashless, vegan-friendly space within Torry Battery (page 298). With a strong environmental focus, the café uses local suppliers and small-batch coffee roasters, plus seasonal ingredients and reusable serving options wherever possible. It's geared towards connecting the local community with Aberdeen's marine environment through year-round events and educational programmes. These include weekly coffee mornings and beach cleans on the first and third Sundays of each month.

Mackie's 19.2 Marischal Sq, AB10 1BL ☎ 01224 518252 ⏰ noon–21.00 daily. Mackie's ice cream is a Scottish staple and this is its first parlour, so named because it's 19.2 miles from the farm. Take your pick of more than 20 flavours in a tub, cone, sundae or, as I did, slathered all over waffles.

Monsoona Healthy Indian Cuisine Bridge St, AB11 6JJ ☎ 01224 590030 ⏁ monsoona. co.uk ⏰ noon–14.00 & 17.00–23.30 daily. This restaurant's vivid red décor and warm lighting complement its vibrant dishes. Some Indian food can be heavy, but Monsoona uses low fat yoghurt and cream and sunflower oil, which is low in saturated fat, to create healthier dishes without compromising on flavour.

Sweet Mumma's Kitchen Palmerston Rd, AB11 5RE ☎ 07595 452621 🅵 ⏰ 09.00–14.00 Mon–Sat. Decorated with hanging flowers, faux chandeliers and pastel shades, this dog-friendly café serves breakfasts, paninis, bagels, mac & cheese and more. It occupies the next railway arch along from the City of Aberdeen Gin Distillery (page 296).

THE CITY OUTSKIRTS

⌂ **Cove Bay Hotel** (page 320) ⛺ **Deeside Holiday Park** (page 320)

The boundary of Aberdeen City stretches outside the central hub into several surrounding neighbourhoods. To the north, the zigzagging River Don flows southeast, eventually reaching Donmouth Local Nature Reserve at the tip of Old Aberdeen (page 284). Beside one of its curling loops further upstream is **Dyce Military Cemetery** (🏴 nanny.news.slice), 2½ miles north of Aberdeen International Airport.

"Every now and then you might catch the splash of a leaping fish or the flash of a rabbit's tail."

The ruined shell of a 13th-century church stands in the centre of the cemetery, dedicated to the Pictish missionary St Fergus. Inside the church, sheltered from the elements under a wooden porch, are the **Dyce Symbol Stones**. There are six of varying sizes and they were all discovered either inside or near the churchyard. The Celtic cross slab, showing Pictish crescents and double discs, and the Pictish symbol slab are the largest, at around

5ft tall. On the latter, a Pictish beastie and Z-rod overlapped by a double disc are clearly visible. Four smaller grave marker stones, each with their own intricate carvings, are mounted into the stone wall beside the larger slabs.

Aside from the occasional Easyjet passing over, this is a peaceful spot. I noticed the view over the river from the church and wandered down for a look, ending up spending several hours ambling along lightly trodden trails beside the river bank. The herons aren't shy and will fish in plain sight, close to mallards perching on rocks and swallows skimming the surface while they're here in summer. Every now and then you might catch the splash of a leaping fish or the flash of a rabbit's tail as it plunges into the bracken.

Hazlehead Park

AB15 8BD

Granted to the city in 1319 by Robert the Bruce and covering some 400 acres, Hazlehead is Aberdeen's largest park and lies four miles west of the city centre. It has an intriguing mix of features, such as Scotland's oldest maze, although my favourites are the beautiful sculptures and gardens that you could easily spend an hour exploring. I've never seen so many memorials and commemorative sculptures together, and they make Hazlehead Park a really reflective place. Kids and dogs have open space to run around, but away from the play park area you can sit in a variety of gardens and hear nothing but birdsong.

Just past the café is a series of squat stone cairns known as the **Bruce Cairns** after Robert the Bruce. Each one features a carving by local sculptor Richard Ross Robertson (1914–2007) of a different scene, including Robert the Bruce's coronation and the Battle of Bannockburn. If you scan the QR codes on the plaques beside each cairn, they pull up an accompanying illustration by Gabrielle Reith and poem written by Sheena Blackhall, recited by pupils from Hazlehead Primary School.

Elsewhere in the park, look out for: a memorial garden dedicated to the 167 men who died in the Piper Alpha North Sea Disaster on 6 July 1988; a memory path laid with inscribed slabs for lost loved ones; and a group of standing stones in the azalea garden called Hazlehenge, which form part of the Sculpture Trail. My favourite piece is *Fleeting* by Maja Quille – a bench created from dozens of metal birds, their interlinked wings outstretched in flight.

REBECCA GIBSON

REBECCA GIBSON

VISITSCOTLAND/KENNY LAM

1

2

3

Gordon Highlanders Museum

Viewfield Rd, AB15 7XH ⊘ gordonhighlanders.com ⊙ 10.00–16.30 Tue–Sat

You can easily spend two hours at this fantastic museum that tells the story of the Gordon Highlanders, one of the best-known regiments in the British Army. Exhibits travel through Napoleonic, Victorian and Edwardian times, both World Wars and into the 20th century. The regiment has been awarded 19 Victoria Crosses, 11 of which are on display here. As you approach the entrance you'll see the Gordon Highlanders' crest with a stag's head on the wall outside. Beneath the stag is the word *Bydand*, which means 'steadfast'. This is a contraction of the Scots phrase 'bide and fecht', meaning 'stand and fight'.

Visitors can take a self-guided tour of the museum using an audio headset, which offers a simpler version for children as well as the classic tour. However, I recommend requesting a volunteer-led guided tour at the welcome desk – my guide Jim had amazing tales to tell of soldiers and battles that really enhanced the experience. I particularly loved the story behind a tam-o'-shanter hat with a bullet hole in the top, worn by Private Davey Davidson while on patrol in Ireland in 1973. Regimental Magazine reported that the bullet 'parted his hair'.

"As you approach the entrance you'll see the Gordon Highlanders' crest with a stag's head on the wall outside."

One of the downstairs rooms is full of regimental silver, presented in square cabinets with smoky blue backdrops. The armoury has a vast collection of swords, knives, muskets, revolvers and drawers full of medals. My highlight was walking through the replica World War I Moffat Trench, where you can peer into the officer's dugout and see examples of food, gas masks and equipment that were used in the trenches. Note that you can't access the trench without a guide.

Much of this museum has been designed with children in mind. There are wooden tabs to pull out and read, 3D displays, a Lego figure treasure hunt and miniature dioramas showing battle scenes in amazing detail.

For a truly immersive experience, you can book a Waterloo Regimental Dinner for a minimum of eight guests. The package includes champagne and canapés, a four-course menu with regimental silver

◀ **1** The David Welch Winter Gardens. **2** Gordon Highlanders Museum. **3** The interior of Drum Castle.

on the table, a guided museum tour, a piper on arrival and a dram of Gordon Highlanders whisky.

Once you've visited the museum, it's worth wandering through nearby **Johnston Gardens** (AB15 7XE ☺ 08.00–dusk daily). This 2½-acre park contains shrubbery, mossy rockeries and a mini waterfall tumbling down rocks into a pond crossed by a periwinkle blue bridge, as well as a small play area for children. In spring and summer, the gardens bloom with rhododendrons, blossom, bulbs and aquatic plants. You'll see mallards and moorhens on the water all year round – if you're going to feed them, bring peas, corn or oats, not bread.

Tollohill Wood

/// flute.saying.plans

This secluded wood lies 3½ miles southwest of the city centre. With its deep rocky dells and hip-high bracken, it's what I call a Jurassic forest because it doesn't take an overactive imagination to picture a dinosaur poking above the foliage. There are no waymarked trails, but an established track runs around the perimeter. After first heading into the trees from the car park, bear right at the fork and follow it north. Beeches, birches and rowans are all mixed together, separated from an adjacent open field by a mossy stone wall.

The perimeter path almost breaks out of the trees at the northwest edge of the wood, but bends back in up a rocky incline. Shortly, you'll pass a **Neolithic cairn** next to the path. Measuring about 6ft wide and 3ft tall, it consists of a ring of mossy boulders with a flatter slab placed over the top, creating a tiny cave now stuffed with beech leaves.

"Beeches, birches and rowans are all mixed together, separated from an adjacent open field by a mossy stone wall."

When the path forks some 100yds further up from the cairn, turn left and continue uphill – you might have to duck under low-hanging branches. After about 40yds, look right and you'll see a narrow stone **monument** on the crop of the hill, commemorating a visit from Prince Albert in 1859. Once you reach it, you can peep north over the trees towards the centre of Aberdeen.

With so many interweaving tracks curling back on each other, it's easy to lose your sense of direction here, but stick to any of the established paths heading east from the monument and you'll soon emerge at the car park. As you drive back north towards Aberdeen you can admire the distant city view, which will have been behind you on the approach.

To get here, follow the B9077 on the south side of the River Dee, then take the unnamed lane on the left signposted for Causey Mounth Road. Tollohill's car park is another half a mile along here.

Drum Castle

AB31 5EY ⊙ Jun–Aug 10.30–16.00 daily; Sep–May, check website for hours; National Trust for Scotland

Thirteen miles west of Aberdeen is one of Scotland's oldest tower houses. Made of pink and grey granite, Drum Castle combines a Jacobean mansion house, a Victorian extension and a medieval tower. Its name derives from the Gaelic for 'ridge' or 'knoll', referring to the castle's elevated position. Its spacious rooms are dominated by an abundance of family portraits in gilded frames, Victorian high-backed armchairs and oak-panelled ceilings.

Drum Castle was owned by 24 generations of the Irvine family (1323–1976). The 17th Laird was Alexander Irvine, who fought for Bonnie Prince Charlie. After the Battle of Culloden, he escaped and was kept hidden at Drum by his sister Mary. His survival and that of Drum's ancient oak wood is largely thanks to her – when the king's men arrived demanding to search the castle, she let them. If she'd refused, they would have destroyed the castle and killed the family. While her brother hid, Mary managed the estate and continued to do so after Alexander's death. There's a portrait of her in the drawing room, painted by Henry Raeburn, and the onsite Mary's Larder café is named after her.

"Outside the walled garden is a smaller pond garden where you can look for newts and dragonflies in summer."

As well as exploring the castle, it's possible to walk several short circular trails through the grounds, passing through manicured gardens, farmland and woodland. On the one-mile Farmland Walk is a walled area called the **Garden of Historic Roses**, where a wooden platform provides a vantage point over square beds of roses and shrubs with a grid of grass paths passing beneath arched trellises.

Each quarter of the garden has been laid out in the style of a different century, researched using historic photographs from the 1600s to the 1900s. Styles transition from knot gardens and formal box parterres to informal mixtures of shrubs and herbs for the most modern quarter. Roses didn't feature in the parterres and knots seen in 17th- and 18th-century gardens, so the current roses need to be regularly pruned to keep this modern adaptation within tight borders.

Outside the walled garden is a smaller pond garden where you can look for newts and dragonflies in summer. Although unsuitable for wheelchairs, the one-mile Woodland Walk trail passes spectacular mature oaks, rowans, beeches and birches. I glimpsed a roe deer with a bright orange summer coat trotting through the trees.

STONEHAVEN & AROUND

Fifteen miles south of Aberdeen is the coastal town of Stonehaven. It's perhaps best known for its Hogmanay Fireball ceremony, where a team of seasoned 'swingers' march down the high street, bringing in the new year by whirling wire mesh balls of flame around their heads.

Further south along the coast from Stonehaven are two excellent wildlife reserves. RSPB Fowlsheugh has a cliff-nesting seabird colony known for its puffins, while St Cyrus National Nature Reserve, the most southerly point of interest in this book, offers a contrasting mix of windswept dunes, towering crags and wildflower meadows humming with insects.

STONEHAVEN FIREBALLS

⊘ stonehavenfireballs.co.uk

As the midnight bells chime on 31 December, around 40 men and women march along Stonehaven's High Street swinging flaming balls over their heads, each one weighing some 14lbs. Legend has it that this wards off evil spirits for the year ahead.

The Fireballs contain any non-synthetic, combustible materials and must be dense enough to burn for a 25-minute procession. Graeme Cusine, who has been a Fireball Swinger since 2009, uses old jeans, socks and bits of firewood.

The first official record of the Fireballs is as recent as the early 20th century, but it's firmly planted in Stonehaven's identity and even inspired the name of local brewery Reids Gold's (⊘ reidsgold.com) vegan Fireballs Session IPA beer.

Women began participating from 1935 and it wasn't until 1991, once the event started attracting much bigger crowds, that barriers were put in place. Now people begin to gather as early as 10pm, so plan ahead if you want good views.

2 STONEHAVEN

On every other day of the year but Hogmanay (see opposite), Stonehaven has a tranquil, relaxed atmosphere. Visitors tend to congregate around the harbour, picnicking on a tiny beach by the stone jetty or perusing a waterfront museum. The town is also known for Dunnottar Castle, a sprawling ruin on a platform of cliffs.

The harbour and beach on the town's eastern side are within the 'Auld Toon', where Stonehaven originated before expanding inland into what is now largely residential. There's a footpath called **Bay Walk** all the way along the beach promenade, stretching for one mile and alternating between a concrete or wooden surface. The beach changes as you walk, with sand, grit and pebbles merging together. Both ends of the walkway have a bridge over a river joining the sea: Cowie Water to the north and Carron Water to the south.

In 2003, a **fossil** of the oldest known air-breathing land animal in the world was discovered within the sandstone rocks near this beach by amateur geologist Mike Newman. The creature was a millipede arthropod that lived 428 million years ago and was named *Pneumodesmus newmani*. I don't think there's any greater brag than having an animal named after you. You can learn more about the millipede in the Tolbooth Museum (page 309), but to see the original fossil you'll have to trek 112 miles south to the National Museum of Scotland in Edinburgh.

Bay Walk follows the curve of the beach all the way to the harbour at Stonehaven's southeast corner. Before you reach it, there's a semi-circular picnic area with curved wooden plank benches and a life-size sculpture of a dolphin, made of wire and filled with shingle. From here, you can cut south through one of several narrow walkways leading to Old Pier.

Stonehaven's harbour originates from before the 17th century, but was reconstructed after storm damage and the present harbour dates to 1908. It's separated into several basins and some of these permit aquatic activities such as paddle boarding. Lessons, coastal tours and social paddles are available with Stonehaven Paddle Boarding (⊘ shpb.co.uk). The harbour is sheltered, flanked on its southern side by a steep hilly promontory leading to Dunnottar Castle (page 310).

Shorehead, the narrow road running around the harbour's western perimeter, is cobbled and lined with large stone houses. There's a sandy beach by the slipway, which is a popular spot for building sandcastles.

To the right of this slipway is Duthie's Well. Named after Stonehaven merchant Captain William Duthie, it's the last of the five wells that served the Auld Toon in the 19th century.

With your back to the harbour, look west up High Street and you'll see a skinny spire with a weathervane 100yds up the road. This is the **Clock Tower**, a square sandstone structure constructed in 1790 with both French and Dutch influences. It has two bells, the second added to commemorate Queen Victoria's Golden Jubilee. Now they are only rung on special occasions like Hogmanay, just as the Fireballs procession kicks off.

On the harbour's northern side is the **Tolbooth Museum** (✐ 07512 466329 ◌ stonehaventolbooth.co.uk ◔ Apr–Sep 13.30–16.30 Fri–Mon; Oct–Mar 12.30–15.30 Sat & Sun; free entry) – the oldest building in Stonehaven. You'll hear sea shanties drifting out the door as you stand outside. Said to have been founded by George Keith, 5th Earl Marischal, and originally intended as a storehouse, the museum is stuffed with Stonehaven's past. There are sections on farming, maritime history, geology and its days as a prison – you can walk into a cell, complete with its original door. Dotted around the museum are QR codes where you can listen to volunteers talking about the collections and their experiences. A range of local interest books are for sale, including highlighted walks and trails.

Dunnottar Woods

Carved animal sculptures, a bed of orange beech leaves and the whispering Burn of Glaslaw all make Dunnottar Woods a photogenic patch. It's possible to walk a circular loop through its mixed patches of spruce and beech, as well as branch off on numerous overlapping trails.

I love a forest with secrets, and one of the highlights of this wood is a concealed stone igloo called **The Shell House** (▨ jabs.plankton. remedy), located beside the burn near the centre of the forest. Peer inside and you'll see its walls are encrusted with thousands of seashells, from tiny periwinkles to blushing pink hand-sized conches. Topped with moss, it looks like a house for fairies, but was more likely built to amuse the children of Lady Eleanora Kennedy, a member of the

◀ **1** Stonehaven. **2** Stonehaven Fireballs. **3** Exhibits in Stonehaven's Tolbooth Museum. **4** The Shell House, Dunnottar Woods.

prominent Kennedy family who lived in nearby Dunnottar House in the 19th century. The house was demolished in 1959, but luckily the tiny shell-filled shelter still stands.

Dunnottar Woods aren't all fairytale though. Partway along the waymarked History Trail is **Gallow's Hill**, where condemned criminals were hanged. These gallows were built on a 3,000-year-old Bronze Age burial mound. Stand on top of the mound and look over the forest below – it's hard to believe now that this peaceful spot with its soundtrack of birdsong was once a site of execution.

The northern fringe of Dunnottar Woods is half a mile from Stonehaven Harbour. The most direct walking route here begins by heading west on High Street and joining Dunnottar Avenue after 350yds. When the road bends left, branch slightly right to continue on Dunnottar Avenue, then turn left on to Carron Gardens and walk to the mini turning circle at the end. You'll see the green Forestry Commission sign straight ahead.

¶¶ FOOD & DRINK

Old Pier Coffee House Old Pier, AB39 2JU ✆ 01569 766035 ⏏ theoldpierstonehaven. com. In the perfect location for enjoying a take-away lunch with your legs swinging off the harbour wall. Choose from toasted baguettes with creative veggie options, soup, brunch and fresh cakes and pastries. You'll know where it is in summer when you see the queue of people outside.

The Ship Inn Shorehead, AB39 2JY ✆ 01569 762617 ⏏ shipinnstonehaven.com ⏱ daily; see website for hours. Specialising in fish and seafood but also with a variety of vegetarian options, The Ship Inn has a warm, friendly atmosphere and a nautical theme to reflect its prime position on the harbourfront. Enjoy lunch and dinner made from locally sourced produce in the dog-friendly lounge bar, the Captain's Table restaurant, or outside during summer – perfect for watching boats come and go while sipping a drink.

3 DUNNOTTAR CASTLE

AB39 2TL ⏏ dunnottarcastle.co.uk ⏱ Apr–Sep 09.00–18.00 daily; Oct–Mar check website

This spectacular ruin perches on 160ft-high craggy cliffs, 2½ miles south of Stonehaven via the A957 and A92. There's a car park 500yds away, but it's far more enjoyable to reach the castle via a clifftop walk from town (see opposite). The castle and the coast path can be popular; for a quieter visit with people-free photos, I recommend visiting earlier in the morning so you're just finishing as everyone else shows up.

CLIFFTOP WALK TO DUNNOTTAR CASTLE

It's roughly a 2½-mile round trip from Stonehaven Harbour to Dunnottar Castle via the coast-path route, and you'll probably want to allow at least three hours for both the walk and a decent amount of exploring time at the ruin.

To get there, walk south on Shorehead and follow a brown sign to the castle, pointing up pedestrianised Wallace Wynd. The path climbs steeply away from town and on to the Coastal Tourist Route, heading southeast. Look back for views over the harbour and town centre. Once the road bends to the right, join a concrete footpath branching left to begin the clifftop trail.

You'll see a **war memorial** standing prominently to the right, 200yds up a side path that pops with daffodils in spring. This striking monument consists of eight round pillars connected by an octagonal stone border at the top. Walk up some stone steps for a closer look at stone slabs bearing the names of those lost during World War I.

There's a wooden model of the memorial in the Tolbooth Museum, created by retired civil engineer Colin Sandeman and donated to the museum in January 2020.

Return to the cliff path and continue south. The track curves around Strathlethan Bay, which shines turquoise even on an overcast day. The formidable rock formations on the southern side of this bay are known as the **Dunnicaer Sea Stack** – spot the cave opening that looks like a door for giants. Past the bay, cross a bridge over a stream. From here you can appreciate the vastness of the castle ruin ahead.

Once you arrive at the castle, you'll see a path turning right towards the road, leading to the car park and a hut with refreshments. Descend a stone staircase to the castle itself. It begs to be photographed, stood as it is on a craggy outcrop jutting into the sea. As you pass the cliff, look up and you might see nesting fulmars perched on grassy shelves in spring, cackling to each other.

Dunnottar's name comes from the Celtic Dùn Fhothair, meaning 'the fort on the shelving slope'. The rock it stands on is believed to have been occupied as far back as the 5th century, when St Ninian built a missionary station there. According to legend, Sir William Wallace trapped an English force at Dunnottar during the Wars of Independence in 1297, although there was no evidence of a castle on the site at the time. It's said the English took refuge in a chapel but Wallace burnt it to the ground. Fifteenth-century poet Blind Harry wrote about these events in his poem *Wallace* – rather than the historical events themselves, this was apparently the inspiration for the 1995 film *Braveheart*.

You can get great views of the ruin's exterior without paying for entry, but it's worth going in for all the nooks and crumbly crannies you can explore inside. My inner child was boggle-eyed at the warren of cool chambers, lit only by daylight seeping through slits in the stone. The bakery is particularly fun, with a low, arched ceiling and echoing water drips.

A section known as the Lion's Den is where George Keith, 5th Earl Marischal, kept a pet lion in 1593. Now the distorted cooing of rock doves nesting in the chambers above is the only sound like a roar. Elsewhere on the ruin site, up a steep stone staircase, is a tiny museum containing displays of 19th-century musket balls and a miniature replica of what the castle may have looked like while under siege by Oliver Cromwell's troops in 1651.

Towards the southern side of the castle, you can see behind the fulmar cliff you passed on the way in and admire another bay to the left. Straight ahead, a waterfall threads between two cliffs, its course cutting a winding runnel into the grass below.

4 RSPB FOWLSHEUGH

AB39 2TP rspb.org.uk/reserves-and-events/reserves-a-z/fowlsheugh

The name of this clifftop nature reserve, 4½ miles south of Stonehaven, comes from a Scots word literally translating to 'bird cliff'. A narrow path hugs a cliff edge where over 130,000 seabirds nest on crevices and rock ledges during spring and summer, including guillemots, razorbills, fulmars, kittiwakes and puffins. The adjacent grassland habitat attracts meadow pipits, skylarks, linnets and a variety of butterflies and moths foraging among sea thrift and sea campion.

When you smell that fishy pong, you know you're in a good place. Walk right from the car park and follow the road for 160yds until you reach a wooden puffin beside the information board. Steps cut into the hill lead up to the unprotected cliffs – this is definitely a place to watch your step! During summer, the sights, sounds and smells of thousands of breeding seabirds are overwhelming.

You can walk for about a mile along an out-and-back trail to a tiny hide at the far end, ideal for sheltering in less desirable weather. For your safety and to avoid disturbing the nesting birds, stay back from the cliff edge and watch from a respectable distance. Fowlsheugh is a lot quieter from late August through winter, as most seabirds leave the cliffs

---

1 St Cyrus NNR. 2 Dunnottar Castle. 3 RSPB Fowlsheugh. ▶

to spend winter at sea. Still, there are chances of spotting distant seals and dolphins throughout the year.

Before you leave, turn left past the wooden puffin and walk to the end of the road, without crossing into the private driveway. Look left over the bay and you'll see **Crawton Waterfall** peeking behind the rocks. This is the end of Crawton Burn as it topples over the cliffs into the sea.

Note that parking is very limited at Fowlsheugh, with only twelve bays stacked beside an unnamed road to the tiny hamlet of Crawton. Don't block the road or its verges – if there's no space, you'll have to return another time.

5 ST CYRUS NATIONAL NATURE RESERVE

/// signature.conducted.corporate & nature.scot

Nineteen miles south of RSPB Fowlsheugh via the A92, St Cyrus National Nature Reserve (NNR) is on Aberdeenshire's southern border. For me, its appeal comes from its diversity – despite barely stretching two miles, this packed reserve contains grassland, cliffs, sand dunes and the mouth of the River North Esk. Its small size makes its abundance of wildlife even more impressive; over 300 plant species have been recorded here, protected from the elements by the cliffs and steep sand banks. As well as the whisper of the sea, I hear skylarks, chiffchaffs and chaffinches on spring visits, and there's always the possibility of seeing bottlenose dolphins from the beach. Look out for the Pollinator Trail information boards dotted around the reserve, which tell you about the bees, flies and wildflowers you might find.

The reserve has something for a variety of different interests, including a hide for birdwatchers, an ancient kirkyard for history enthusiasts and the beach for everyone to enjoy. These are all linked up by several waymarked trails branching in different directions from the visitor centre. Heading north is the one-mile **Tyrie Trail**, following a combination of gravel and compacted mud paths through grassland. Shortly after beginning this trail, a boardwalk forks off to the beach. If you continue straight, the path passes **Nether Kirkyard** after 400yds, appearing on the left behind bracken. It's surrounded by a stone wall, but you can step off the Tyrie Trail and climb a set of stone steps over the wall and down again for a closer look.

Flanked by shaggy cliffs covered in sea thrift and fulmars, the kirkyard now mostly contains 19th-century headstones, with no trace of a church, although the remains of a roofless stone burial enclosure stand in the centre. The site is also known as Ecclesgreig Old Church and Burial Ground, linked to a 9th-century Pictish ruler called Grig who established a place of worship here. The name of the nature reserve and neighbouring village, also called St Cyrus, originates from one of many variations of Grig's name: Ciric.

Beside the kirkyard, the Tyrie Trail turns 180° and returns to the visitor centre along a rockier path parallel to the outward route.

In the opposite direction to the Tyrie Trail is the 1½-mile **Estuary Walk**, which begins in a fenced field often bursting with rabbits. Follow a grass path between gorse bushes and cross a small wooden bridge at the end of the field. On the other side, a grass track lined with driftwood leads to a wooden hide overlooking the estuary. Like all good hides, it's equipped with illustrations of birds and cetaceans you might see.

¶¶ FOOD & DRINK

Old Bakery Coffee Shop Beach Rd, St Cyrus DD10 0BJ ✆ 01674 850930 🇫. With indoor seating or the option to take-away, this little café serves sandwiches to order, soups, fresh home bakes and ice cream.

ACCOMMODATION

The following list is my recommended selection of B&Bs, self-catering lets, hotels and camping options across the North East. I've chosen them based on their location, character, friendliness or how Slow they are in terms of facilities and ethos. It's also refreshingly easy to find dog-friendly places around here, so I've included a diverse range. Rates vary seasonally – if you're visiting in summer, I recommend booking well in advance, especially for smaller villages. For more information and longer reviews, go to ⊘ bradtguides.com/nessleeps.

Within the guide chapters, hotels and B&Bs are indicated by 🏠 under the heading for their nearest town or village, self-catering by 🏡 and camping and glamping sites by ⛺.

Obviously, there are far more options to choose from in the North East than I can list here. Check out **Visit Moray Speyside** (⊘ morayspeyside.com/find/places-to-stay-in-moray-speyside), **Visit Aberdeenshire** (⊘ visitabdn.com/plan-your-trip/where-to-stay) and **Visit Cairngorms** (⊘ visitcairngorms.com/plan-your-visit/places-to-stay) for more recommendations.

1 CAIRNGORMS NATIONAL PARK: WEST

Hotels

The Boat Country Inn & Restaurant
Boat of Garten PH24 3BH ⊘ 01479 831258 ⊘ boathotel.co.uk. Like its dining area (page 48), the dog-friendly rooms at this hotel have plenty of tartan furniture, stag-themed décor and warm lighting, providing a cosy place to rest after a long day exploring. It's well-placed for forest walks, with Loch Garten less than three miles away. You can also catch the Strathspey Steam Railway from right outside.

The Grant Arms Hotel Grantown-on-Spey PH26 3HF ⊘ 01479 872526 ⊘ grantarmshotel. com. Known for its celebrity-guided wildlife holidays, the 'UK's Wildlife Hotel' welcomes dogs and offers a blend of modern comforts and traditional character, all with a nature theme.

B&Bs

Nethy House Café & Rooms Nethy Bridge PH25 3EB ⊘ 07963 217793 ⊘ nethyhouse. co.uk. Five spacious and stylish rooms, just a stroll from Abernethy Forest. The ground floor room is wheelchair-accessible and dog friendly.

Ravenscraig Guest House Aviemore PH22 1RP ⊘ 01479 810278 ⊘ ravenscraighouse.co.uk. A combination of modern amenities and stylish décor in a traditional Victorian building, with dog-friendly cabins and small wooden chalets also available in an annex at the back of the building. Walkers are well-catered for.

Self-catering

Aviemore Youth Hostel Aviemore PH22 1PR ☎ 01479 810345 ♂ hostellingscotland. org.uk/hostels/aviemore. Offering simple and practical accommodation in shared dorms or private rooms, with the added bonus of Craigellachie NNR right outside. As well as a self-catering kitchen, there's the option of Continental breakfast served in the dining room (pre-booking essential).

Glentruim Lodge Newtonmore PH20 1BE ☎ 07712 589042 ♂ glentruim.com. A large detached house at the end of a private track. Guests can hire the whole property as a self-catering let for up to 12 people, or hire one of three bedrooms on a B&B basis, sharing a lounge and kitchen with the owners and any other guests. Also available on-site is a tiny self-catering ecopod with everything you need for cosy, secluded glamping.

Camping

Dalraddy Holiday Park Alvie PH22 1QB ☎ 01479 810330 ♂ campinginaviemore.co.uk. Open all year round, this dog-friendly campsite offers wooden chalets and pitches for tents and caravans, right next to Torr of Alvie and the Speyside Way.

2 CAIRNGORMS NATIONAL PARK: EAST

Hotel

Loch Kinord Hotel Dinnet AB34 5LW ☎ 01339 885229 ♂ kinord.co.uk. Praised for the quality of its locally sourced food, this small, family-run hotel welcomes dogs and provides the kind of caring service you'd expect in a B&B. Guests can also stay in a self-catered woodland lodge in the grounds.

B&Bs

Argyle House Tomintoul AB37 9EX ☎ 01807 580766 ♂ argyletomintoul.co.uk. Small, dog-friendly guest house with an impressive breakfast menu, just 100yds from Tomintoul's central square.

Cranford Guest House Braemar AB35 5YQ ☎ 01339 741675 ♂ cranfordbraemar.co.uk. Close to Balmoral, this dog-friendly B&B is run by knowledgeable hosts who are happy to advise on local walks. Outdoor enthusiasts are catered for with bike and ski storage space.

Self-catering

Ballater Hostel Ballater AB35 5QJ ☎ 01339 753752 ♂ ballater-hostel.com. Friendly, spacious hostel offering dorms and private rooms – owners Daniel and Dominique often drop in for a blether while you cook in the communal kitchen.

Camping & Glamping

Howe of Torbeg Ballater AB35 5XL ☎ 01339 756262 ♂ howeoftorbeg.co.uk. Offering simple home comforts in the wilderness of Royal Deeside, this small-scale site has several glamping pods and an off-grid shepherd's hut with environmentally conscious features, including low-flush toilets and solar lighting.

3 CENTRAL MORAY

B&B

Dunvegan B&B Dufftown AB55 4AA ☎ 01340 821124 ♂ dunvegan-dufftown. co.uk. Within walking distance of several of Dufftown's distilleries, this stylish B&B offers a complimentary dram in each room.

Self-catering

Duke Cottage Fochabers IV32 7DN ♂ dukecottage.com. Just a handful of steps from the village square, this cosy, dog-friendly cottage sleeps up to four people and has a fenced garden with a barbecue.

The Milking Sheds Dufftown AB55 4AR
☏ 07801 350723 ⌖ speysidecottages.com. Two semi-detached stone cottages offering a fully equipped kitchen and patio area. For families and groups, there are two larger properties next door: a Victorian villa and Scotland's first luxury self-catering Smart Home. This property's swish interior is kitted out with automated light features, including Night Mode to guide you when it's dark, and the freedom to control music and also the colours and intensity of the light from most rooms. All four properties welcome dogs.

Camping & Glamping

Ace Adventures Forres IV36 2QL ☏ 01309 611729 ⌖ aceadventures.co.uk. Choose from woodland camping pitches, bell tents with wood-burning stoves and luxury shepherd's huts at this secluded site in the Findhorn Valley, which also offers white-water rafting.

Hideaway Under The Stars Aberlour AB38 9NL ☏ 07786 225639 ⌖ hideawayunderthestars. co.uk. Combining touches of luxury with lots of bespoke wooden elements, this rustic, dog-friendly holiday home has a domed roof with a circular window for cosy stargazing. You can swim in a private fairy pool and pick your own organic food from the garden.

4 THE MORAY COAST

Hotel

The Victoria Hotel Portknockie AB56 4LQ ☏ 07834 589868 ⌖ thevictoriahotelportknockie.co.uk. Traditional stone building with a small pub and just seven peaceful rooms, some of which allow dogs. Host Paul offers a warm welcome and cooks a fabulous breakfast.

B&Bs

Moraybank B&B Elgin IV30 1QT ☏ 01343 547618 ⌖ moraybank.co.uk. Located within a handsome 19th-century house set back from the road behind a stretching lawn, this refurbished

B&B has maintained many period features, including a striking Gothic bathroom in one of its three rooms.

Stravaig B&B Cullen AB56 4SW ☏ 07985 412387 ⌖ stravaigcullen.com. Named after a Scottish word meaning 'to wander aimlessly', this family-run B&B has excellent rates considering its central location right on Cullen's high street. Beyond its stone wall exterior, a comfy guest lounge and two bedrooms (one dog friendly) with en-suite bathrooms, houseplants and lots of cupboard space all provide a homely feel.

Self-catering

Covesea Lighthouse Keeper Cottages Lossiemouth IV31 6SP ☏ 01343 810664 ⌖ covesealighthouse.co.uk. Once home to lightkeepers, these modernised dog-friendly cottages offer visitors the unique opportunity to stay at the foot of Covesea Lighthouse, right next to a sprawling sandy beach and The Moray Coast Trail.

Mossyards Holiday Cottages Roseisle IV30 5YD ☏ 01343 830250 ⌖ mossyards.co.uk. Close to Duffus Castle, these two dog-friendly cottages both have a sunlit patio with farmland views, as well as floor-to-ceiling windows for when you'd rather cosy up inside in a high-backed armchair. Enjoy complimentary organic produce from the garden when it's available too.

Camping & Glamping

The Loft Glamping & Camping Forres IV36 2UD ☏ 01343 850111 ⌖ theloft.co.uk. A rustic farmland glamping experience with pitches for tents and campervans as well as snug wigwams and dog-friendly cabins with a wood-fired hot tub.

5 ABERDEENSHIRE: THE NORTHEAST COAST & BUCHAN

Hotel

The Garden Arms Hotel Gardenstown AB45 3YP ☏ 01261 851260 ⌖ thegardenarms.

com. More like a home than a hotel, this low-ceilinged, wonky-floored 18th-century building is famous for welcoming Bram Stoker on one of his visits to the area.

B&Bs

Aden House B&B Old Deer AB42 5LN ✆ 01771 623195 ⌂ adenhouse.info. Close to Aden Country Park and Deer Abbey, this dog-friendly B&B is praised for its helpful hosts and Scottish breakfasts. A clincher for me were the rooms – cosy, good value and named after birds.

Cruden Bay B&B Cruden Bay AB42 0NJ ✆ 01779 812215 ⌂ crudenbaybedandbreakfast.com. Overlooking Cruden Bay Golf Club and a mile from Slains Castle, this family-run B&B offers a relaxed atmosphere and warm hospitality.

Self-catering

Driftwood Cottage Portsoy AB45 2QR ✆ 01261 843386 ⌂ moraycoastcottages.com/portsoy. A coastal-themed dog-friendly cottage containing a jumbled back garden with three terraces, a summer house, pond and lots of driftwood decoration.

Mill of Nethermill Holidays Pennan AB43 6JA ✆ 01346 561482 ⌂ nethermillholidays.co.uk. Located beside a secluded pebble beach between two headlands, these four luxurious properties welcome dogs and have exposed stone walls, modern kitchens and rustic wooden furniture. Also on-site is Millshore Pottery (⬛) showcasing local crafts and hand-thrown stoneware pottery by owner Lynn.

Wildflower Eco Lodges Fraserburgh AB43 8XT ✆ 07717 376194 ⌂ wildflowerecolodges.co.uk. Two open-plan self-catering lodges in Aberdeenshire countryside, where you can bring your dog and warm up by a wood-burning stove.

Camping & Glamping

Down on the Farm Rosehearty AB43 6JY ✆ 07954 989737 ⌂ downonthefarm.net. Coastal dog-friendly glamping accommodation

on a working farm that actively promotes agritourism with its lambing and sheep-shearing tours. Choose from Hideaways shaped like Pringles tubes, an off-grid converted carriage or a farmer's hut.

6 ABERDEENSHIRE: FORMARTINE & THE GARIOCH

Hotel

Banks of Ury Inverurie AB51 3XQ ✆ 01467 620409 ⌂ banksofuryhotel@gmail.com ⬛. Family-run bar and hotel perfectly located in the centre of Inverurie, a five-minute walk from the train station.

B&B

Edgehill B&B Insch AB52 6YB ✆ 07796 448158 ⌂ edgehill-bandb.co.uk. This small B&B lies on the border between the Garioch and Marr, making it well-placed for exploring sites of interest in either direction. Its four rooms are simply furnished with spacious, modern bathrooms and under floor heating.

Self-catering

Goukstone Methlick AB41 7HP ⌂ goukstone.com. Luxury dog-friendly shepherd's huts with a solar-powered shower and eco-toilet, sheep's wool insulation and wood-burning stove; a sustainable Slow experience without compromising on comfort. E-bike hire also available.

Camping & Glamping

Ythan Valley Campsite Ellon AB41 7TH ✆ 01358 761400 ⌂ smithfield.ythanvalley@gmail.com. A small number of non-electric grass tent pitches for tents only, offering a quiet, stripped-back retreat in rural Aberdeenshire. Campers can also order homemade bread, delivered warm to their tent each morning. Open April to September. Two-night minimum stay.

7 ABERDEENSHIRE: MARR

Hotel

The Commercial Hotel Tarland AB34 4TX
✆ 01339 881922 🖰 thecommercial-hotel.co.uk.
With only nine dog-friendly rooms and warm
hospitality offered to both staying guests and
visiting diners, this family-run village inn offers a
personal touch and excellent cooked breakfasts.

B&B

The Boat Inn Aboyne AB34 5EL ✆ 01339
886137 🖰 theboatinnaboyne.co.uk. 'Dogs, kids
and muddy boots welcome!' is the website's
tagline, providing an insight into the relaxed and
friendly experience you'll have at this inn that
has overlooked the River Dee since 1720.

Self-catering

Glen Dye Cabins & Cottages
Banchory AB31 6LT ✆ 01330 850689
🖰 glendyecabinsandcottages.com. This mini
village of characterful properties is tucked away
within a quiet glen, just half a mile from the
start of the walk up Clachnaben. It offers both
big and small hideaways (all dog friendly), plus
access to a wood-fired sauna and the BYOB Glen
Dye Arms pub.

Camping & Glamping

Feughside Caravan Park Banchory AB31 6NT
✆ 01330 850669 🖰 feughsidecaravanpark.
co.uk. Located in a quiet corner beside the Water
of Feugh on its way to Banchory, this small,
dog-friendly campsite is just a few miles from
Clachnaben and all the tasty treats on offer at
Finzean Farm Shop.
Tap o'Noth Forest Garden Farm Rhynie AB54
4HH ⬛ Tap:Retreat 🖰 tapfarmrosa@gmail.com.
Cook campfire-style and soak in a wood-fired hot
tub while listening to the birds or watching bats
skim overhead at this off-grid shepherd's hut
next to Tap o'Noth Hillfort, located on a working
permaculture farm.

8 ABERDEEN CITY & STONEHAVEN

Hotel

Cove Bay Hotel Cove Bay AB12 3NA ✆ 01224
897211 🖰 covebayhotel.co.uk. Close to
Aberdeen while still offering coastal solitude,
this hotel in the small suburb of Cove Bay
sits near the Aberdeen Coastal Path and has
contemporary bathrooms and sea views.

B&Bs

Alba Guest House Aberdeen AB24 3BS ✆ 01224
625444 🖰 albaguesthouse.co.uk. Simply
decorated with block colours and striking artwork
on the walls, this dog-friendly guesthouse is well-
positioned for exploring Old Aberdeen. Breakfast is
fantastic, cooked and served by the proprietor who
was once a restaurant owner.

Self-catering

Skene Terrace Apartments Aberdeen AB10
1RN ✆ 01334 470711 🖰 lawsonlets.com/
aberdeen. Just half a mile from Aberdeen's train
station, these two self-catering apartments are
on a quiet street in a striking Georgian building,
providing an ideal base for short stays in the
city. Both flats have an open-plan living and
dining area with a fully equipped kitchen, and
bright bedrooms offering lots of wardrobe and
cupboard space.

Camping & Glamping

Deeside Holiday Park Aberdeen AB12 5FX
✆ 01250 878123 🖰 woodleisure.co.uk/
our-parks/deeside. A variety of dog-friendly
accommodation available throughout the year,
including en-suite glamping pods and luxury
caravans with hot tubs, as well as pitches for
caravans, motorhomes and tents.

INDEX

Entries in **bold** refer to major entries; *italics* refer to walk maps.

THE BRADT STORY

In the beginning

It all began in 1974 on an Amazon river barge. During an 18-month trip through South America, two adventurous young backpackers – Hilary Bradt and her then husband, George – decided to write about the hiking trails they had discovered through the Andes. *Backpacking Along Ancient Ways in Peru and Bolivia* included the very first descriptions of the Inca Trail. It was the start of a colourful journey to becoming one of the best-loved travel publishers in the world; you can read the full story on our website (bradtguides.com/ourstory).

Getting there first

Hilary quickly gained a reputation for being a true travel pioneer, and in the 1980s she started to focus on guides to places overlooked by other publishers. The Bradt Guides list became a roll call of guidebook 'firsts'. We published the first guide to Madagascar, followed by Mauritius, Czechoslovakia and Vietnam. The 1990s saw the beginning of our extensive coverage of Africa: Tanzania, Uganda, South Africa, and Eritrea. Later, post-conflict guides became a feature: Rwanda, Mozambique, Angola, and Sierra Leone, as well as the first standalone guides to the Baltic States following the fall of the Iron Curtain; and the first post-war guides to Bosnia, Kosovo and Albania.

Comprehensive – and with a conscience

Today, we are the world's largest independently owned travel publisher, with more than 200 titles. However, our ethos remains unchanged. Hilary is still keenly involved, and **we still get there first**: two-thirds of Bradt guides have no direct competition.

But we don't just get there first. Our guides are also known for being **more comprehensive** than any other series. We avoid templates and tick-lists. Each guide is a one-of-a-kind expression of an expert author's interests, knowledge and enthusiasm for telling it how it really is.

And a commitment to wildlife, conservation and respect for local communities has always been at the heart of our books. Bradt Guides was **championing sustainable travel** before any other guidebook publisher. We even have a series dedicated to Slow Travel in the UK, award-winning books that explore the country with a passion and depth you'll find nowhere else.

Thank you!

We can only do what we do because of the support of readers like you – people who value less-obvious experiences, less-visited places and a more thoughtful approach to travel. Those who, like us, take travel seriously.

Bradt GUIDES

TRAVEL TAKEN SERIOUSLY

INDEX OF ADVERTISERS